ABUSE *and* POWER

ABUSE
and
POWER

HOW AN INNOCENT AMERICAN
WAS FRAMED IN AN ATTEMPTED
COUP AGAINST THE PRESIDENT

CARTER
PAGE

REGNERY
PUBLISHING
A Division of Salem Media Group

Regnery® is a registered trademark of Salem Communications Holding Corporation

ISBN: 978-1-68451-120-4
eISBN: 978-1-68451-121-1
Library of Congress Control Number: 2020934512

Published in the United States by
Regnery Publishing
A Division of Salem Media Group
300 New Jersey Ave NW
Washington, DC 20001
www.Regnery.com

Manufactured in the United States of America

10 9 8 7 6 5 4 3 2 1

Books are available in quantity for promotional or premium use. For information on discounts and terms, please visit our website: www. Regnery.com.

To the honest members of the U.S. Intelligence Community, law enforcement, and the media—may their brave professionalism continue to shine as a beacon of hope amidst the destruction

CONTENTS

CHAPTER ONE

THE BEST OF TIMES, THE WORST OF TIMES

*"And ye shall know the truth and the truth
shall make you free."*

—*John 8:32, engraved on the wall of CIA headquarters*[1]

At the time, August 5, 2016, seemed like a routine Saturday. I was visiting Washington, D.C., for a meeting of the Trump foreign policy advisory team, as our limited work together had become a bit more frequent in the summer leading up to the election. I was staying for five nights at the Grand Hyatt Washington, located just a few blocks up Tenth Street from FBI headquarters. Overall, things were going well that summer, and I was happy to spend more time with our Trump campaign volunteer team. But despite getting to know some of the best international relations and national security professionals I had ever worked with over the course of my long career, there was mounting evidence that the good times would not last. Things were starting to go off the rails.

That morning's *Washington Post* included a long story about how my presence on the advisory team had somehow "[stirred] unease in both parties."[2] Apparently, Democrats and Republicans alike took issue with my volunteer role. I didn't take the criticism seriously. As the big media companies became more detached from reality and the truth, I still considered most of these leading pundits and other reporters to be a complete joke. It was no secret that members of "both parties" opposed then-candidate Trump's presidential bid, and amidst these minor early salvos which quoted many of candidate Trump's critics, I started to understand the media's underhanded tactics firsthand.

That morning's article for the *Post* could have been worse, I thought. Tom Hamburger and Steven Mufson, who wrote the hit piece, were among the very first operatives to ask me about the Democrat-funded opposition research that would dominate the headlines for years to come. They had contacted me to discuss alleged clues surrounding bribes that I supposedly might have been offered by top Russian officials. The phrasing alone showed how baseless the accusations were. Their outrageous questions came not long after high-priced political operatives had misled the *Wall Street Journal* enough to inquire about these very same partisan lies. None of these larger news organizations could be convinced to print them. At least not yet. While I knew the article could have been worse, I couldn't possibly have imagined how nefarious the campaign would end up being.

I had invited Professor Stefan Halper as my guest to the Trump team party happening that evening. Years later the world would learn that that summer, Professor Halper had been working as a U.S. Intelligence Community source who spied on myself and other members of the Trump campaign.[3] Luckily, he declined my invitation. After a long workout at the hotel gym, I headed over to the evening event.

When I arrived at the Trump foreign policy house party, two retired U.S. Army generals from our team greeted me at the door. Although many members of our group had been libeled by the press earlier that year after being identified as Trump campaign supporters, the focus of these latest attacks started to take an unexpected turn. A new Cold War had begun to heat up, and we joked that night about how my Russia connections might have made me a more natural target for these baseless political attacks. But as time started to run out on the final months of the Obama administration, none of us could have realized the dramatic scheme that was already being planned at the highest levels of government. Nor could we fathom the extraordinary dishonesty of the Intelligence Community, the media, and the Democratic Party that allowed the scandal to continue.

Aside from the Trump campaign volunteer meeting, my August 2016 visit to Washington offered me opportunities to catch up with several other foreign policy experts with whom I had recently spent time at the Republican National Convention in Cleveland. One day I had lunch with James Carafano, the Heritage Foundation's director of foreign policy studies. I also met with Iceland's ambassador Geir Haarde and the Hungarian ambassador Réka Szemerkényi. My relatively ordinary meetings were inconsequential in comparison to another series of high-level briefings occurring in Washington that month. Just a few weeks later, Senate Minority Leader Harry Reid and other members of Congress received an infamous series of briefings from CIA Director John Brennan "that intelligence officials had evidence of Russia's intentions to help Mr. Trump."[4]

Enabling these fabricated spy stories later earned Brennan an opportune career transition. After leaving government, he eventually became a national security and intelligence commentator on NBC and MSNBC.[5] Previously unimaginable for former senior intelligence officials, his new role as an emerging media pundit was defined largely by a range of spirited attacks on President Trump.[6] In 2018, as countless fictitious stories about the Mueller investigation continued to clap like thunder on television each night, Brennan even called the president's actions "nothing short of treasonous."[7]

When Brennan was head of the Central Intelligence Agency under President Obama, he avoided speaking like that—at least in public. The CIA's standard operating procedures forbid agency officials from conducting domestic spy operations. Certainly one of the top spies in the nation's attacking a major party's nominee for president would violate every norm.

But norms did not dissuade Brennan from taking proactive steps against Donald Trump from the shadows during campaign season. His hatred for Trump would eventually grow into one of the defining traits of his career. When meeting with Senate Minority Leader Harry Reid in late August 2016, Brennan allegedly "indicated that unnamed advisors to Mr. Trump might be working with the Russians to interfere in the election." Brennan went on to suggest financial dealings between Russian affiliates and advisors to Mr. Trump might be behind the conspiracy.[8]

A few days after meeting with Brennan, Senator Reid fired off a letter to FBI Director James Comey: "questions have been raised about whether a Trump advisor who has been highly critical of U.S. and European economic sanctions on Russia, and who has conflicts of interest due to investments in Russian energy conglomerate Gazprom, met with high-ranking sanctioned individuals while in Moscow in July of 2016, well after Trump became the presumptive Republican nominee."[9]

This supposedly conflicted individual was part of a Trump campaign with "significant and disturbing ties to Russia and the Kremlin."[10]

That individual was me. Or more accurately, a fictional representation of me.

Based in part on his briefing from Brennan and other political operatives in the Intelligence Community, practically every statement Senator Reid made about me was untrue. As Kimberley Strassel of the *Wall Street Journal* correctly wrote years later, "The Reid letter marked the first official blast of the Brennan–Clinton collusion narrative into the open."[11] It also marked the moment that Donald Trump and supporters of his campaign like myself would be plunged even deeper into a shadowy world of spies and intrigue. Later, our predicament would worsen with countless physical and judicial threats. Like an ever-strengthening drumbeat, the initial attacks that labeled us "traitors" were among the smears we heard coming from over the horizon. There would be much more to come.

It took tireless reporting, legal battles, and political dogfights to unearth a string of revelations about once "Top Secret" official acts. Thanks to those efforts, the wrongdoing of the most powerful men and women in our nation's capital would begin to be exposed. The depth and coordination of their scheme was incredible, even to the people it targeted. What happened to me could happen to any American. That's why I'm telling my story. The continuing cascade of revelations about this wrongdoing makes it clear that every American remains at risk, including and especially President Donald J. Trump.

■ ■ ■

I had long known that America's establishment politicians and their elite advisors were out of touch with the rapidly evolving world. Donald Trump was the first prominent national figure to stand up and say what many of us had seen with our own eyes. Most of America's foreign policy mistakes during the post–Cold War era had been led by supposedly first-rate people whose decisions were often exempt from rigorous scrutiny. Candidate Trump recognized the mistakes repeated by Washington's foreign policy mandarins and called for accountability.

As a longtime student of foreign policy, I found Trump's call for change refreshing and long overdue. While establishment politicians pushed ideological policies that only served the interests of Washington insiders, Donald Trump soberly assessed America's place on the world stage and put the interests of the American people first.

I was also pleased to hear candidate Trump call for a new relationship with Russia and other states of the former Soviet Union. "Wouldn't it be nice if we could actually get along with Russia, wouldn't that be a decent thing?" he asked.[12] I agreed. I thought it was in America's interest to engage with Russia as an international partner where there was common ground, perhaps in taking steps to address the China threat.

My experience with Russia largely stemmed from my work in the energy sector. I had spent time with some of the industry's greats like oil and gas investor T. Boone Pickens, and George P. Mitchell, the Texas oilman whose modest investment in hydraulic fracking technology had helped unlock trillions of dollars' worth of domestic oil and gas reserves and catapulted the United States to the forefront of world energy production.

I also maintained connections in Russia, where Gazprom, the largest publicly listed natural gas company in the world held 17 percent of global gas reserves. Gazprom alone was much larger than ExxonMobil, Shell, Chevron, Total, BP, and several other supermajors combined.

Opportunity to get involved with this strategic sector drew me to Moscow as an international energy financier. Living among the Russian people for a few years convinced me that the United States and Russia could forge a better relationship—that both our countries would benefit if we cooled down the level of hostility.

At the same time, I didn't—as they say in the State Department—go native. I recognized that our countries had different histories, different political systems, and different interests. As I had done throughout my career, I put America's interests first.

Patriotic service is fundamental to who I am. When I was in Moscow, the only government that "recruited" me as "an asset" was the United States government. I was a longtime source for the Central Intelligence Agency (CIA) and other American spy units, providing information on evolving energy markets and Russia's ever-shifting business and political cliques. As I'll explain later in this book, my service to the CIA extended far beyond Russia.

As a private figure in academic and U.S. government and business circles, I found a lot of hard evidence that Russia was less of an enemy than many foreign policy pundits often made it out to be. After decades of debate with international relations scholars, diplomats, intelligence officers, and other government officials, I knew my views would never be popular among foreign policy elites. In 2010, the *Washington Post* reported that the Intelligence Community included 854,000 people holding top-secret clearances.[13] That gigantic intelligence bureaucracy largely relied on Cold War thinking to justify its existence. It represented a steady part of the foundation upon which the CIA and other agencies were constructed since the struggle with Moscow began after World War II.[14]

I knew my views went against the grain of the "interagency consensus." But I felt foreign policy, like any other political issue, deserves a debate, and I was open in my desire to present another side of the argument. I never realized, however, that the foreign policy establishment would be so vengeful in punishing dissenters.

In 1998, after my service in the U.S. Navy during the Clinton administration, I became an international affairs fellow at the Council on Foreign Relations, an institution sometimes viewed as synonymous with the foreign policy establishment. Throughout most of the Obama administration, I served as a fellow with the Center for National Policy in Washington. Originally finding some level of peaceful discourse with these people, I mistakenly assumed license to debate issues freely in public. Wow, was I wrong.

A few days before Donald Trump announced my name to the *Washington Post*, I received a message from the Center for National Policy saying that Maureen Dowd of the *New York Times* wanted to ask about my volunteering for the Trump campaign. I never spoke with Ms. Dowd. On March 23, 2016, less than forty-eight hours after the *Washington Post* announced that I was among the campaign's volunteers, I received another email from the Center for National Policy. There was, you see, a very timely "streamlining and consolidation" taking place.[15] My fellowship was officially over.

■ ■ ■

As the world now knows, things like losing a fellowship were the least of the headaches that I, as an unpretentious supporter of candidate Trump, would begin to experience. At the behest of the Democratic Party and the Intelligence Community, the media established the narrative that I was a rogue actor operating in conspiracy with a foreign power, sent to conduct criminal acts. I sometimes wonder if the ranks of the political class and their media acolytes are filled with frustrated novelists. Of course, and as would eventually be proven after years of investigations, the reality was that they needed this narrative to make me a convenient portal through which to surveil the Trump campaign.

Throughout the ordeal of the next few years, I never tried to disguise who I really was. Although almost entirely unknown to much of the outside world, I had regularly participated in foreign policy debates for years. Though I was never integral to the Trump campaign, I viewed volunteering in 2016 as a way to remain engaged in this kind of intellectual dialogue. I was nothing more than an unpaid member of a volunteer team, and I never pretended to be anything else. As if my peripheral role on the campaign couldn't be clearer, I had to miss our advisory committee's only meeting with candidate Trump because of a previously scheduled engagement on the other side of the country.

In a previous era, when Richard Nixon's administration was using the Federal Bureau of Investigation (FBI) and even the CIA to spy on domestic opponents, journalists built their careers on exposing illicit domestic surveillance. Average Americans of all political stripes took risks to stand up for the U.S. Constitution and the right of free thinkers like myself to offer dissenting opinions. As I soon discovered, things had changed. In the twenty-first century, somehow, most self-styled media watchdogs acted more like Intelligence Community lapdogs. The mainstream media today are all too happy to wag their tails and do as told when the "IC", or U.S. Intelligence Community, starts giving orders—especially when offered special treats in the form of leaked information for headline stories.

I came to appreciate that despite their different functions, elite Washington journalists and the IC leadership are often the same type of people. Upper middle-class, socially well-connected professionals, they congregate in tony suburbs like McLean, Virginia, or Potomac, Maryland, or the more upscale neighborhoods of the District of Columbia. They have earned degrees from the same universities, send their children to the same schools, go to the same events, seminars, and parties, and (as we will see) sometimes share the same beds. So when the Intelligence Community determines that one political figure or another is a problem, it is easy to gin up a story line with their friends and neighbors in the media. Intelligence agents who purported to be concerned about Russian influence in American politics themselves used powerful spy agencies to interfere in American politics—which was just about the most prototypically "Russian" thing any American could do.

If I had not joined the Trump campaign, if I had not deviated from the establishment's foreign policy positions, I never would have had to endure the subsequent years of harassment—and worse. But if it hadn't been me, it would have been someone else instead. I was targeted by Donald Trump's political foes within the FBI, the Justice Department, and elsewhere, who decided to make me Exhibit A in an imagined Trump–Russia conspiracy story line.

CHAPTER TWO

WHO IS MALE-1?

*"He was recruited as an American asset by Russian spies
in New York City in 2013. He was successfully recruited.
He handed them documents and information to help them
out and was enthusiastic about their relationship...."*

—*Rachel Maddow, MSNBC*[1]

What happened to me—a series of malicious attacks by politicians and their consultants, with criminal leaks from intelligence officials to back up their character assassinations—can happen to anyone. False spin can quickly redefine a lifetime of patriotic service into explosive ammunition for the advancement of partisan objectives.

Here is how Rachel Maddow of MSNBC introduced me to the American public as the "Male-1" intelligence asset:

> That advisor, Carter Page, met with a Russian intelligence operative named Victor Podobnyy, who was later charged by the U.S. government alongside two others, for acting as unregistered agents of a foreign government...apparently an unwitting American source for a Russian spy ring that was operating out of New York City.[2]

Since an infamous Yahoo! News article by Michael Isikoff broke, I've been variously described in the media and by some of the most powerful politicians in this country as an intelligence asset for a foreign power, a go-between in an effort to corrupt an American presidential election, an "idiot" by a Russian spy,[3] and in the words of Adam Schiff, chairman of the House Permanent Select Committee on Intelligence, I am someone who doesn't deserve sympathy because I, apparently, "admitted to being an adviser to the Kremlin."[4]

In various public accounts, people who don't know me or much about me have felt free to characterize my life and behavior to the English-speaking world. And if that wasn't enough, my own government's propaganda outlets, including Radio Free Europe, helpfully translated these smears into a diverse array of foreign languages and rebroadcast the lies across much of the globe, ensuring that anyone I had ever worked with in my global consulting business would hear it all.[5] Somehow, I've been characterized as both a naïve stooge of manipulative secret agents and an international Machiavel who helped Vladimir Putin rig a presidential election. Quite a feat.

So who really is this Male-1 guy?

■ ■ ■

When you take the Hudson Line commuter train north out of Manhattan, the large windows on the left side of the train frame the cliffs on the other side of the river, giving you the sense, at times, that you're rolling past an enormous Hudson River Valley School painting. Your last stop is in Dutchess County.

First settled by Dutch farmers, Dutchess County and its surrounding area is steeped in colonial and modern history. There you'll find Hyde Park, the estate where Franklin Roosevelt was born, where he graciously received King George VI and Queen Elizabeth. That town is just north of Poughkeepsie, where I grew up. Needless to say, it wasn't Hyde Park, and we weren't Roosevelts.

My father, Allan, was an executive at the local power company. My mother, Rachel, was a financial planner. My sister and I grew up in a strict and devoted household. I joke with my father today that he was a hardcase. He kids me back that I was a risk-taker and habitual prankster who needed him to keep things from getting too out of control. My mother agrees with both of us. So as I tried to meet the high expectations of my teachers at Our Lady of Lourdes High School, I had to conform to the even higher expectations of my parents. Some kids might get angry with that kind of pressure, but for some reason, I flourished. I was a cross country runner, a Catholic altar boy, and an Eagle Scout. Part of my summers were spent at a strict local Dominican camp, which I actually considered a fun way to spend my break.

My two grandpas loomed large in my youth. Most grandfathers are remembered as indulgent, affectionate figures in one's early life. Mine were role models, two men who left deep and lasting impressions on me as to how a man should approach life. They were a part of their times, but they had also stayed true to themselves.

My mother's father, Grandpa Joe, was a Minneapolis grocer and city council member. He left school in the eighth grade but became a compelling public speaker who effortlessly displayed deep knowledge about social and urban issues. His constituents adored him because he was so passionate about advancing policies that brought them better opportunities. He was equally passionate in opposing the sweetheart deals that are a staple of urban politics. Grandpa Joe's habit of exposing insider dealing earned him a number of powerful enemies. They eventually used their power to gerrymander him out of the neighborhoods where he had enjoyed support, reshaping his ward to straddle both sides of the Mississippi River. For good measure, they also made sure to include the University of Minnesota in his district, where he could never be liberal enough for his new constituents.

My paternal grandpa, Andy, studied Russian at Cornell University, served in World War II, and used his language skills as an army liaison to Soviet officers and diplomats. After the war and a period toying with

another degree in the city, he moved to Ohio where he spent years as a
civilian contract officer, purchasing supplies for the Air Force. After his
retirement, Andy settled deep in the heart of upstate New York. Working
on his farm, he ended each day of hard work by voraciously reading
books. Grandpa Andy derived a youthful enthusiasm from almost any
chore, and he ended up doing a lot more than farming. I remember him
soldering old radios, carefully whittling down pieces of wood that would
become a door or a post, and lying on the ground, his feet sticking out
from under his 4-wheeler Power Wagon plastered with stickers as he
changed the oil.

Any car Grandpa Andy owned needed to have a trailer hitch, just in
case he happened to find some treasure along the road. I once went with
my grandpa on a trip to Montana and had to talk him out of hitching a
trailer to our car so he could pick up extra fossils like the ones he'd
scoured from cliffs in the badlands of South Dakota.

Despite charting his own course, Grandpa Andy never retreated from
society. He was a gregarious and outgoing man who liked to go into
town. He enjoyed meeting new people, and he liked good conversation.
He was a rare person, a highly self-educated man who was proud of
achieving whatever he set his mind to—often doing so with his own
hands.

From both my grandfathers, I inherited a sense of independence and
integrity, a willingness to swim against the tide. Like them, I've found
that these attributes sometimes come at great personal cost. But just like
them, I never let those costs prevent me from doing the right thing.

■ ■ ■

During my high school years, despite never having traveled overseas
before, headlines awakened me to new possibilities for adventure. I remember a fascinating lead story one night in October 1986 that showed the
Reykjavik Summit, where Ronald Reagan escorted Mikhail Gorbachev
to his car after some tough negotiations. The theatrics that reporters

focused on, such as whether or not President Reagan or the younger Gorbachev decided to wear a coat in the frigid cold, were of no interest to me.[6] From my perspective, that all seemed like trivia when compared to the hard-core negotiations about the future of nuclear weapons that had just taken place indoors.

As I learned more about the transformational changes in government policy that were then happening, I became hooked on delving deeper into the concepts that were redefining international relations. While the possibility of travel to far-off lands and different cultures held its attractions, the substance of the negotiations that could take place there was infinitely more compelling to me. I would learn foreign languages and appreciate, though not always agree with, foreign ways of looking at the world. Long before political differences at home would divisively prevent people from constructively engaging with each other, I wanted to help America overcome the greater divisions that had long afflicted our country.

During my sophomore year of high school, the older brother of a close friend of mine graduated from the U.S. Naval Academy, and his career brought the possibility of military service onto my radar screen. A student of history, I also came across a speech that President John F. Kennedy gave at the U.S. Naval Academy in Annapolis just a few months before his assassination: "I can assure you in 1963 that your services are needed, that your opportunities are unlimited, and that if I were a young man in 1963 I can imagine no place to be better than right here at this Academy or at West Point, or in the Air Force."[7] With all the changes happening in the world in the 1980s, those principles stated by a U.S. Navy veteran rang especially true when I was in high school.

I wanted to serve my country, and Annapolis was the best path towards that goal. As a practical matter, it was more difficult for locals from the Hudson River Valley towns to get in to neighboring West Point. And since I had practically no firsthand exposure to the military, the fact that Annapolis offered a diverse range of service selection possibilities from aviation to the U.S. Marine Corps made it an attractive alternative.

I was drawn to the Naval Academy not by the romance of the sea, but by the wide array of opportunities it afforded midshipmen to serve their country. So I applied to the selection committee of my local congressman, Representative Hamilton Fish IV, for an appointment to the United States Naval Academy.

Weeks after sending in my application, I was diagnosed with a medical condition which, while not life threatening, would have made me ineligible for an appointment to any service academy. Instead of giving up my dream, I elected for a surgery that could remedy the condition. I remember while I was recovering at the hospital, my parents stepped toward my bed with serious looks on their faces. For a moment, I thought they were preparing themselves to tell me I had a serious medical complication. To the contrary, they informed me that I had received a letter of acceptance from the United States Naval Academy. Their serious look had been one of pride.

I was to report for Plebe Summer in July, the season in which the Navy promises to transform civilians into midshipmen. Like so many other plebes, my parents drove me to Annapolis. Excited for what lay ahead, I could hardly sleep the night of my I-Day or Induction Day at the Naval Academy.

Maryland's capital in the summer is a place of spectacular color. Flags of the nation, state, and Navy flap above the streets, and flowers spill out of window boxes. Out on the dark waters of the Severn River, the white triangular sails of the yachts of the leisure class slide by. Tourists and locals hang out in outdoor cafes downtown, sipping cocktails all day long and into the night. But even on liberty or shore leave, I would have absolutely no time for any of that. I planned to work around the clock.

Plebes officially begin their "Plan of the Day" in the early morning, but many of us stealthily started it earlier and well before 5:00 a.m. Eventually the official daily program began. Running and calisthenics. Marching to the tunes of the Drum and Bugle Corps after the noon meal formation. Reciting from memory passages of the de facto Fourth Class midshipman's handbook, *Reef Points*. Lots of practice with marching in formation with our rifles in close order drill.

For most, no amount of advanced mental preparation can soften the shock of the strict regimentation of life in the military. From the moment you feel the cold metal of the electric razors shaving your head on Induction Day, a new and unique way of life begins. Many outsiders are even more shocked to hear about when Detailers—or the upper-class trainers— "snipe" at Fourth Class midshipmen for not addressing them with a Yes Sandwich ("Sir, yes sir").

From my perspective, Plebe Summer seemed more like summer camp than a torture chamber. I had been preparing for it throughout most of my life. The discipline I had experienced in more than a decade of Catholic school education had been multidimensional, much like the Navy's. Used to being "sniped" at for some perceived deficiency? Check. Used to spot checks of my knowledge under pressure? Check. Used to positive high standards? Check. Used to being supported while I strived to do my best? Check and double-check. And when it came to sniping, the upper-classmen had nothing on the nuns of my early Catholic education. Over the summers, I had experienced a Dominican camp training regimen near home in Dutchess County. In many ways—and especially given the high level of enthusiasm I had for being at Annapolis—those prior experiences seemed tougher.

I had the advantage of having learned something important early in life. If you are faced with a tough, all-consuming challenge, a half-hearted approach doesn't make it easier. Actually it tends to make things infinitely harder. If you go in with a positive attitude and remind yourself that there is nowhere else you would rather be and nothing else you would rather be doing, things generally go a lot easier, and the time passes quickly. Dedicating myself 110 percent was always the key to success, whether it was staying on the good side of Sister Hubertine in third-grade or at the Naval Academy years later.

I'll never forget one thing my high school varsity cross country coach told me, which I think has summed up much of my life: "You're not that good of a runner, Carter, but you have an extraordinary tolerance for pain. That largely helps to make up for your deficiencies."

Initially, I found it difficult to keep up playing sports at the Naval Academy. I struck out after a short stint on freshman crew, in part because I was working almost around the clock on my studies. But my prior athletic experiences, which included track and swimming in high school, had prepared me to join the Academy's Triathlon team. Just like my cross-country coach said, my high tolerance for pain helped me do pretty well with the combination of running, cycling, and swimming. As much as the races themselves, I found the preparation for these competitions an essential outlet that centered me and released the stress of the rigorous life at the Academy. I continued to participate in these endurance races throughout much of my life, competing in Ironman triathlons until June 2016. After the 2016 presidential election interference escalated, the countless threats meant to terrorize me and so many other innocent Americans effectively made it impossible for me to continue. But along the way, triathlons reinforced some lessons that my high school cross country coach helped me learn about myself. I am not a powerlifter or an explosive sprinter, but I've persevered as an endurance athlete. I can take punishment, survive, and finish the race.

With my success as a triathlete and my high rank in the Class of 1993, I originally wanted to become a Navy SEAL. I applied for a thirty-day summer submarine assignment dedicated to the Navy SEAL mission that midshipmen could select for their "summer cruise." Someone in the application process, however, focused on the word "submarine" and left out the SEAL part. So when my third-class summer came, I was assigned to the USS *Alabama* for a seventy-day cruise. This *Ohio*-class submarine was bristling with sea-launched, intercontinental ballistic Trident missiles tipped with nuclear warheads. I stood port-and-starboard watches for twelve hours a day for over two months under the waves of the Pacific Ocean. I never did become a Navy SEAL, but it was an educational summer at sea, and I earned an enlisted submariner pin on the USS *Alabama* in my free time before coming ashore.

My approach to academics was similarly idiosyncratic and equally intense. The Naval Academy focuses largely on science and engineering, the two disciplines most responsible for winning wars. Many administrators at the Academy tended to look down on those of us who were "poets" studying such "soft" subjects like language, history, and political science. I majored in the latter and earned a Bachelor of Science with distinction, also improving my high school Spanish and beginning to learn Russian.

In the classroom, I had a wide variety of strong professors who gave rigorous but often entertaining lectures. One was a U.S. Marine officer named Captain Jackson who taught economics. He led us through all the standard concepts of supply and demand, the price mechanism, inflation, and monetary supply. But he also did something that many of us wished more professors would do. In his popular class, he worked on our personal development too. Though some of his faculty peers might have blanched at the thought of assigning a popular self-help book, my professor defied convention by adding Napoleon Hill's 1937 book, *Think and Grow Rich,* to our assigned reading.

I read the works of some of the greatest writers deeply, philosophers and economists, profiting from them all. A motivational speaker in his own right, Captain Jackson encouraged us to make *Think and Grow Rich* a part of our lives. At least a few of us did, as the self-improvement book resonated in a way that the works of great economic thinkers like Joseph Schumpeter or Robert Heilbroner could not. "Tolerance and an open mind are practical necessities of the dreamer of today. Those who are afraid of new ideas are doomed before they start," Hill wrote.[8] My professor, for one, knew intuitively that young men and women needed knowledge about themselves and about how to navigate the challenges of life as much as they needed to be able to calculate a price point or explain GDP growth.

Midshipmen must adhere to a strict code of honor. The raucous bars not far beyond the Academy's gates were a constant temptation. As if to test us, we could hear the music drifting from them as we completed four-mile outer-perimeter runs. The problem with the bars of course was that you had to be twenty-one to get inside. Midshipmen who used fake IDs risked their Navy careers. A minor infraction—even a "white lie" about your weekend activities—could be an honor code violation that sent you packing. In this and many other ways, a Naval Academy midshipman is held to a much higher standard than a James Comey or an Andrew McCabe, one FBI leader who leaked sensitive information, and another who lied to the FBI, both without immediate legal consequences.[9]

■ ■ ■

I first visited Russia in June 1991. As a high-performing student with knowledge of the Russian language, I was selected to join a historic delegation representing the Academy in sessions with our counterparts from the Soviet Naval Academy. For around three weeks, we lived in Moscow, surrounded by the onion domes and communist architecture of that metropolis. Moscow seemed mysterious to a young man whose previous foreign travel had been limited to a road trip across Canada with my father and Grandpa Andy, and much later a quick trip to Rome and the Vatican with other Catholic midshipmen over spring break.

We met a number of senior government officials in the Russian White House. It was a classic piece of Soviet architecture, an imposing white monolith. At that time, it had an enormous clock at its apex that looked like the face of a Bulova wristwatch. The Soviet officials we met were curious and friendly. There was little doubt that major change was afoot in their country.

Spending time with average citizens helped dispel many of my preconceived notions about Russia. During my month in Moscow, I found that shopping and conversing with people on the street was infinitely more useful for learning the language than my three years of sitting in Russian classes at Annapolis. I experienced Russians as a friendly, gracious people. They reminded me, in fact, more of Americans than most other Europeans did. The Moscow subway system reminded many of us of the one we knew from New York City. Even those commuters with modest means managed to dress well and present themselves with dignity despite the challenges of the Soviet economy. I always found that somewhat poignant and endearing.

As I spoke with people in restaurants and shops, I was peppered with questions about the United States. When I asked questions, I was surprised by the openness of some Russians in criticizing their government. I doubt I would have heard such unguarded comments just a few years prior, during an earlier phase of the Soviet era.

Just a month after we left Moscow to return to Annapolis, Gorbachev was "detained" in his dacha by a conspiracy of hardliners who wanted to undo his reforms and return the Soviet Union to the days of Brezhnev and Andropov. In August 1991, when the news of a communist coup d'etat broke, Boris Yeltsin led a group of determined young democrats to stage a demonstration in front of the Russian White House. When tanks rolled in, Yeltsin and the reformers climbed atop them and invited the Soviet soldiers to come out of their turrets and join the revolution. When the soldiers emerged smiling and accepted bouquets from Russian students, it was clear that the Soviet Union was creeping toward its end. Just a few months later in December 1991, the Soviet era officially ended, and each of the individual republics including Russia gained independence.

My final year at Annapolis, I was named a Trident Scholar, which allows students to dedicate their senior year to independent study and research. Even though I was in the top 10 percent of my class, this was a relatively rare honor, especially for someone not majoring in the hard sciences, mathematics, computer science, or engineering. The Trident program allowed me to conduct a year of independent research on Capitol Hill.

I became a research fellow on the House Armed Services Committee, where I worked on my senior thesis while serving under the committee's chairman, Congressman Les Aspin. Aspin had won his first election by a dozen votes in a recount in 1970, running as a peace candidate against the Vietnam War. From those inauspicious beginnings, Les Aspin rose to become, improbably, the Hill's leading defense intellectual. Possessing degrees from Yale, Oxford, and MIT, Aspin was rumpled, charming, and incisive. An odd duck in the world of military affairs, but deeply respected for his knowledge of weapons systems and the odd process of government procurement, his ability to analyze the effectiveness of defense programs was exceptional. During the Spring semester of my First-Class year, Congressman Aspin served President Clinton as secretary of defense. Just over a year after taking office in the Pentagon, he was forced to resign from the cabinet after denying a request to back up U.S. troops in Somalia with heavy armor. That decision was seen in a poor light after the Battle of Mogadishu, in which two Army helicopters were downed and nineteen American servicemen were killed. Vilified for this mistake and designated as the fall guy for a series of broader national security failings of that young administration, Les Aspin died from heart disease a short time later.

I already had some Capitol Hill experience before I started working for Aspin. As part of the Naval Academy's political science honors program, I had been named an intern in the office of another Democratic politician, known for being a prolific author and former professor with a powerful intellect: Senator Patrick Moynihan. In many ways, that was as memorable as my time with Congressman Aspin, though my duties were far less intellectually demanding. I was given a perch in the mail room, where I helped respond to constituent mail. I jumped at every chance to perform a research assignment for one of Senator Moynihan's legislative assistants, while keeping up with my research for my coursework.

Daniel Patrick Moynihan is remembered today as a man for all seasons, a distinguished scholar, a former White House aide to President Nixon, an acerbic observer of social trends, a principled diplomat, and a memorable senator. He is still celebrated for his many witticisms with the bite of truth, popularizing the phrase, "defining deviancy down," as well as the aphorism, "Everyone is entitled to his own opinion, but not his own facts."[10] The former vice chairman of the Senate Select Committee on Intelligence, he represented an exceptionally high level of integrity that puts many of his successors from more recent years to shame.

Alas, my encounters with this great man, which included a treasured photo, were limited. But listening to the senator's incisive floor statements left a lasting impression on me, as did reading his books. One of his books was in a personal sense premonitional. That book was *Pandaemonium*, Moynihan's classic take on the central role of ethnic hatred in motivating conflict. A decade before, Moynihan had predicted the fall of the Soviet empire and anticipated the crises of the post-Soviet era. His new book, by which I was particularly fascinated, subsequently described how the end of the Cold War would release ethnic tensions and civilizational fault lines to create new threats to the United States and world peace.

In Milton's *Paradise Lost*, Pandaemonium was the capital of hell. That dark city, Moynihan had written, was "inhabited by creatures quite convinced that the Great Satan had their best interests at heart. Poor little devils."[11] The creatures of the Union of Soviet Socialist Republics had learned that Moscow did not always have their best interests at heart, especially after the Chernobyl disaster.

"The Soviet Union came apart along ethnic lines," Moynihan wrote. "The most important factor in this breakup was the disinclination of Slavic Ukraine to continue under a regime dominated by Slavic Russia. Yugoslavia also came apart, beginning with a brutal clash between Serbia and Croatia, here again 'nations' with only the smallest differences in genealogy; with, indeed, practically a common language. Ethnic conflict does not require great differences; small will do."[12]

Following some of Moynihan's research methods and cutting across a few of his other eclectic areas of focus, my Trident Scholar project took an internal focus on procedural tactics in Washington.[13] Along the lines of the senator's consideration of how to make the federal government more effective, I concentrated on the impact of government secrecy in congressional decision-making. The substantive focus of my project was the development of the Strategic Defense Initiative (SDI), a hot topic during the Reagan administration and good preparation for the arms control work I would later do in the Pentagon.[14] I studied prior battles between the legislative and executive branches over government secrecy including the Iran–Contra affair. Foreshadowing some of the problems that I would experience a few decades later with the U.S. Foreign Intelligence Surveillance Court, I determined that, "the political nature of the balance of secrecy makes it an issue that has received little attention from the courts."[15] Amidst various abuses and related scandals over the decades, I also concluded that, "secrecy was found to be a political question which has variably shifted in favor of the Congress and the Executive throughout American history."[16] In essence, it often became a struggle for power between the two branches of government.

World events were very much on my mind when the new administration rolled into town. As a Trident Scholar, I was in Washington, D.C., for the swearing in of Bill Clinton as the forty-second president, and as a member of congressional staff, I received a ticket to the Arkansas Ball for the presidential inauguration and watched Bill and Hillary twirl on the dance floor. Looking back at that peaceful time, a quote from Henry Kissinger comes to mind: "History knows no resting places and no plateaus."[17] As I watched a new president ready to preside over a more peaceful world, it might have seemed that for once Kissinger was wrong. The next few years would be a kind of plateau. There was only one superpower in the world. The American Way had triumphed.

Thanks to Moynihan's book and contrary to the more commonly cited work by Francis Fukuyama, I was aware, as many others were, that the "end of history" could not last.[18] History would resume soon enough.

By the middle of the 1990s, small differences at the seams of ethnic and civilization boundaries, from the Balkans to the Middle East to Central Africa, erupted into conflict and genocide. And as nationalism swelled, the calm relationship between the United States and other great powers, Russia and China foremost among them, turned gradually to competition and enmity. Dr. Kissinger was perhaps too categorical, but he would ultimately be proved right as history resumed, rather than ended.

■ ■ ■

After graduation from the Academy, I received a commission in the U.S. Navy. I served as a junior officer from 1993 to 1998, before transitioning to the Navy Reserve.

My first stop was the Pentagon, where I spent eighteen months occupied with doomsday doctrines and foreign affairs with the Navy's Nuclear Affairs and International Negotiations branch as an arms control action officer—office code N514 and personal designation N514G. I held a Top Secret/Sensitive Compartmentalized Information clearance, which exposed me to some of the nation's most sensitive secrets. Though a junior officer, I was introduced to the military's Strangelovian situation rooms and visited CIA headquarters for the first time, where I paused for a moment out of respect for the names of fallen agents on the Memorial Wall. The following year, after less than twelve months of studying at night and on the weekends, I received a Master's in national security studies at Georgetown's National Security Studies Program.

As interesting as all that was, I was thrilled to receive my orders to report to Surface Warfare Officer school in winter of 1994. Like most officers stuck pushing paper in the Washington bureaucracy, the privilege of serving at sea or in other operational commands seemed like a major leap forward. At my going away party at Legal Sea Foods near Crystal City, the N514 team gave me a copy of Mark Riebling's book, *Wedge: The Secret War between the FBI and CIA*.[19] Lieutenant Commander George Jackson, another one of the action officers in my office, might have summed things up best when he included the following above his signature inside the front cover: "Believe it or not, there is something to the phrase 'the only way is underway.' I hope you get the chance to appreciate that. Facta non verba."

At the time, I was busy getting ready for Surface Warfare Officer School in Newport, Rhode Island, and didn't have the opportunity to read the thick 563-page *Wedge* in full. But once I began serving with members of the CIA, I became familiar with Riebling's thesis about their "*Secret War*" with the FBI. The international aspects of my recent work in the Pentagon meant I had limited contact with officials at the FBI. Through interaction with professionals on the National Security Council in the Old Executive Office Building next to the White House and other bureaucratic agencies, I had become accustomed to some of the infighting that often characterizes the relationship between different government bureaus. Although the book helped me appreciate the downside of such rivalries, I never imagined the far worse implications of peaceful accord amongst the bureaucracy. Decades later, President Trump and I would experience firsthand that intelligence agencies working together towards one goal can be more dangerous than petty competition.

During my hectic move to Newport in late 1994, I didn't make it to Chapter Fifteen of *Wedge*, which details the events surrounding Watergate. Reading that section many years later, I understand how the story of the Nixon administration's illegal domestic surveillance of their political rivals was actually less egregious than what the Obama administration did to Donald J. Trump, myself, and others. Rather than operatives breaking into the offices of the Democratic National Committee, the DNC and their party used law enforcement and its statutory powers to organize the political surveillance of the Trump campaign via a federal court order. It would take far longer for members of Congress and the public to begin uncovering the details of that political surveillance. The CIA first learned about the Watergate incident involving low-level operatives James McCord and Howard Hunt when they got a call from Bob Woodward of the *Washington Post*.[20] In this more recent instance, the would-be Woodwards failed to ask the key perpetrators tough questions and wound up shilling for the Intelligence Community. And instead of a group of covert "plumbers," this conspiracy involved the highest levels of the CIA, including Director Brennan, as well as the leader of the Democrats in the U.S. Senate, Harry Reid.[21]

But those events were far beyond the horizons of what I imagined the future held in store for me. After my training, I began my first seaborne assignment as an officer on the USS *Butte* (AE-27), a *Kilauea*-class ammunition ship. No one would mistake it for the USS *Enterprise* (CV-6), one of the most decorated Navy ships in World War II. *Butte* had a serious, if unglamorous, mission, as we set sail on the ship's final cruise across the Atlantic in September 1995. We supported Operation Deliberate Force, a NATO military campaign mounted against the Republic of Serbia.

The Bosnian Serbs, backed by the Republic of Serbia, had repeatedly threatened safe areas established for civilians in Bosnia and Herzegovina. The massacres of Bosnians, mostly Muslims, in Srebrenica and other places haunted the Western conscience. For the first time since 1945, the world was witnessing a genocide unfold on the European continent. It was, as Moynihan foresaw, a conflict built on small differences. Though the Bosnian Serbs were Christians and their victims were Muslims, the two shared a common ancestry and language. They had lived together in peace for decades as a part of Yugoslavia. But now they were murdering each other.

The Serbs committed the vicious act of deliberately shelling the Sarajevo marketplace in late August 1995, tipping the balance of world opinion from concern to action. From the deck of our ship I had a ringside seat supporting the Operation Determined Force campaign, watching the lumbering minuet of the USS *America* and other aircraft carriers navigating the Adriatic as they enabled one sortie after another against the Serbian forces. In the run-up to that campaign in 1994, NATO had seen its first combat operations when NATO fighters shot down four Bosnian Serb fighters for violating a no-fly zone. In just a few years, NATO would find itself in a long, tough war of attrition in Afghanistan after pandemonium came to Manhattan, the Pentagon, and rural Pennsylvania on September

11, 2001. Although none of us could foresee where the world was going, there was a palpable sense even then that the Pax Americana was fraying and that many strategic surprises lay ahead.

When our mission took a break, we came to port in Cannes. On shore leave, many swam and sunbathed on stony beaches and ate broiled fish fillets with pasta. Our American and French hosts could not have been more hospitable, throwing a memorable reception at the Grand-Hotel du Cap-Ferrat just up the coast in Saint-Jean-Cap-Ferrat. It was a strange juxtaposition, but one that well described the new reality, in which savage war zones and horror were only an hour's flight from where others enjoyed luxury and comfort.

Following our brief shore leave on the Côte D'Azur, I continued my service as *Butte's* navigator while we threaded our way through the Suez Canal. This daunting responsibility would have been nerve-racking without the wisdom of our chief petty officers and other senior enlisted. Their depth of experience helped prevent any mishaps such as the hull's scraping shoal waters or colliding with another ship. On watch, I continuously scanned radar and our surroundings for any ship or object that might constitute a "Constant Bearing, Decreasing Range" or CBDR as it's more commonly known. Relying on a group of highly skilled shipmates, I helped guide the *Butte* through the canal twice without incident. In November, among other tasks, we had one crucial mission to fulfill—the distribution of Thanksgiving turkeys to U.S. diplomatic installations along the Red Sea, including in Yemen and Djibouti.

At one point during our deployment, hostile Iranian patrol boats harassed our ship near the Strait of Hormuz. As the officer of the deck, I spent hours observing the Iranians circling in the water in patrol boats. Any one of them might have been packed with high explosives, able to cut toward us in seconds. Their game was largely one of intimidation; I knew that the odds that they would ever pull anything that stupid were relatively low.

After these adventures, I received orders to report to the USS *Carr*, where I would serve as combat information center officer on this *Oliver*

Hazard Perry–class guided missile frigate. It wasn't exactly the most advanced warship, but it was built for combat rather than logistics deliveries, and just a few years before, *Carr* had had to resort to firing .50 caliber machine guns and a 25mm chain-driven cannon to chase off Iranian boats. Our mission included a range of diplomatic assignments with NATO, the kind of duties I had been looking forward to since high school. Prior to the deployment, I had been awarded the Samuel Eliot Morison Naval History Scholarship to complete independent research on the current naval history of the region, so I was able to use much of my free time to study the current developments that were reshaping countries throughout the Mediterranean basin. As serious as our missions were, our occasional ports of call could have been destinations for a luxury cruise ship... Tunis, Tunisia; Catania in Sicily; Malaga and Barcelona in Spain; Casablanca, Morocco; Odessa, Ukraine; and Haifa, Israel. I enjoyed them all, saw a few ancient ruins, toured venerable churches and mosques, and threaded the labyrinthine souks of Casablanca.

The Navy invested in me once again by sending me to the John F. Kennedy Special Warfare Center and School for anti-terrorist training before sending me to the Western Sahara to support the United Nations mission there. I served there from January through June 1998. It was a decidedly landlocked mission with diplomatic overtones and a change of pace from my previous assignments.

The Sahara is a sea of sorts, but one without a Cannes or a Malaga. I was posted to Tifariti, an oasis town too far from the coast to feel any breeze from the sea. My patrols were mostly across hard clay rather than the desert's characteristic endless waves of dunes as found further east in neighboring Algeria (which I also visited).

The Western Sahara, then as now, is contested territory between the Kingdom of Morocco to the north and the local insurgents, the Polisario Front, which represents the indigenous Arabic–Berber Sahrawi people. Once a colonial possession of Spain, the Western Sahara remains the scene of one of the longest and most intractable low-grade conflicts of our times. It has also remained intensely monitored. While stationed at the UN peacekeeping mission, MINURSO, I reported to a Chinese site commander and a Russian deputy commander. Our resident Arab speakers were Egyptian army officers. They were useful in discussions with the Moroccan and Polisario fighters from whom we occasionally learned about prisoners of war who might be held captive in the immediate vicinity.

Despite the relative isolation, six months in the Sahara Desert offers many opportunities for gaining perspective. An incomparable destination in its own right, it also served as an exceptional jumping-off point for a leave period in other countries across Europe and the Middle East. During those months, I managed to spend more time in Barcelona and returned to Istanbul for the Crossroads of the World Conference in May 1998, where I gained more knowledge about the energy sector of the Caspian Sea region. At the end of my tour in the Western Sahara, I resigned from active duty in the U.S. Navy with the rank of lieutenant. I feel grateful to the United States Navy for educating and training me and for exposing me—even as a minor player—to grand policy in the Pentagon and to diplomacy by other means in Operation Determined Force.

As I returned to the United States amid the run-up to the nation's simmering impeachment controversy, the disparity between many of our leaders and the caliber of our enlisted men and women struck home. Like many in the military, I was disturbed by the sexual harassment scandal of then-President Bill Clinton and a former White House intern who was a few years younger than I. Such incidents were hardly unknown in military ranks, but the light treatment the forty-second president received for his harassment of women surely stands as a premium example of "different spanks for different ranks."

As part of my transition out of the Navy, I had a brief stint in August 1998 at Moscow State University for more language training. Following that, my interest in international affairs led me to New York City, where I was selected as an international affairs fellow with the Council on Foreign Relations. I deepened my focus on the energy-rich Caspian Sea region, presenting original research on the geopolitical tensions of that inland sea bordered by Russia, Iran, and three former Soviet republics in Central Asia. While at the Council on Foreign Relations, I took the Number 6 subway train from my office to New York University where I studied in the Stern School of Business M.B.A. program at night and on the weekends.

During the recent years of controversy, when I was under a government microscope and the target of leaks from the FBI and Adam Schiff, many have wondered if I am a "Russophile"—someone with a deep, romantic attachment to the Russian language, the implication being that perhaps my love of Russia has somehow compromised my love of country. I am not a Russophile. Nor am I a Russophobe. I have a clear-eyed view of the autocratic tendencies of that society and its government and the corruption that can be found in some parts of its system. But I never imagined that the Obama administration and elements of the U.S. Intelligence Community which I had long served would display many of those same habits of governance and official corruption, thereby mirroring other more traditionally authoritarian countries. I have also never been afraid to admit that I manage to get along with Russians and have counted some Russians as friends. This is in keeping with my general posture toward life. I have a talent for adapting to challenging situations and developing constructive professional relationships worldwide. I tend to see the positive side where cynics take a more jaundiced view. Call me naïve, but as both a foreign policy analyst and an international deal-maker, I have successfully worked to improve relationships between Washington and Moscow.

If the FSB (formerly the KGB) and the SVR (the Russian Foreign Intelligence Service) ever evaluated me as a target to cultivate as an intelligence source, they must have written me off as a perpetual Eagle Scout and former Catholic altar boy. For all my contacts with Russian people in Moscow and elsewhere over the course of the past several decades, no one has ever asked me, or even suggested, that I do anything illegal or shady.

■ ■ ■

While I was in business school, Russia was still trying to shrug off the devastation of the 1998 financial crisis. By the turn of the millennium, Russia's prospects had markedly improved. After the devaluation of the ruble, the country's industries eventually stabilized, making them more internationally competitive. Rising commodity prices promised a robust national income stream, while Putin set out to bring new life to the Russian economy by instituting a low flat income tax and an energetic program of deregulation.

I watched these developments with interest from Merrill Lynch's office in London, where I worked with Michael Packer and his team who helped establish the investment management company's equity e-commerce strategy. (Soon thereafter, on 9/11, Michael lost his life at Windows on the World at the top of the World Trade Center.) I advised senior management about assessing private equity positions in Japan. I was promoted to serve as the chief operating officer of the capital markets and financing group in Europe, the Middle East, and Africa, a business with an annual revenue of around $600 million.

While working in these positions, I began a program at the University of London, School of Oriental and African Studies, where I eventually earned a doctorate. Between my work and my study, I noticed significant upticks in the Moscow Exchange and the Russian Trading System. Were these blips or the beginnings of a steep climb?

In 2004, I placed my bet on a steep climb.

Merrill Lynch transferred me to Moscow as a founding member of the firm's representative office in Russia. A vice president, I was tasked with originating and executing investment banking transactions in Russia and the Commonwealth of Independent States. In an advisory capacity, I was involved in a diverse array of deals including Gazprom's $7.5 billion acquisition of a 50 percent stake in Sakhalin-II LNG and a $2 billion gas trading, storage operations, and upstream swap with BASF AG.

As both a practitioner and a scholar, I took a deep dive into the international political economy of the oil and gas industry, as well as the interlacing connections of world finance. I had essentially become a deal-maker and advisor on Russian acquisition targets, learning how to structure deals and helping Western investors build confidence in their holdings in the Wild West environment of post-Communist Russia.

Amidst all my international travels, I spent most of my years in Russia in the capital city of Moscow, where I had a spacious apartment in the Kudrinskaya Square Building, a Stalinist skyscraper once built for the *nomenklatura*. I socialized with a circle of Russian friends from McKinsey & Company on Friday nights, and an circle of American friends on Saturday nights. For a while, I dated a nice lady who was a ballerina at the Bolshoi Ballet. I enjoyed talking with Russians—as I do with people everywhere—and especially liked to practice my Russian on the subway. In conversations with Russian friends from the late-Soviet era until today, I have consistently encountered a desire for building a better relationship with America. For both sets of friends, these were heady times. We were all making money while feeling that we were doing good by helping Russia build its market economy.

I went to the U.S. embassy in Moscow on a regular basis, as I was a member of the gym. I particularly enjoyed Sunday night basketball games with Americans, mostly businessmen like myself and U.S. Marines, as well as other embassy employees. I understand that today, in a slight thaw from the tone of the Obama years, Russian businessmen are joining these embassy basketball games as a way of filling in for missing American talent.

Working around the world and even in our own country, there is often an awareness, like something barely perceived in one's peripheral vision, that a secret world of spies and surveillance is lurking in the backdrop. I have never wanted to be a part of that world. But in Washington, no less than Moscow, you cannot help but sense that it is around you, both everywhere and nowhere.

For me, the secret world in part emerged with an invitation to lunch.
An American intelligence agent wanted to have a friendly chat with me
over food. When I got to the restaurant, I was informed that I was actually having lunch with the CIA. Those lunches would continue throughout most of my years working overseas. We discussed topics that might
have informed my lunch partner's knowledge of how Russia was evolving, which I was happy and proud to provide to my government.

■ ■ ■

The collapse of Bear Stearns in March 2008 signaled the beginning
of the Great Recession. The upward sweep of Russia's equity markets hit
a cliff, as did the New York Stock Exchange, NASDAQ, and London
Stock Exchange. Russian equities would rise again, only to be impacted
one more time by events in the United States—the imposition of sanctions
as punishment for the annexation of Crimea and other acts of aggression,
but even more by the unexpected and relentless productivity of U.S. oil
and gas production enabled by "fracking."

By this time, I was back in the United States, dividing my time
between Oklahoma City and New York. I had served as chief operating
officer of Merrill Lynch's energy and power unit, growing our international and cross-border business. In 2008, I struck out on my own as
managing partner of my own firms, one of which was Global Energy
Capital. I worked with my colleagues to increase our range of business
activities across North America, Europe, Asia, and the Middle East.
My related company Global Natural Gas Ventures considered a few
liquefied natural gas (LNG) projects in China and worked to identify
potential sources of liquefied petroleum gas for one of China's largest
municipal gas suppliers. I had begun to establish an oil trading venture
in the Middle East before the Obama administration allowed the
regional crisis with ISIS to spin completely out of control. I remained
engaged in what many referred to as the new Great Game of regional
energy strategy across this geostrategic region. I began work to help a

subsidiary of Gazprom, the Russian oil and gas behemoth, develop small-scale LNG projects. We shared ideas regarding new financing mechanisms and researched ways to jointly promote gas commercialization in both Russia and the U.S. This would all come to an abrupt end when a manufactured spy scandal against President Trump and myself derailed the project.

■ ■ ■

One of my international business colleagues, whom the CIA had previously expressed a significant level of interest in, invited me to a gathering at the Asia Society on Park Avenue in January 2013. It was at this event that I happened to meet one Victor Podobnyy, a junior attaché at the Permanent Mission of the Russian Federation to the United Nations. We traded contact information and met on one occasion—not a dinner or lunch, just a brief meeting at the lounge at JoJo Restaurant on East Sixty-Fourth Street. He had a tea, and I had a Coca-Cola.

I found Podobnyy, then in his mid-twenties, to be a less than sparkling conversationalist. But I viewed our meeting as a benign opportunity to practice my Russian. Irrelevant as it may be, the obvious reality was that any Russian diplomat might decide to share whatever information we discussed with the government he represented. A year earlier, the FBI had apprehended ten Russian "sleeper agents" in the United States. But to this day, nothing Podobnyy ever said, emailed, or did throughout our limited communications ever showed any evidence of his being a "spy." Russia does, after all, have actual diplomats in its diplomatic corps. Plus, he was so young that I couldn't help but think he sounded like one of the more lackluster students from my NYU class. The idea that this bland diplomat in his mid-twenties was a relevant intelligence operative was not even remotely conceivable. After all, every spy I'd dealt with before tended to ask at least a few pertinent questions from time to time.

Podobnyy and I continued our irrelevant small talk via email and by phone. After we had exchanged a handful of entirely benign messages,

I received another meeting request a few months later. This time, the request came from the FBI. On June 13, 2013, I was invited to the basement of the Plaza Hotel. I met an FBI special agent and his partner, who ushered me to a relatively quiet and discreet corner of the Plaza's lively food court. While I tried to explain to them that my "relationship" with the Russian diplomat was limited to a single Coca-Cola and a handful of emails, they asked me some extraneous questions.

What areas of discussion did Mr. Podobnyy want to pursue?

I laid out for them that we had, in general terms, discussed the state of world and Russian energy markets.

What questions did he ask?

Podobnyy had not asked me any sensitive questions about my firm, our customers, or anything else that would be considered proprietary or relevant information. If he had, I would have walked away. I could only recollect general questions about my take on the future of world energy markets.

Did you give him any documents?

As we talked about Russian energy markets, I decided to share with Podobnyy my completely innocuous lecture notes from a weekend class I was teaching at the Center for Global Affairs at New York University. These notes were based exclusively on public sources. There was nothing in them that one couldn't learn from reading the papers of the International Energy Agency, perusing *The Economist*, or scouring the annual reports of publicly traded companies.

I explained to them how I remembered that when I had told Podobnyy about my lecture, his eyes quickly glazed over. To be honest, Podobnyy bored me as well, and the thought occurred to me that I could find a better partner with whom to practice my Russian.

■ ■ ■

On the morning of January 27, 2015, well before I volunteered with the Trump campaign, I stumbled across a surprising article in the

Washington Post. The seemingly innocuous exposé was an early introduction to something I and all Americans would begin learning a lot
more about in the following year: how the Obama administration could
captivate and manipulate a gullible media. The *Post's* headline reflected
the sensationalist spin: "This Alleged Russian Spy Ring Was Interested
in Some Very Dangerous Things."[22]

Victor Podobnyy had been indicted by the Department of Justice, in
the Southern District of New York, for allegedly aiding some Russian
banker, Evgeny Buryakov. Buryakov was allegedly involved in a conspiracy to act as an unregistered agent of a foreign government. Podobnyy and his co-conspirator, Igor Sporyshev, had already departed
America. Leveraging my prior assistance as they described in the indictment, the FBI had comprehensively surveilled the supposedly secure
office where they met, while also bugging their calls. Buryakov had
already been arrested.

I looked up the indictment. Some of the conversations captured by
the FBI read like self-parody. Podobnyy marveled that he was "sitting
with a cookie" in the "chief enemy spot." But he complained that the
SVR (Russia's foreign intelligence service) was not all he was hoping it
would be. He never expected to be in "movies about James Bond" and
"of course, I wouldn't fly helicopters." But he was disappointed that the
SVR had him traveling under his own name.[23]

Buryakov, however, might have been in a more sensitive spot. It seems
that he may have been what the spooks call an NOC—"non-official
cover."

More alarming was the complaint's description of an American involved
in international energy business, "Male-1," who had been in occasional
contact with Podobnyy and was a previously undisclosed informant for the
FBI. Male-1, as the world would learn a few years later, was me.

After the Justice Department released the sealed complaint to the
public, I read the indictment quoting Podobnyy discussing his irritation
with Male-1 for ignoring an email. Podobnyy complained to Sporyshev
that Male-1 "writes to me in Russian [to] practice the language."[24]

This more or less captured the degree to which Podobnyy occupied my attention, as well as the relative unimportance of our light dialogue.

"He flies to Moscow more often than I do. He got hooked on Gazprom thinking that if they have a project, he could be rise up. Maybe he can."[25]

All of this mouthing off by the young Podobnyy represented little more than sheer bravado and was by all indications completely detached from my real focus. I wasn't "hooked" on Gazprom; I was involved in a lot of energy ventures worldwide.

With this surprise public disclosure and without any warning whatsoever, the Bureau put me in a very bad position. My interactions with the Russian diplomat had been entirely innocuous in every way. But I had done my duty by reporting details of those meetings to the FBI, thereby leaving myself dangerously exposed as an FBI informant. Instead of respecting my service, the Obama administration's Department of Justice had hung me out to dry without even notifying me that my support would be included in the indictment. Years later, the Justice Department, the media, and their political allies tried to use the information in that indictment to paint me as a Russian intelligence asset.

Despite the innuendo promoted by "journalists" such as Rachel Maddow, there was never any talk of any kind of deal with the Russian government, officially or unofficially. As I told the FBI in 2013 and Robert Mueller's investigators years later, Podobnyy never offered me any sort of gift or illicit promise whatsoever. I never gave him any "documents" of any intelligence value, unless you consider information available on Google and at NYU's Bobst Library intelligence sources. Plus, if my interactions with Podobnyy were of any value, the value would have been to the U.S. government, as I was an FBI informant, just as I had been a CIA asset in Moscow and worldwide.

My cooperation with U.S. intelligence, of course, had been a secret until the Obama administration, and its agencies betrayed the trust that had been built over many decades of service. Any person who read the indictment, including Podobnyy and anyone with the most basic level of knowledge within the Russian government, would know I was Male-1. The public exposure of my cooperation with the FBI carried the explosive potential to contaminate my relationships with business associates in Russia and elsewhere, immediately putting my life at risk. After many decades of service, Jim Comey's FBI, Eric Holder's Department of Justice, the special agent who asked me about Podobnny, and the rest of their colleagues lacked the professional courtesy to at least give me a heads up. I was publicly burned by the FBI and DOJ under Obama.

Years later, when Michael Horowitz, the Department of Justice inspector general, issued his report on the investigation of FBI and DOJ malpractice in foreign intelligence warrants against me, he wrote that the confidential informant squad supervisor in New York wanted to open up a counterintelligence case against me. The FBI reported to Horowitz that I had volunteered that I was Male-1 in the indictment to a "Russian minister and various Russian officials at a United Nations event in the 'spirit of openness.'"[26]

This was a complete mischaracterization of my discussion with the alleged "Russian minister." For a long time after Podobnyy's arrest, I avoided Russia, much to the detriment of my business. Eight months after the indictment, I encountered some Russian officials when I was invited to hear President Obama speak at the UN General Assembly on September 28, 2015. In between speeches the delegates and their guests typically mingle in the grand hall of the General Assembly. It was while moving from one of these intermissions back to my seat that I saw a Russian official and set the record straight. I told him that I may have had a conversation with another Russian official who had been identified by the U.S. government as a spy. I did this because in the small network of the Russian energy world, the indictment—which described Male-1 as an American energy businessman living in New York at the time—had essentially unmasked me.

As the Obama administration had gone far beyond the boundaries of common decency let alone national security, I worried that my exposure as a confidential informant on behalf of my country would invite other extrajudicial consequences. Just a few years before, a Russian defector Alexander Litvinenko had suffered a terrible death in the United Kingdom from sipping tea laced with polonium. While I felt safe in New York, would I be safe in Moscow? At the very least, I could certainly be singled out for particularly close surveillance. Though I had nothing to hide, it was still unconscionable that the U.S. Intelligence Community would needlessly put my life at risk. But as Napoleon Hill had written in his book that I studied in Captain Jackson's class at the U.S. Naval Academy: "Those who have cultivated the habit of persistence seem to enjoy insurance against failure. No matter how many times they are defeated, they finally arrive up toward the top of the ladder."[27] I was not about to let these misleading court pleadings endanger my life. These circumstances left me with no choice but to set the record straight.

For someone who works in the interstices between countries, it is important to be seen as trustworthy in business. I was proud to have served my country in uniform and as an asset for the CIA and informant for the FBI. But I was profoundly upset that the government chose to take my cooperation and sweep it off the side like road-kill on a highway. The misleading statements in the federal court document were so preposterous that I never imagined they would have any tangible effect. But given the risks involved on a personal level, efforts to reestablish some basic semblance of truth had to be made.

I did not know then, and would never have guessed, that my own government had become lost in a wilderness of mirrors. The Obama administration and its political loyalists had begun to create the illusion that I was some kind of spy or "agent of influence": a Democrat-funded conspiracy theory that extended across Russia, the United States, and perhaps elsewhere. The idea that my work in Russia might somehow be unpatriotic was beginning to gel in the mind of at least one of my U.S. Intelligence Community handlers. As it turned out, I didn't have any reason to fear polonium tea. Just two years and three months after being named as Male-1, I faced a torrent of death threats not from Russians, but from my fellow Americans, thanks to what would turn out to be a corrupt, partisan scheme to take down the president of the United States.

I eventually came to realize that among the most explosive revelations that I discussed with the DOJ and FBI officials on March 2, 2016, was the fact that I had recently volunteered to help the Trump campaign. While I had loyally served my country in the national security arena throughout the past two decades, I never could have imagined that they would have made much of my support for Donald Trump. Back then, I assumed government officials avoided crossing certain boundaries. The idea that federal intelligence agencies would meddle in the national political process during an election year seemed too audacious for even the most radical imagination. Apparently I miscalculated how partisan and politically extreme many of the operatives within these once-revered organizations had become after seven years of the Obama administration.

CHAPTER THREE

ENTERING THE ARENA

*"She told us that after the March 2 interview, she called
CD's Counterespionage Section at FBI Headquarters
to determine whether Page had any security clearances
and to ask for guidance as to what type of investigation to open on Page. On April 1, 2016, the NYFO CI
Supervisor received an email from the Counterespionage
Section advising her to open a ▮▮▮▮▮▮▮ investigation
on Page."*

—U.S. Department of Justice, Office of the Inspector General (OIG)[1]

Since founding Global Energy Capital in 2008, I headquartered my
business on the twenty-first floor of the IBM Building on Madison
Avenue in New York City. As luck would have it, the building is connected
to Trump Tower via a tall glass atrium, making for a convenient stroll to
some excellent eateries. Having long felt virtually at home in the building
next door, I was surprised when its namesake announced his candidacy
for president on June 16, 2015. An iconic moment, candidate Trump
famously descended the escalator I had often ridden on the way to lunch
in the food court. I had never met Donald Trump, but like many New
Yorkers his distinct imprint had long been a presence in my life. Love him
or hate him, Donald J. Trump's ubiquitous presence on television and
across the media spectrum would soon take a higher position in the minds
of just about everyone, across the United States and the world.

Donald Trump's celebrity was never what attracted me to him as a
presidential candidate. During my studies and work in policy think

tanks, I had written in favor of new strategies for America's approach to the world. I had long believed that the foreign policy establishment needed a shake-up. Donald Trump's candidacy was a unique opportunity to do precisely that. In candidate Trump, I finally saw someone who was reaching for a credible strategy to change the direction of our country.

My sole prior experience in a presidential campaign reinforced those views and was one of the catalysts for my excitement about then-candidate Trump. I had volunteered for only one other presidential campaign, that of Senator John McCain in 2008.

Years before he turned on me, I volunteered for John McCain's presidential campaign more out of a sense of respect for the man than a belief in his policy vision. I first met McCain when I was still a Second-Class midshipman, during my political science honors internship on Capitol Hill. The following year, I shook his hand again as I received my diploma at Navy–Marine Corps Memorial Stadium in Annapolis. I had long studied his work and remember reading a book about his connections with other fellow Naval Academy graduates from the same era, many of whom I also admired. When Senator McCain ran for president in 2008, it almost felt as if an uncle had decided to join the race for the White House. Though I often disagreed with him, I supported John McCain out of personal respect. Relatively late to the party, I served as an alternate member of the New York State delegation during the Republican National Convention in early September 2008.

Volunteering for the campaign gave me the chance to engage in a few conversations with the senator's top foreign policy advisor, Randy Scheunemann. McCain was surrounded by the supposed best and brightest of the GOP's foreign policy advisors, and in interacting with those supposed experts, I couldn't help but think that their neo-conservative takes were reflexively belligerent—an even more extreme version of the posture that had led George W. Bush's administration into a desert ravine. Years later and not surprisingly, Scheunemann and other McCain alumni would join in signing a March 2016 letter from a group of self-proclaimed "members of the

Republican national security community" who were "united in [their] opposition to a Donald Trump presidency."[2]

While I had volunteered for McCain out of a sense of personal duty and was often frustrated by his policy positions, I offered my services to the Trump campaign because of a genuine alignment on the issues. My ears perked up when I heard candidate Trump say in September 2015 that Ukraine was not being "given the proper respect from other parts in Europe."[3] For reasons candidate Trump described in that speech to the Yalta European Strategy Forum as well as many other addresses on the campaign trail, it was clear that he was advancing new standards of mutual respect in world politics.

The fact that Donald Trump had other advisors who brought different perspectives from the usual D.C. bureaucrats and think tank mandarins was another plus. Throughout his career, Donald Trump had long valued those with military service and business experience. My prior contributions in the U.S. Navy and the financial arena made me think that my unconventional background would be a good fit. Candidate Trump didn't seem to prefer comfortable minions who fit the standard mold long valued by the Washington establishment (including resumes packed with failure at one cushy bureaucratic job after another). The range of ventures I had dedicated decades of my life to were linked to the real world and the real economy. Meanwhile, my policy experience closely correlated with goals that candidate Trump advocated for. Plus, many establishment think tanks, as well as those dedicated "members of the Republican national security community," thoroughly opposed candidate Trump's perspectives on the issues. So if I could make some modest contribution by throwing my hat in the volunteer ring, it would be an honor to do so. Especially since the ring was right next door.

Over the years, I had come to know Ed Cox, a wise man of the foreign policy world and Republican establishment stalwart in New York State. Though still often referred to as President Nixon's son-in-law, Ed is very much his own man. He is a highly accomplished, hard-working, and thoroughly generous person, too. We had had various spirited conversations during the McCain campaign on the need for a new approach in foreign policy. In December 2015, I wrote to him saying that I found reason for renewed hope in candidate Trump's statements throughout the past half year. I attached a copy of a recent op-ed I had drafted that referenced the game-changing détente achieved by Richard Nixon and Leonid Brezhnev, as well as the more recent personal diplomacy between Ronald Reagan and Mikhail Gorbachev. Based on first-hand experience, I knew for certain that the same types of accomplishments were now well within reach.

Ed Cox helped open the door for me to meet Corey Lewandowski, Donald Trump's campaign manager at the time. Lewandowski agreed to meet, making it clear he would do so out of respect for Ed. I made an appointment for the morning of Tuesday, January 12, 2016, and waited on the fifth floor of Trump Tower for a long time before being ushered into the campaign manager's office—a brief glimpse into the immense workload of the top job in the Trump campaign.

Corey was juggling countless things, evident during the few minutes I spent in his office. We would exchange a few words before he stopped to answer a phone, respond to an urgent request from a staffer who ran into his office, and then return his attention to me. We'd start again, and Corey would listen for a moment before his other phone would go off, and he would make a quick decision, hang up, and look at me as if to say, "now, where were we?" I'd start to talk again, and then a campaign aide would stick a head into his office with an urgent question, or Corey would bolt to his laptop when another urgent email arrived. After about five minutes, I had apparently managed to say enough to convince Corey that I was worth considering for a volunteer role. He referred me for a meeting with Sam Clovis, who was sitting at a desk outside.

Sam and I met briefly that day, and over months of informal communication, I came to gain a deep respect for him. A native of Salina, Kansas, Sam Clovis had earned a degree in political science from the U.S. Air Force Academy. Among many other similarities in our respective careers, our service academy background helped us establish an immediate bond. Sam's depth of heroic accomplishments made my relatively short stint in the U.S. Navy pale by comparison. Sam had a storied twenty-five-year career in the Air Force, serving as a fighter pilot, commander of the Seventieth Fighter Squadron, rising to the rank of colonel, and retiring as inspector general of the North American Aerospace Defense Command and the United States Space Command.

In 1978, Sam had pulled a fighter from 3Gs to 12Gs in an instant, losing his wing tanks and wing tips and punching holes in his fuel tanks. The hard landing crushed his cervical vertebrae, causing him to lose 1.5 inches in height. This was on top of thousands of hours in the harness of a fighter pilot. Sam developed severe stenosis from his dedicated military service.

But always a true inspiration with incomparable perseverance, Sam did not allow his disabilities to slow him down. Like me, he was a lifetime student in his free time, collecting an array of degrees including an M.B.A. from Golden Gate University and a doctorate in public administration from the University of Alabama. A true renaissance man, he generously imparted his insight to the next generation of leaders in years as a tenured full professor and a dean of a college of business and management science. Other diverse aspects of his career included his time as a radio talk show host and as a fellow at the Homeland Security Institute. He served as the Trump campaign's national co-chair and chief policy advisor, a post he held until Donald Trump's victory.

In early March 2016, Sam called on me to take on an informal role in the campaign. A Who's Who of senior GOP foreign policy officials had signed an open letter declaring that the Republican nominee was supposedly so unfit that they could not support him.[4] In the wake of this belligerent act of defiance, the media began to drill in: "So who are your foreign policy advisers, Mister Trump?" While crisscrossing the country, Sam had stopped at his home in Iowa when he received a call from Jared Kushner. Sam knew that the candidate's daughter Ivanka and son-in-law Jared were helping him to bring greater discipline on the campaign.

"We need a foreign policy advisory team," Jared said. "Can you help put something together?"

"Yes," Sam answered.

■ ■ ■

Senator Jeff Sessions of Alabama of the Senate Armed Services Committee, who had once distinguished himself by his early endorsement of Donald Trump, was selected to chair the campaign's foreign policy and national security advisory committee.[5] In February 2016 as part of my discussions with Sam about the possibility of my helping as an informal foreign policy advisor, I had written him an e-mail:

> Sam, I heard on Mr. Trump's MSNBC Town Hall tonight that he's in the process of putting together a foreign policy advisory team...I'll once again be departing for meetings in the Middle East tomorrow, so just wanted to express my interest in contributing as a member of that team.[6] Although I have little to gain from this personally, I'm committed to supporting Mr. Trump's efforts to make America great again and I would like to contribute anyway I can. Having directly seen the extensive damage of U.S. foreign policy mistakes through my service overseas both in the military and in private-sector ventures, I know first hand how high the stakes currently are for the future of the world and our country.[7]

Sam assembled a list for the candidate's approval. It included Lieutenant General Keith Kellogg, who had been the chief operating officer for the Coalition Provisional Authority in Iraq; Major General Gary Harrell, who had commanded the 1993 Battle of Mogadishu; Rear Admiral Chuck Kubic, who had commanded the Navy Seabee Division attached to the Marine Expeditionary Force during the 2003 invasion of Iraq and follow-on battle in Fallujah before going on to develop, build, and lead a major international construction company; Major General Bert Mizu-sawa, who commanded a joint task force in Afghanistan and was a Harvard MacArthur Fellow in international security with a Silver Star; Dr. Walid Phares, a highly respected academic and advisor to Congress and government agencies.[8]

Another senior member of our team was a fellow Annapolis gradu-ate, Joseph Schmitz. During President George W. Bush's administration, Joe had held a top position in the U.S. Department of Defense. During the campaign, I knew relatively little about the job responsibilities that his prior four-star-equivalent position as an inspector general (IG) entailed. But only a few years later, the severe civil rights violations that our volunteer committee suffered would eventually become an explosive national drama as the Department of Justice IG investigated the unprec-edented FISA abuse against the Trump campaign.

I was fortunate to count myself among this uniquely distinguished group.

The last-minute nature of the still-growing Trump campaign meant that I was already heading to a seminar in Hawaii by the time I learned of our first official meeting. Too late to change my schedule, the advisory committee met with the candidate at the Trump International Hotel in Washington on March 31, 2016. Many of the other members of our volunteer committee were in attendance, along with assorted scholars from think tanks, the candidate's trusted speech writer Stephen Miller, and communications aide Hope Hicks.[9] Some attendees would later tell me that the meeting lasted about an hour.

■ ■ ■

Though I never met the candidate or advised him directly, I did forward ideas up the chain, sometimes to Corey Lewandowski, Stephen Miller, or through Sam Clovis to one or another aide. Candidate Trump's willingness to buck the stale consensus that had formed around U.S. foreign policy was a primary reason I was motivated to support his campaign in the first place. I also did some research on Hillary Clinton's track record as Obama's first secretary of state. Many of the core facts about her approach to foreign policy and her shortcomings that were drawn from scholarly publications might otherwise elude a typical opposition research investigator's search results.

Other Republican candidates were offering more of the same Cold War rhetoric that one might expect from Beltway experts. Over more recent years, I have come to respect Senator Ted Cruz after following his advocacy on many issues including national security threats and our constitutional civil rights. More specifically, he has become an important voice for U.S. Intelligence Community reforms following the FISA abuse.[10] But in 2016, I disagreed with many of his ideas regarding U.S.–Russia relations. When asked in 2015 if we should cooperate with Russia, for example, Senator Cruz responded: "Of course, we shouldn't be [partnering] with the Russians. Look, this is a great example of the utter failure of the Obama, Clinton foreign policy. This void in power has let Putin step in there...And anyone who believes Russia is fighting against terrorism, I got a bridge to sell 'em."[11]

That sort of saber-rattling towards the Russians wasn't just dangerous, it was wrong. Over the years, my study of U.S.–Russian relations led me to believe that American experts had repeatedly squandered golden opportunities to form a productive partnership with the Russian people. During the early Yeltsin era, when it seemed like Russia might become a stable democracy, Russians complained about the continuation of the Jackson–Vanik Amendment. This U.S. legislation had sanctioned the Soviet government for its harsh treatment of Jewish citizens and refusal to allow them to emigrate. Upon its implementation, Jackson–Vanik was deemed by many to be a success, leading to the eventual liberation of hundreds of thousands of Jews, as well as evangelical Christians and Roman Catholics. But after the fall of the Soviet Union, we kept Jackson–Vanik and other legacy policies in place. Such early slights did a lot of harm, showing a lack of reciprocity and what the Russian people understandably interpreted as a desire to humiliate them. Jackson–Vanik continues today in another form, the Magnitsky Act, which imposed sanctions after the death of a Russian accountant of that same name. These sanctions are aimed at the government, but they are felt by the people. And they have served to concentrate growing anti-Americanism and a sense of distrust of Washington across much of Russia, most especially in Moscow.

I circulated a piece I wrote for the campaign noting some of the lessons I had learned from Jack Matlock, who had served as U.S. ambassador to Moscow 1987 to 1991. As one of the key negotiators who helped bring the original Cold War to an end, he confirmed something that Mikhail Gorbachev often says, namely, that a "clear commitment" had been given by the West to Russia that NATO would not expand eastward.[12]

What happened next? Germany was reunified under NATO during the presidency of George H. W. Bush.[13] The Czech Republic, Hungary, and Poland joined NATO under President Bill Clinton.[14] Bulgaria, Estonia, Latvia, Lithuania, Romania, Slovakia, and Slovenia joined under George W. Bush.[15] And under President Barack Obama, Albania and Croatia joined.[16] NATO's armed forces and pledges of mutual defense had come up to the very borders of Russia. What were the Russians to think?

In the run-up to the 2016 election, antagonizing Russia still garnered bipartisan support. At a New York event in 2014, U.S. ambassador to the United Nations Samantha Power described for an audience how she tries to teach her five-year-old son "the truth about her work": "One of [my son's] very dear friends was trying to take the toys he was playing with and my son said—and I never guessed he would be capable of this— 'You're just like Putin!'" According to the *New York Times* coverage, "The audience howled in appreciation."[17]

Other senior officials in the Obama administration didn't just talk an anti-Russian game, they often took similar needlessly aggressive action against the Russian government. Before Russia seized control of Crimea and prior to the escalation of a low-grade military conflict in

Eastern Ukraine, Obama's assistant secretary of state Victoria Nuland played a visible role in support of a popular uprising to overthrow Ukrainian President Viktor Yanukovych, whose election was deemed by international observers to have been fair.[18] Yanukovych had provoked the ire of Western officials by rejecting an association agreement with the European Union while seeking Russian help in buying $15 billion in Ukrainian government bonds and reductions in the price of gas.[19]

Nuland and other Americans publicly fanned the flames of protest. A call between Nuland (a former top foreign policy advisor to Vice President Dick Cheney before working in the Obama administration, married to arch-neoconservative scholar Robert Kagan) and U.S. ambassador to Ukraine Geoffrey Pyatt was intercepted and leaked to the media.[20] The call shows that Nuland and Pyatt freely discussed barring Ukrainian opposition leaders from accepting government posts, as if the United States had the right to dictate to foreign leaders the composition of their government and their foreign policy.

"Fuck the EU," Nuland profanely said of undermining the European Union's more subtle tactics in favor of a more nakedly hawkish approach. Then serving as the U.S. assistant secretary of state for European and Eurasian affairs at the State Department, these comments understandably didn't sit well with many of her counterparts overseas.[21]

Childish tendencies of aggression and belligerence such as these made it clear to me that America's leadership in Washington had lost the capacity to look at themselves from the outside-in. Consider the more mature approach of Winston Churchill: "There is no doubt that trying to put oneself in the position of the other party to see how things look to him is one way, and perhaps the best way, of being able to feel and peer dimly into the unknowable future," the once and future British prime minister said as leader of the opposition of the Soviet Union in the early days of the Cold War.[22] Churchill showed that a degree of understanding is necessary to properly gauge world events.

Now try to put yourself in the position of the other party, as Churchill would say, and see how things look from Moscow. The United

States filled the vacuum of Eastern Europe with powerful NATO forces from countries that boast a combined economic might more than thirty times the size of Russia's, placing forces right up to their borders, and overthrowing a flawed but democratically elected government. They did all this while preaching to Russia and the world about the need to be peaceful and respectful of democracy. If one goes by Churchill's direction to put oneself in the position of one's opposition, how do we look?

From the Russian point of view, the United States was guilty of violating spoken and written agreements that were designed to ensure Russian security. Russia hawks like to point to the Budapest Memorandum of 1994, in which Ukraine voluntarily gave up its nuclear weapons (it had for a short time the world's third-largest nuclear stockpile after the fall of the Soviet Union) in exchange for a signed agreement from Russia, the United Kingdom, and the United States to respect Ukraine.[23] Hawks may point to the language in the Memorandum that forbade aggression against Ukraine, which is certainly happening now in the eastern Donbass region of the country's border with Russia. But one of the conditions of the Memorandum was to also refrain from using economic pressure on Ukraine to influence its politics.[24] Considering the strong-arm tactics of American officials in Ukrainian politics, it would seem to a Russian that we violated the agreement as well.

Or consider Vice President Joe Biden's public boasts that he held up a loan to force the Ukrainian government to fire a prosecutor investigating government corruption (and possibly Hunter Biden's role in the natural gas company Burisma Holdings).

"You're not getting the billion," Biden recounted his actions before a session of the Council on Foreign Relations in 2018. "I'm leaving in six hours. If the prosecutor is not fired, you're not getting the money. Well, son of a bitch. He got fired."[25]

This is what Putin, his inner circle, and countless other Russians mean when they bitterly denounced the hypocrisy of the Obama administration and many of their predecessors in Washington. It would lead anyone to be deeply suspicious or distrustful about the designs, real and imagined, of American neoconservatives embedded in both parties. Rightfully so as they proved themselves worthy of deep suspicion and distrust, as I would subsequently learn from their misdeeds against Trump supporters like me.[26] At a Brookings Institution event, Victoria Nuland declared that America's allies: "[M]ust contribute to new 'spearhead' force, which will allow us to speed forces to trouble spots."[27] The alliance's easternmost member states—Estonia, Latvia, Lithuania, Poland, Romania, and Bulgaria—all either border Russia or share the Black Sea with annexed Crimea.

I am not suggesting we need to worry about these actions as a matter of good manners, and certainly not out of a sense of moral equivalency. But is this a smart way to treat a country that spans eleven times zones and bristles with nuclear weapons? Do we need to be at odds with such a great world power when tensions are rising with another great world power, the People's Republic of China? Might we consider working just a little harder to find common ground with the Russians?

Donald Trump instinctively voiced similar questions when he launched his presidential campaign. As a low-level advisor, I tried to provide the campaign with the resources to translate that common-sense appraisal of the situation into a fleshed out policy vision. I was hardly the only voice in that growing crowd—candidate Trump had dozens of advisors providing his campaign with memoranda and research documents. And while my ideas were certainly unorthodox when compared to the dogmas of the foreign policy establishment, they hardly justified the terrible actions members of the press corps and IC would take against me.

■ ■ ■

While I happened to share a broader policy vision with candidate Trump, I certainly did not whisper in his ear. That being said, I did try to help the campaign in a number of concrete ways.

Sam Clovis and I met with Jon Huntsman, the former Utah governor who served as U.S. ambassador to China under President Obama, for his thoughts on reforming the structure and processes of the National Security Council, which started out as a small secretariat and had bloated to more than 400 people. We scheduled our meeting for August 3, 2016, upstairs in a conference room at my 590 Madison Avenue office. Jon had specific ideas for streamlining the staff and performance of the NSC. As the world would later see during the Trump administration, the bloat and dysfunction would continue to be a source of trouble for the administration.[28]

I also provided background on statements made by some of his Republican challengers during the primary debates. As candidate Trump prepared to pivot from the primary to general election debates against Hillary Clinton, I provided ideas and facts for the campaign team to consider. I did further, deeper research on Hillary Clinton's track record as Obama's first secretary of state, focusing on the contradictions in her policies and statements, or places where she or President Obama had contradicted their stated policies. Little did I know at the time, but this same cast of characters and their Democratic operatives were secretly working to undermine some of the core principles of the U.S. Constitution. Both inside government and in the private sector, it may stand as the biggest contradiction of all. Years later, the foreign policy ramifications of these historic abuses live on.

Before getting incessantly chased by false allegations from reporters, I had a final chance to offer my ideas on September 19, 2016. Following candidate Trump's call for the United States to "take the oil" from ISIS, he was widely criticized by mainstream media commentators for taking a mercenary view of the struggle against Islamic extremism. I worked to offer a few facts that provided a fuller picture. The Islamic State of Iraq and Syria raked in up to $1.2 billion in 2014 from oil and refined products.[29] A significant proportion of that money was suspected to be used in support of terrorism. I offered a bit of context and related background on the range of policy mechanisms by which the U.S. government had historically treated the assets of our enemies during past skirmishes.

■ ■ ■

Although I was just a junior unpaid advisor, I did gain a few privileges. The best ones typically involved engaging in intellectual debates. One of those opportunities came in June 2016, when I was invited to Blair House, known as the U.S. president's guest house. Built in 1824, Blair House is an old brick Federal-style mansion sitting in Lafayette Park. Indian Ambassador Arun Singh and his diplomatic staff asked me to join a roundtable discussion with other foreign policy experts during the Washington visit of Narendra Modi, prime minister of India.

Before we met the prime minister, I congregated with my fellow invitees and milled around Blair House. Between the sashed curtains, the large windows of the room overlooked the green of Lafayette Park on a summer afternoon. In one of the side rooms in the mansion, I happened to see Strobe Talbott, president of the Brookings Institution. A well-known Washington insider, former *Time* magazine columnist, and deputy secretary of state under President Clinton, Talbott had been a close friend and ally of Bill Clinton for decades, going back to their time together as graduate students at Oxford University in the United Kingdom. The group had entered into a robust exchange of views, as they say in diplomacy. Neera Tanden, president of the leftist Center for American Progress and another Clinton ally, sat next to Talbott. Another Washington Beltway presence and former Obama administration official, Kurt Campbell joined the group that was now well stocked with Democrats. Fairly quickly, Strobe began tearing into Donald Trump. This kind of exchange would have been expected of a typical gathering of Trump critics at the Brookings Institution, but such belligerent rhetoric seemed decidedly inappropriate for an event where the Indian prime minister had tried to gather varying perspectives. I countered that an essential issue in the upcoming election would be whether American foreign policy had been wisely managed or needed a thorough rethinking.

After we made our way into the main conference room with Prime Minister Modi, I was able to weave some talking points I'd prepared into conversation with the prime minister.

First I suggested that the United States might view ensuring stability in Pakistan as more important to the future security of America and India than a continued focus on the many conflicts of the Middle East. I immediately saw that Modi's line of thinking intersected well with candidate Trump's. Both saw the logic in adopting integrated approaches to global economics, trade, and security to create greater stability in the world. There was no reason each of our countries couldn't live peacefully and in friendship with other emerging powers, including Russia and China. The full extent of any mention I made of Russia or China was: "If we create smarter ties between New Delhi and Washington, we are not bound to be adversaries with these other emerging powers." That was it.

I also noted that building upon and leveraging the close alignment of our shared national interest was paramount. We needed to avoid unnecessary distractions, implying that the snares of Iraq and Afghanistan kept us from more important priorities. A posture of mutual respect could help South Asia, and indeed America, overcome decades of enmity.

I brought up some of my other points in our group conversation. During the meeting with so many old "Beltway" insiders from the Washington set, it became clear that the United States' foreign policy was at an inflection point. American voters would soon choose between the Democrats' foreign policy as displayed by the Obama administration and former secretary of state Hillary Clinton, and a completely reevaluated set of priorities and methods from Donald Trump.

■ ■ ■

There were other innocuous events on my schedule from this time that would come back to haunt me and members of the Trump campaign for many years to come.

Shlomo Weber, a professor of economics in Russia and at Southern Methodist University in Dallas, invited me to speak to the graduating class of 2016 at the New Economic School in Moscow—an event independent of my work with the campaign. The school was founded soon after I had first visited the Soviet Union, and many of its graduates have distinguished careers in the private sector, academia, and government. To an American capitalist, this young institution stood as a symbol of Russia's thrilling departure from the Communist economics of the Soviet era and Cold War.

I ran the invitation by Corey Lewandowski to make sure that the campaign didn't see any issues with it and suggested that perhaps Donald Trump might want to speak in my place. It was a well organized venue in which the candidate could display his foreign policy credentials. Presidential candidates often use foreign trips to showcase what they would look like as America's head of state abroad. Barack Obama himself had held a European rally before an ecstatic crowd in Berlin when he was still a presidential candidate. If an American citizen's addressing this particular institution seemed controversial, it certainly hadn't impeded another one of the school's former speakers: President Obama had given an address there seven years earlier, and no one had seemed to mind. But I mistakenly assumed that candidate Trump and his supporters would be subject to the same standards as conventional politicians. As the world would soon learn from the two-tiered justice system of the subsequent years, nothing could be further from the truth.

Corey replied to my email: "If you want to do this, it would be outside of your role with the DJT for President campaign. I am certain Mr. Trump will not be able to attend."[30]

I asked Shlomo to note in his introduction of me as a speaker that I came to the New Economic School as a private citizen and a business executive. I also stressed the same point at the top of my remarks, adding that I found it encouraging to be among many students who studied after hours and on weekends while holding down demanding jobs, just as I had done.

My July speech was similar to the seminars and presentations I had delivered at various top academic institutions in Moscow long before my involvement with the Trump campaign. I spoke about the nexus of energy and security concerns at the heart of Eurasia in the Central Asian republics, as well as in Russia and China. My speech lasted more than thirty-nine minutes. I harkened back to the seminal Long Telegram of February 1946, in which diplomat George Kennan famously argued that, "At bottom of Kremlin's neurotic view of world affairs is traditional and instinctive Russian sense of insecurity."[31]

While the main topic of my speech was international political economy, I did mention in passing:

> While the perspectives of leaders in Russia and the CIS countries have fundamentally advanced in recent decades, the West's combination of a nearly universal critical tone and continued proactive steps to encourage leadership change overseas may understandably advance a residual level of insecurity. Today, a broad Western consensus has defined these societies as largely state-controlled, ridden with corruption or both. Although that may in some ways be partially true in any country including in the United States, recent history has exposed opportunities to build upon mutual interests in ways that are often hidden by this intolerance.

I noted that in President Vladimir Putin's executive order on foreign policy, signed the day he began his third term on May 7, 2012, his first point called for policies based on, "principles of equality, non-interference in internal affairs and respect for mutual interests" with the United States.[32] I suggested that was a good place for both sides to start. This statement subsequently proved to be more than a bit prophetic. If Russia did interfere in U.S. elections in 2016 through social media, as some would later allege, the government in Moscow was simply treating our politics as our diplomats and NGOs had treated theirs.[33] You don't have to agree with that judgment or hold our systems to be morally equal. But seeing our apparent hypocrisy through Russian eyes helps one understand why the Russian government might sometimes react the way it does.

One bit would later stand out to critics: "Meanwhile, the United States and other developed powers have often criticized these regions for continuing methods prevalent during the Cold War. Yet ironically, Washington and other Western capitals have impeded potential progress through their often hypocritical focus on democratization, inequality, corruption, and regime change."

Some failed foreign policy makers on the way out of the Obama administration might have taken offense at that. But it seemed to me then, and even more now, completely evident. As would again arise during the American policy elite's multiple Ukraine debacles, the desire to interfere in the regimes of other countries often makes the United States appear supremely hypocritical. Inequality? Until the economy began to boom in the early years of the Trump administration, inequality at home had been steadily increasing.

I can understand why my viewpoint might rankle and disturb some, including people in the comfortable policy circles of Washington. No one ever died from being rankled and disturbed. In fact, as public figures, foreign policy practitioners in the government should expect criticism when they fail to advance the public interest. Immediately following my talk, I heard from someone in the audience that the former U.S. ambassador to Russia Michael McFaul had been writing snarky tweets about my remarks. Unlike McFaul, the Obama/Clinton architect of the disastrous "reset" policy, I wasn't so thin-skinned as to take his critiques personally.[34] I didn't see it as a big deal. I was, after all, nothing but a private citizen exercising my freedom of speech in a benign academic institution. As journalists began spinning McFaul's remarks into hit pieces against myself and the Trump campaign, I decided to give Hope Hicks a heads-up that a few voices had latched onto some fabricated story lines. Although a little blowback from the likes of McFaul might be conceivable, what I got was, of course, much more than a bit of simple blowback.

Instead of taking my criticism like professionals, McFaul and other members of the foreign policy establishment decided to tar and feather me. Thanks to their actions, I was being watched by some of their former colleagues in the Obama administration. How closely, I had no idea yet.

For inviting me to give the speech, Shlomo Weber would later be interrogated by the FBI at "Madeline's Cafe" [*sic*] in Dallas.[35] The following July he joined a long list of other academics, many holding American passports, who would be interrogated about their interactions with the infamous Carter Page.

■ ■ ■

On the evening of Saturday, July 9, 2016, just one night after my second Moscow speech as a private citizen, I flew back across the Atlantic from JFK airport in New York to London's Heathrow airport. I was there to attend a Cambridge University conference, "2016's Race to Change the World." Like on my trip to Moscow during the prior week, I was not acting as an official representative of the Trump campaign but participating in a private capacity as a foreign policy scholar. The program's declared intent was to bring together several influential U.S. practitioners of international relations to discuss the embryonic foreign policies of the 2016 campaign season. Coming just before the two-party nominating conventions, the speeches and white papers of the two campaigns might have begun to take on some real substance. Unfortunately, it proved to be an experience similar to the Washington insiders' meeting with Prime Minister Modi just a month earlier. Although I personally tried to laugh off the unbecoming partisanship, the level of disdain directed at candidate Trump by many of the attendees limited the potential for robust and open debate.

The event began with a welcoming dinner and discussion at Magdalene College as guests of Rowan Williams, the former Archbishop of

Canterbury and liberal theologian. I found the Most Reverend Williams to be friendly and engaging, a Welshman whose conical beard and chevron eyebrows made him the very appearance of an Oxford don. Most everyone at the dinner was quite friendly, though the sometimes-irritable former secretary of state Madeleine Albright occasionally peppered the evening's conversation with her characteristically dismissive remarks about Donald Trump. These stemmed both from specific policies she disliked and a personal loathing for the Republican candidate. I found it both amusing and appalling.

Also at the dinner was the event's organizer, Steven Schrage. Steve is a former official in the White House, Congress, and State Department who went to teach at the Harvard Institute of Politics. He's a good, smart guy who—not unlike my hosts a week earlier at the New Economic School—would subsequently be repaid for his hospitality by being swept up in Washington and the media's Russia hysteria.

Spending a few days at Cambridge listening to debates and participating in discussions is idyllic for a foreign policy enthusiast like me. Albright and former Republican congressman Vin Weber were the headliners, and both gave pretty good presentations in one moderated discussion with Steve Schrage.[36] Most people in the audience assumed that the foreign policy priorities they were debating would eventually be executed by a President Hillary Clinton. Although he was more subtle in some of his private comments to me on the sidelines, Weber would later say in August 2016 that he could not imagine remaining a Republican if Trump were to win.[37]

We also heard Sir Malcolm Rifkind, former UK minister of defence and foreign secretary describe the global challenges the next president would face. Former U.S. assistant secretary of state Jamie Rubin gave a less-than-inspired talk on Brexit. I didn't speak with Richard Dearlove, former director of MI6, but I did hear him give a strong anti-Trump speech. If I ever cross paths with Dearlove again, I'd like to ask him about his former employee Christopher Steele and the quality of his intelligence during their MI6 days together.[38]

And then there was Professor Stefan Halper.

Halper has a long and somewhat mysterious pedigree at the intersection of foreign policy, politics, and intelligence. He served in senior positions in the White House and State Department, as well as the presidential campaigns of George H. W. Bush and Ronald Reagan. He was close to members of the Bush family and had ties to the CIA. He has been accused, though he denies it, of having some involvement in the purloining of President Carter's debate briefing book for the Reagan campaign.[39] He was the former chairman of a bank in the Washington area said to have tight political connections.[40] Halper was not often in the news himself at the time, but he later told me a lot about his contacts in the media. So he was sometimes in the shadow of the news. A sturdy man with a wide face, Halper is known affectionately (and not) in some circles as "the Walrus."[41]

When I showed up for that welcoming dinner at Magdalene College, Halper was nearby, and we struck up a nice conversation. It was the first time I had ever spoken with him. After the official start of the conference the following morning, Halper gave a detailed talk on the impact of presidential decision-making on global dynamics. Speaking of Trump's "maverick candidacy," Halper, seemingly alone among most of the speakers, appeared to be open to the possibility that Trump could win. Halper marveled that Trump was able to convince a hostile media to give him, in effect, $2 billion worth of free advertising.

Towards the end of the conference, Halper seemed to be especially friendly with Dearlove. Before the former MI6 head's session, I remember the two of them huddling alone together near a window. I didn't eavesdrop on his whispered conversations with Dearlove in the bright passageway of Cambridge's modern Alison Richard Building, but I would later learn that Halper recorded his conversations with me without my consent during the next month.[42]

I eventually came to learn that Halper had a longtime connection to the intelligence world and to MI6. What I did not know until years later was that Halper would work as an informant for the FBI—Source 2, as he is identified in Horowitz's FISA Abuse report—and was tasked with explicitly investigating Sam Clovis, myself, and other supporters of the Trump campaign.

In 2018, Senator Chuck Grassley, then chairman of the Senate Judiciary Committee, began investigating the Department of Defense's Office of Net Assessment (ONA), the Pentagon's internal think tank, for awarding contracts to Halper between 2012 and 2018.[43] Grassley and his congressional staff looked into Halper's work with a range of individuals, including a Russian intelligence official listed as an advisor, who was later allegedly used for the discredited Steele report.[44]

"Given Professor Halper's intelligence connections and government funding, it is reasonable to ask whether he used any taxpayer money in his attempt to recruit Trump campaign officials as sources," Grassley said.[45] A lot of open questions remain about the details of the relationship between Halper and the FBI.

I saw Halper off and on throughout the conference, but the main substantive conversation we had at Cambridge came on my final day there. He invited me to his faculty home, cluttered with books like most of the academics I've known. Halper offered me his thoughts on the Trump campaign. He said that Trump's policy-making was too much on the fly, was disjointed from expertise, and that there was a need to build relationships with policy experts who could smooth the rough edges of Trump's proposals. While he spoke and offered specific names and events, I cracked open my laptop and took some notes. Halper also asked me several questions about membership in the Council on Foreign Relations. I told him I would be happy to help him seek a membership. I kept my promise and sent an email to the CFR on Halper's behalf.

After leaving Cambridge for the Republican National Convention in Cleveland, I thanked Halper by email for his insight. A few weeks later I received a response from Halper, in which he expressed interest in meeting with Sam Clovis the next time he was in Washington, D.C.[46] Hoping to be of service to the campaign, I put Clovis and Halper in contact. Halper again asked me for more information about becoming a member at the Council of Foreign Relations, before inviting me to lunch at the Cosmos Club the next time he was in Washington.[47]

Sam would later meet Halper at a Doubletree Hotel near Washington, D.C., for a chat. The Cambridge professor offered to provide research on China and handed over a few papers. Years later when I asked him how it went, Sam told me: "We talked like two professors in the faculty lounge sharing coffee. I immediately assessed I didn't need him and I didn't want him."

■ ■ ■

Moscow, Cambridge, and now a flight to Cleveland to attend the Republican National Convention. I travel a lot, but July 2016 was particularly busy.

The main week of the convention came after the party platforms had already been drafted. Having completely missed that prior week, I joined some of the final week's events. Upon my arrival that Monday afternoon, I was immediately immersed in a whirlwind of panel discussions. Along with many "global ambassadors" I attended the "Global Partners in Diplomacy" events sponsored by Global Cleveland and the Republican National Convention on Tuesday, July 19, 2016.[48] I listened to my colleagues from the Trump campaign volunteer committee, including Walid Phares, make excellent contributions during various panel discussions on terrorism and other topics.[49]

While attending this almost week-long event, a few final whimpers from the sidelines in the Quicken Loans Arena sporadically flickered across our screens and into the various events. Never Trump Republicans, including many Romney loyalists, mounted half-hearted efforts to un-bind the RNC delegates and change the supermajority rules.[50] I guess they imagined that the convention might somehow turn on the clear winner of the 2016 primary, disenfranchising millions of Republican primary voters in order to make Mitt Romney, Jeb Bush, or some other establishment stalwart the nominee. That effort at undoing a democratic outcome was skillfully blunted by Donald Trump. It was good practice for the challenges he would continue to face over the years that followed.

The Obama-friendly media fixated on a brief controversy over the Republican platform and Ukraine. Before I arrived in Cleveland, delegate Diana Denman allegedly attempted to insert amendment language calling for the United States to "provide lethal defensive weapons" to the Ukrainian government in an RNC platform subcommittee meeting.[51] J.D. Gordon, a member of the campaign's national security team and others realized that this went against the grain of Donald Trump's oft-spoken constructive desire to explore a better relationship with that region. J.D. persuaded the sub-committee co-chairman to table the amendment and replace "lethal defensive weapons" with "appropriate assistance." It was a welcome nuance that the media falsely tried to spin as a Chamberlain-in-Munich sell-out.

But the campaign stayed firm. Like so many others, it seemed to me to be a mistake for a new administration to come to power with a closed fist instead of an openness to negotiation. Before I had even arrived in Cleveland, J.D. Gordon had sent an update email to the members of our advisory team: "We are proud to say it is the strongest pro-Israel policy statement in the history of the Republican Party. We are also pleased to say we defeated red-line amendments like providing lethal assistance to Ukraine."[52]

After the decision had already been made in Cleveland, I would later tell the FBI agents at one of my interrogation sessions that I enthusiastically agreed with the change. About this, I had no reservations and no regrets. My emailed response to Gordon was unequivocal, "Fantastic, J.D., thanks a lot for the useful insights and context. As for the Ukrainian amendment, excellent work."[53]

The FBI's sworn filing against me would later assert that I "helped influence" the Republican Party "to alter [its] platform to be more sympathetic to the Russian cause."[54] Again, my denial and the easily verifiable facts that proved my non-involvement were not included. If the FBI had checked or listened to me, they would have learned that I arrived in Cleveland after the debate over the Ukraine platform plank had already taken place and been decided.[55] I simply wasn't in place to influence these meetings or anything related to the Republican platform. I wasn't even in the same state.

The new campaign chairman Paul Manafort supposedly worked to tamp down various disagreements among Republican delegates. Aside from some news articles, most of the people I knew both with and without connections to the Trump campaign had little sense of who exactly Manafort was. The one exception was Professor Halper, who told me during our July 13, 2016, meeting at his faculty home in Cambridge: "Paul is an old friend."[56] Though Manafort's earlier dealings abroad would later become common knowledge, he didn't seem to have any interaction with our volunteer foreign policy team that I could see. In fact, he had primarily been brought on board to manage the logistics of a national convention and presidential campaign—purely matters of domestic politics. The campaign must have realized it needed someone who understood the mechanics of the nomination process, as the rumblings of a Never Trump delegate-push swirled around the media. Manafort benefitted from previous experience in Republican party politics and seemed like someone who could help get the Trump campaign over the line. But apparently there may have been a lack of trust among some of these various political operatives. Just a few weeks after he joined the campaign, a recording emerged of Manafort telling RNC members that Trump was more sophisticated in person.[57]

When that recording was released, I sent an email to Stephen Miller and a few others that while Manafort "is clearly providing important assistance to the campaign regarding convention rules, tactics, etc., I firmly disagree that a fabricated image makeover is necessary. To the contrary, I strongly agree with what may perhaps be Corey's most famous quote: 'Let Trump be Trump.'"[58]

As I had written to members of the campaign back in April 2016: "One aspect of letting Trump be Trump has been his tendency not to shy away from taking on his opponents who have attacked him...."[59] I can't remember even hearing of Manafort before 2016 and certainly never met him, though that would not keep us from being falsely linked to some grand conspiracy.

Donald Trump did not disappoint when it came time for him to give his acceptance address in Cleveland. When he strode onto the stage on the evening of July 21, he took the podium, took command of the Republican Party, and prepared to take on Hillary Clinton.

As Mr. Trump contended for the presidency with Hillary Clinton, he also acquired secret enemies in the upper echelons of the bureaucracy: politically motivated FBI and Department of Justice officials who were preparing a convenient target to help them enact their "insurance policy."[60]

CHAPTER FOUR

THE START OF THE INTERNATIONAL FUGITIVE YEARS

"...efforts to influence the 2016 U.S. presidential election represent the most recent expression of...longstanding desire to undermine the U.S.-led liberal democratic order, but these activities demonstrated a significant escalation in directness, level of activity, and scope of effort compared to previous operations."

—Central Intelligence Agency (CIA), Federal Bureau of Investigation (FBI), and National Security Agency (NSA), January 6, 2017[1]

SEPTEMBER 2016

While I remained busy with my regular activities during the summer of 2016, strange questions from the media began to clutter my cell phone.

During the second day of the DNC Convention in Philadelphia, July 26, 2016, Damian Paletta of the *Wall Street Journal* texted me that: "We are told you met with Igor Sechin during your recent Moscow trip and discussed energy deals and the possibility of the U.S. Government of lifting sanctions on him and others."[2]

I had never met Sechin before. Not only did I not know the man, I began to wonder who was feeding these lies to the media. Rex Tillerson, future secretary of state, had developed a close business relationship with Sechin during his time as CEO at ExxonMobil. Later that year, Paletta wrote that Tillerson had received a high state honor from President Putin, Russia's Order of Friendship.[3] As I had noted that week in my slide presentation for another speech under the auspices of the New Economic School, Tillerson's appointment offered a great contrast to the relationship between Obama's first secretary of state Hillary Clinton and President Putin who, "[e]ffectively gave each other a de facto Order of Mutual Distrust."[4]

It seemed that conspiratorially minded pundits could still conceive that Tillerson might have a connection to the false allegations that had been bandied around the past several months.[5] As this new Red Scare heated up, any American who had legitimately achieved success in Russia at some point in his career was often immediately considered a suspect.

Reporters from the *Washington Post*, the *New York Times*, *Politico*, CNN, and others all began contacting me during the summer of 2016. I didn't know it then, but like rodents on a running wheel, they were all furiously trying to verify false claims fed to them by the Democrats' opposition research team. Many months later and well past the election, these falsehoods would be revealed in their entirety when BuzzFeed published the now infamous "Steele Dossier" in January 2017.[6] But at the time, I had no idea why reporters kept calling me with ludicrous questions that were remarkable in their detail.

The *Washington Post* began filling in my portrait in early August with a profile by Tom Hamburger and Steven Mufson. Like Paletta, they were among the first journalists to ask about the false allegations regarding Igor Sechin and Igor Divyekin. Those fell flat, and I quickly dispelled the lies from the Democrats' consultants, but the *Post* didn't stop there. Instead, they highlighted one quote from my New Economic School speech about the West's "hypocritical focus" on democracy.

A rare exception of truth in a sea of falsehoods, the *Washington Post* did correctly note that my Moscow speech had suggested that investment might be the key to better relations. They accurately reported that I had said the United States should provide Russia with "emerging technologies and potential capital market access contingent upon the U.S.'s refocus toward resolution of domestic challenges," while Russia would approve "collaborative partnerships in the energy industry and other diversified sectors."

But these *Post* reporters relied on false witnesses and creative writing when reporting about my meeting with Prime Minister Modi. Mufson and Hamburger reported that this "little-known adviser to Donald Trump stunned a gathering of high-powered Washington foreign policy experts meeting with the visiting prime minister of India, going off topic with effusive praise for Russian President Vladimir Putin and Trump.

"The adviser, Carter Page, hailed Putin as stronger and more reliable than President Obama, according to three people who were present at the closed-door meeting at Blair House—and then touted the positive effect a Trump presidency would have on U.S.–Russia relations."[7]

I never mentioned Putin to Modi or put down the current president, and I only mentioned Russia once in passing. I spoke of generally building friendships with emerging powers, including India. And the "three people who were present"? Who was this objective group sufficiently alarmed to go running to the *Washington Post*? Could they by any chance be Strobe Talbott, then president of the Brookings Institution with whom I had exchanged views before the Modi meeting began? Or Neera Tanden, the president of the Center for American Progress who was sitting next to him? Or Kurt Campbell, who had been an assistant secretary of state under President Obama?

If the incestuous nature of how these stories were constructed is not yet clear, consider another source for the story.

Of my supposed nefarious activities, Mufson and Hamburger quote foreign policy expert David Kramer saying, "It scares me." Kramer oversaw aspects of Russia and Ukraine policy at the State Department during the George W. Bush administration.[8] He told Mufson and Hamburger that my speech in Moscow and recent comments by Trump on the possibility of lifting sanctions against Moscow were "deeply unsettling."[9]

Kramer was later forced to admit in federal court in Florida to discussing the contents of the Dodgy Dossier not just with the *Washington Post*, but with many other journalists, including Carl Bernstein.[10] He shared information from the report with Victoria Nuland, whose policies as assistant secretary of state I had previously criticized in academic forums.[11]

That federal deposition in Florida also revealed that David Kramer had walked out of a room in 2016, leaving BuzzFeed reporter Ken Bensinger alone with the Steele document and a camera phone. Kramer testified: "I said, 'you know, I got a phone call to make, and I had to go to the bathroom, so I'll let you be because I don't read well when people are looking at me breathing down my neck,' and so I left him to read for 20, 30 minutes." Following all his spreading of the salacious material, Kramer later expressed shock that the document appeared in BuzzFeed.[12]

As allegations from Steele's Dodgy Dossier were being spread around town, the coordination between the media, the Obama administration, and other leading Democrats had already begun. By the end of August, Senate Minority Leader Reid issued his public letter to James Comey asking that I be investigated for public comments I had made in Moscow.[13] It was upon similar false premises from the Democratic hit squad that Adam Schiff, then the ranking Democrat on the House Intelligence Committee, claimed the "Kremlin has its tentacles into the Trump campaign."[14]

As the abstract dots accumulated to fill out my fictional portrait, I emailed Hope Hicks clarifying that I had been grossly misquoted by the *Washington Post*. I wrote to her: "I'm disappointed that this has become a frequent hassle for you, but disclosing the full truth in some format might help finally put these conspiracy theories to bed."[15]

■ ■ ■

As this scandalous public relations campaign gained full stream—promoted by Steele and paid for by the Democrats—the FBI began the process of secretly surveilling me under the Foreign Intelligence Surveillance Act (FISA). They wiretapped my phones. They read my emails. I learned in 2020 that when I was hiding out from the media and the death threats in a hotel in Princeton, New Jersey, agents rifled through my personal effects while I was out. They took cellphone pictures of my personal items, then stored those images without the proper procedures required by law to protect a target's privacy.[16]

Thanks to a few of the subsequent investigations by U.S. Department of Justice Inspector General Michael Horowitz and others, I now know that I was also being recorded when I met with the FBI's confidential informant, Stefan Halper, in August. When I visited Dr. Halper at his home in a Northern Virginia suburb of Washington, I never expected anything but an innocuous visit and an interesting conversation.

Back on that hot August day in 2016, I had no reason to be suspicious. After passing a horse farm, I remember a long driveway leading past a security gate to a big country home. I received a warm welcome from Dr. Halper and his partner, Lezlee. They had previously co-authored a book about Tibet, which the professor gave me a copy of.[17] When we sat down to talk, Halper expressed interest in the inner workings of the campaign and ideas for what a Trump foreign policy might eventually look like. We talked about the Trump campaign's prospects and a range of other topics. It was the first of several meetings I'd have with Halper over the next eight months. After the attacks by the Democrats and the media escalated dramatically in September 2016, I met with Halper at his home again. In December, Halper invited me to lunch at the Cosmos Club, a prestigious social club for the Washington elite. Other meetings continued throughout the months that followed, including in January 2017, when Halper made a special trip from his home in Virginia to visit me for coffee at my hotel a few blocks from the White House. We would continue our conversation at the Cosmos Club again on April 6, 2017.

By that time, I was subject to nearly constant attacks from the media and federal authorities. I told the professor about the crush of media and death threats that were pouring in. Halper was well aware of these challenges. Portraying himself as a kind and sympathetic supporter who understood the life-threatening risks I continued to endure, his benevolent generosity with his time and hospitality didn't seem out of place. After becoming an international pariah, I appreciated someone from the Washington establishment who would still dare to speak with me.

Over fifteen months after first visiting his house, I began to realize that there had been something odd about Halper's continued eagerness to talk. Far from the kind soul that he had portrayed himself to be, Halper was out to entrap me. It had never occurred to me to question his motives.

At that first meeting back at home in the U.S., I'd responded to Halper's prompts by telling him that I had "literally never met" or "said one word to" Paul Manafort, who had not responded to a few emails I had sent him. The dishonest FBI case agent overseeing my surveillance did not find it necessary to share my truthful denials with the Office of Intelligence attorney overseeing a secret warrant against me as a suspected agent of a foreign power (in which I was supposedly in league with Manafort).[18]

I talked with Halper about Igor Sechin and Igor Divyekin, whom the DNC consultant Steele had falsely named as my two Putin-connected handlers. As I told Halper, I had never met either of them. In fact, I told him I didn't even know who Divyekin was. When the FBI submitted sworn testimony before the Foreign Intelligence Surveillance Court that must approve all FISA surveillance applications, the FBI claimed I did not "provide any specific details to refute, dispel, or clarify the media reporting" regarding my contacts with the two Igors.[19] There was no mention of my answer to Source 2, nor did the application, presented as sworn testimony before this secret court without any opportunity for review or any semblance of due process rights, disclose that I had denied having any knowledge about the WikiLeaks hack of the Democratic National Committee. My conversation with Halper was chock-full of such exculpatory evidence; it was systematically excised from the record. The FBI wanted to conduct surveillance on me, and the leaders of Crossfire

Hurricane were willing to toss aside facts from sworn testimony in their continuing efforts to build their case.

■ ■ ■

Meanwhile, the crush of unwanted attention continued. Looking to get away from the constant buzz of the media, I planned a vacation in eastern Pennsylvania starting in late September 2016. I was looking forward to bike rides and continuing my work in relative peace amidst the chaos of a presidential election year. Instead, what I got was a dramatic escalation in attacks that would eventually force me to flee the country, relegated to the life of an international fugitive.

Late morning on September 23, 2016, I saw Michael Isikoff's Yahoo! News article with a doctored graphic superimposing me in front of a Russian flag. The hit piece described me as Donald Trump's "back channel" to senior Russian officials. If true, Isikoff was exposing a collusion conspiracy between a campaign promising to lift sanctions in exchange for, say, more hacking of the Democrats, or more social media posts by Russian trolls. Yahoo! News included a light sprinkling of "allegeds" and "if confirmeds" throughout the piece, but flooded my story in an egregiously false light.[20]

As I already noted, Radio Free Europe—paid for by my own government—helped the Democrats' election interference campaign by broadcasting the Yahoo! News story to the entire world. For all practical purposes, it effectively burned every business relationship I had built in Europe, Russia, the Middle East, and Asia.

I went from being a private person to suddenly having my name "trending" on Twitter. Two and a half days after Yahoo posted the Isikoff article, I sent a letter to FBI Director James Comey. I thought that if I could reason with the FBI, after working to support the Bureau for many years, this might be resolved easily.

"I have not met this year with any sanctioned official in Russia despite the fact that there are no restrictions on U.S. persons speaking with such individuals," I wrote. "I understand that my stake in PJSC Gazprom has also been brought to your attention. For your information, last month I sold my American Depository Receipts and at this time maintain no holding in the company within any of my investment entities or personal accounts."[21]

I had, in fact, divested my small stake in Gazprom in August 2016, for $798.98—a net loss of $5,110.02.

"In bothering the Bureau with such repeated appeals, the parties who have requested my investigation clearly fail to appreciate the risks they create for America with these shenanigans," I wrote to Comey. "Instead of allowing the staff of the FBI to focus the nation's limited resources on real threats, these desperate and unfounded calls for my investigation as a private citizen to advance political interests based on nothing more than preposterous mainstream media reports is a true disgrace.

"Having interacted with members of the U.S. Intelligence Community including the FBI and CIA for many decades, I appreciate the limitations on your staff's time and assets. Although I have not been contacted by any member of your team in recent months, I would eagerly await their call to discuss any final questions they might possibly have in the interest of helping them put these outrageous allegations to rest while allowing each of us to shift our attention to relevant matters."[22]

I had made one of the most important decisions in my life. I decided early on that since I had nothing to hide, and corrupt forces in Washington had already effectively shredded my privacy, I would welcome the FBI's treating me as an open book. Later I hired attorneys to advise me at key inflection points, especially after the Rosenstein–Sessions DOJ allowed Mueller's team of Democratic-donor prosecutors effectively to take the reins of the witch hunt.[23] But for the most part, I went through this gauntlet without any legal advice at all. My strategy was simply to try helping the FBI refocus on the truth. I offered to meet with Senator Reid or anyone else. I would not run. Aside from the extensive personal security precautions necessary due to the terror threats I continued to

endure, I would not shelter-in-place behind a phalanx of lawyers whenever federal or Congressional authorities wanted to interrogate me. I
would stand my ground and answer any question, even if it was under
oath and under the always lurking threat of a perjury trap.

Along the way, I found some reporters who were occasionally willing
to give me a fair shake. One of them was Josh Rogin of the *Washington
Post*. Denying the meetings, I told Rogin over the days after the Isikoff
article broke that: "All of these accusations are just complete garbage."[24]
That word "garbage" made it into the headline.

I opened the door to my accusers, but James Comey and his minions
chose instead to continue focusing on the Democrats' Steele Dossier. As
the Democrats continued to press their narrative with their journalist
pals, the FBI would eventually be forced to terminate its relationship with
Steele because he bragged to the media about being an FBI informant.
They let him run with it for a long time though, using a willing and
uncritical media to craft a public indictment of my character. It wasn't
until Steele explicitly disclosed his relationship with the FBI to David
Corn of *Mother Jones* in late October that the FBI finally fired him.[25]

We now know that Steele's Dodgy Dossier had been helped along by
Bruce Ohr, an Obama-era Justice official.[26] Ohr served as a go-between
for the Democrat-hired consultants at Fusion GPS and the FBI. He took
Steele's opposition research from his wife Nellie, who worked for Fusion-
GPS, and passed it along to FBI agents on the Russia case. He did not
properly inform his supervisors of his role as self-appointed intermediary
between Steele and the FBI.[27]

The dossier would reach the highest rungs of FBI leadership. We
know from the loquacious Mr. Comey himself that the then-FBI director
deliberately discussed the Steele Dossier with Donald Trump days before
his inauguration and later handed off other confidential information to
a friendly law professor to leak to the media.[28]

DOJ Inspector General Horowitz concluded in an earlier investigation that, "Comey set a dangerous example for the over 35,000
current FBI employees—and the many thousands more former FBI

employees—who similarly have access to or knowledge of non-public information."[29]

The Department of Justice declined to prosecute James Comey for the earlier leaks, even though his actions may have been a violation of his FBI employment agreement and the clear standards set by the DOJ and FBI.[30] Nor would the fired FBI acting director Andrew McCabe be prosecuted for lying to the FBI about leaking to the *Wall Street Journal* for a story about the Clinton Foundation.[31]

■ ■ ■

As the torrent of news broke, I could see the problems and distractions that all this was causing the Trump campaign. Already overloaded with her daily responsibilities, Hope Hicks had accurately told Mufson and Hamburger that I was an "informal foreign policy adviser" who "does not speak for Mr. Trump or the campaign."[32]

Realistically speaking, it is hard to think of anything more the Trump campaign might have done in the face of these incessant false allegations from the Democrats and their allies in the media. I would have done the same thing in their position. The maxim is always to protect the candidate, and they were faced with a constant barrage of bad press that extended far beyond the lies in the Dossier. The election was just weeks away, and the ability to refute such wide-ranging accusations against me would take, as it turned out, years. It's never a good thing for a campaign staffer—or, in my case, an unpaid advisor—to become a story. To mitigate the incalculable damage stemming from the predicament, I told everyone that I was taking a leave of absence from working with the campaign. "This is another distraction that's been created here," I similarly told Rogin. "There's so little time between now and the election, this is in the best interests of the candidate."[33]

Following my first truncated escape to Pennsylvania and as all this continued to unfold, I decided to leave the United States on a prolonged business trip. The FBI had refused to heed my pleas about death threats, so I traveled abroad in part to avoid risking my life at home. Apart from this existential motivation, I had financial reasons to travel to South Africa. Thanks to Christopher Steele's work with his Democratic and government sponsors, my business prospects in Europe and Russia were dim to non-existent. South Africa is a resource-rich country with the kinds of extractive industries in which I had a great deal of experience, so I flew to Johannesburg to meet with intermediates of a large integrated chemical and petroleum company. While nothing ultimately came of it, the meetings were long and substantive. Insulated from most of the hysteria created by the U.S. media and their political partners, I never got the sense that I was "radioactive" in that part of the world.

During this first international trip post–character assassination, the Geiger counter began to click again. In October 2016, I was subjected to an interrogation by British Customs at Heathrow about the purpose of my visit. Their former MI6 officer Steele and their colleagues from the U.S. Intelligence Community had likely helped to convince them that I might be meeting my Russian handler, some fictional Igor or another, outside the British Museum on a park bench. Tired from the flight and a little rattled by my treatment at the airport, I showed up at the door of a friend of mine, a woman in London who had often invited me to stay at her house while I was in town.

She seemed deeply concerned from the moment I arrived. "I'm sorry Carter," she eventually explained after some time catching up. "I just don't need this kind of drama in my life right now."

Of course, I couldn't blame her. Who wants to attract MI5, MI6, GCHQ, or any kind of surveillance into one's home, which my brief presence almost surely had already caused? Comey and Co. had helped the Democrats successfully ruin my business and forced me to solidify my existence as an international fugitive.

In the weeks leading up to the 2016 election, I began receiving a string of terror threats, many of them picking up on the theme of my being some kind of traitor. A series of these death threats echoing the "treasonous" language came from the 918 area code—Tulsa and north-eastern Oklahoma. Consider this sample voicemail from early 2017:

> We know what the fuck you've been doing, you piece of shit mother fucker. You think you're not, you know you're not in fucking in cahoots with fucking Rosneft and every fucking Russian oligarch over there? You fucking half-wit, fucking piece of shit. You deserve everything you fucking get. Every fucking thing you get. If it was up to me, after we fucking tried you for treason, we'd take you out in the street and beat the fucking piss out of you with baseball bats, you cock suck-ing mother fucker. Next time you turn your back on your fucking country, you'll fucking regret it.

Only one thing truly frightened me about his call. The caller had somehow got hold of my personal number. If he could do that, what else could he do to track me down and carry out his threats?

■ ■ ■

Even before I took my leave of absence from the Trump campaign in September 2016, I was contacted by a man from a research firm with deep ties to the intelligence agencies.

"You're being set up my friend," he told me.

"By whom?"

"The Clinton campaign and a law firm affiliated with them are pay-ing very expensive, London-based private investigators to go after you and other Trump supporters."[34]

I heard similar things from other friends in the Intelligence Com-munity. They all told me what I had already guessed—it was almost certain that I was being watched and listened to at every turn. I realized that the FBI, armed with the ability to retroactively look at my commu-nications and contacts within the campaign, had found me a convenient platform from which to mount a political investigation and smear job of Donald Trump in the last weeks before the election.

It is against my nature to sit still and say nothing in the face of such attacks. By mid-October, just weeks after the Isikoff story broke, I had already begun to put together a picture of the scale of this shadow campaign against the Trump campaign. With the full weight of the U.S. government looming over me like a silent monolith, I decided to write to Frank-Walter Steinmeier, chairman of the Organization for Security and Cooperation in Europe (OSCE) in Vienna. A distinguished statesman, Steinmeier became president of Germany in March 2017 while I was being grilled by Comey's FBI agents.[35]

I was familiar with OSCE's predecessor organization from my days as an arms control action officer in the Pentagon during my Navy service. I knew that the OSCE took a deep interest in human rights, including political rights and freedom of speech. I also knew that the OSCE had an Election Observation Mission in the United States, which suggested there might be an opportunity for civil rights protection after the Obama administration's failure.[36]

"I am not currently affiliated with any political campaign, but the continued personal attacks by the 'Hillary for America' campaign against me based on completely fabricated, inaccurate information help to clearly demonstrate these violations," I wrote to Steinmeier.[37]

I set out the litany of attacks I had received, from Senator Harry Reid to the whisper campaign against me behind the media attacks after giving a speech that was unpopular in Washington policy circles. I wrote that not all journalists bit the story, but noted that the Clinton campaign's decision to put out a media release not long after the filing of the Isikoff article suggested a high degree of coordination between that campaign and friendly journalists.[38]

I wrote to Steinmeier that the "European Court of Human Rights has called for governments to 'display restraint' and to accept that even offensive, shocking, and disturbing speech can contribute to pluralism and must usually be tolerated in a democratic society. This is especially true during electoral campaigns and of speech that 'targets' government authorities, elected officials, and candidates for office.

"Notwithstanding these basic human rights principles, I have included my July Moscow speech for reference as an Appendix. I am confident you will agree that it is not offensive, shocking, or disturbing in any way, except perhaps from the perspective of those hawkish parties which maintain a preference for what I have previously pointed out to be failed interventionist approaches…

"All of the available evidence makes clear that I have been targeted for potential reprisal merely for vocalizing my thoughts in a free academic forum," I wrote.

I did not write to this international organization lightly. Nor did I write out of despair or personal pique. While I wasn't sure if any action would be taken, I wanted to create a record of the historic wrongdoing in Washington. I wanted to throw into stark relief the hypocrisy of the agents of our own government violating the very precepts we so intently preach to others. And I wanted, frankly, to let them feel the sting of being exposed a bit before an objective party, and perhaps to take a second look at themselves and what they were doing to a presidential election in the process.

Like so many supporters of the Trump campaign, I watched election night in delight as one mainstream news anchor after another displayed visible shock on the air as one state after another went red, contrary to all predictions. I heard Hillary Clinton say in her concession speech the next day, "Donald Trump is going to be our president… we owe him an open mind and a chance to lead."[39] As I heard her words, I wondered if that was it. I regained confidence that the extraordinary saga of the seven weeks since the Democrats' Isikoff article might be over. I should have asked myself instead: When does a shark let go of your leg? Answer: when it wants to.

Contrary to Mrs. Clinton's press conference, I soon learned that this particular shark was only just beginning to chew on me and its growing list of victims. After the election, Clinton supporters turned their rage on me as a scapegoat for their loss. It was Russia, not their hero's bad campaign, that landed Trump in the White House. I became a household name as the media reports multiplied.

My continuing notoriety worried some political operatives from the incipient administration. The incoming White House counsel, Don McGahn, fired off a letter in December telling me to "immediately cease" saying I was a Trump advisor and to stop suggesting that I was more than a short-lived advisory council member "who never actually met with the president-elect."[40]

I wrote McGahn back a letter of my own, strongly agreeing with many of his points. But I explained to him the reality that I had never tried to inflate my role. I made it clear to Don McGahn as well as Hope Hicks that the real issue was the media and their political partners, which continued to inflate my role in the campaign.

"On countless occasions throughout this year, Mr. Trump has correctly alluded to the severe dishonesty in the mainstream media and pundit class," I wrote McGahn. "By all indications, the highly damaging statements that have continued to be cast against me personally to this day are part of a last-ditch effort by the corrupt Clinton regime to delegitimize the new Administration…

"This approach is closely consistent with past tactics that investigators affiliated with Mrs. Clinton have historically taken toward their targeted victims: 'Impugn…character and veracity until…destroyed beyond all recognition.'"[41] My letter cited a *New York Times* article that described similar tactics while her husband was still in the White House.[42]

I often wrote Hope Hicks to help provide some correct data amidst a sea of disinformation. I gave her information about my whereabouts in Hawaii when the first advisory meeting with Donald Trump had taken place, and in the Middle East when Donald Trump gave his biggest foreign policy address during the campaign. I hoped it would be useful to her to be able to tell journalists that I had often been on the other side of the planet while candidate Trump led his successful campaign for the presidency.

I did everything I could to explain that my role was being inflated not by myself, but by the enemies of Donald Trump. In my letters to Don McGahn, I made it clear that the mantra candidate Trump had coined on the campaign trail was now more relevant than ever—*this really isn't about me, it's about us.* I did my best to follow candidate Trump's positive example of putting America first despite the incessant stream of attacks against me.

And perhaps for that reason, the attacks just kept on coming. Robert Mook, campaign manager for Hillary Clinton's failed 2016 presidential race, told *The Hill* that Trump campaign aides should be "prosecuted for treason" if the FBI could prove collusion.[43] The narrative that the Clinton campaign and other Democrats had lost because of Russian collusion was, I suppose, comforting to Mook. It was better than admitting that he had blundered spectacularly by taking Michigan and Wisconsin for granted.

On *Meet the Press* in December 2016, former Clinton White House chief of staff John Podesta said: "Carter Page, one of Trump's foreign policy advisors, went to Russia before the Republican convention and met with the person in the Russian hierarchy who was responsible for collecting intelligence."[44]

It really takes a lot of chutzpah to say something like that, considering that Podesta's brother Tony and his top-flight lobbying firm would later be cited as "Company B" in the indictment of Paul Manafort for his work for Russia. Paul Manafort was sentenced to prison for tax and bank fraud unrelated to his limited work for the Trump campaign, and the Podesta Group went out of business.[45] It took a double dose of chutzpah for John Podesta to make untruthful statements about Russia and myself considering that Podesta's former boss, Bill Clinton, received a $500,000 honorarium from a Russian investment bank connected to the Uranium One deal while his wife was secretary of state.[46] Or that the Clinton Foundation received $145 million from interests linked to Uranium One.[47]

While Donald Trump was preparing his inaugural address and assembling his government, a growing cacophony of voices accused him of being in "collusion" with the Russian government. Intelligence figures and journalists were working around the clock to buttress the Russia story that leading Democrats had put forward.

On January 10, BuzzFeed decided to publish the Steele Dossier. It was the full compilation of Steele's fraudulent source documents, including dozens of smears that had made their way into the press several months earlier in the false Yahoo! News article about me before the election. In his last days as the director of National Intelligence, James Clapper released a report on Russian cyber attacks on the DNC that proved tremendously useful to the Russia–Trump collusion narrative.[48] According to original reports in the days before the inauguration, all seventeen intelligence agencies agreed that the Russians had interfered in the 2016 election to benefit Donald Trump. (That misleading story would eventually have to be clarified by Clapper.[49])

Other reports cracking open Trump's connections to Russia were coming out at breakneck pace. The day before the inauguration, I got a call from a new team of reporters at the *New York Times* whom I'd never spoken with before. On Inauguration Day, their story appeared on the front page under the headline, "Intercepted Russian Communications Part of Inquiry into Trump Associates." They reported: "The continuing counterintelligence investigation means that Mr. Trump will take the oath of office on Friday with his associates under investigation and after the intelligence agencies concluded that the Russian government had worked to help elect him."[50]

Between attacks by the media, the BuzzFeed publication of the Steele report, and the Washington establishment's efforts to frame the president, the new situation became increasingly clear. Something very much like a deep state was working hard to discredit the results of the 2016 election and set up the president for impeachment. Few of us could have imagined that senior officials in U.S. intelligence and law enforcement would so deliberately sandbag an incoming U.S. president, forcing him to publicly deal with degrading, pornographic accusations. Years later, the origins of those false stories would be confirmed by the Horowitz investigation as originating in comments made in "jest" over beers.[51]

Wary of the growing chaos, I stayed far away from Washington on Inauguration Day. I spoke with Steve Bannon for the first time on January 17, 2017, and started to tell him what I thought of the Russia stories. I sent two texts to him following up three days later, a few hours before the inauguration:

"As predicted on our call, this news cycle isn't retreating; see p. 1, today's NYT. The IC pulled this with MLK & Ali too. I'm eager to fight back against the liars that are trying to tear down DJT."[52]

And then: "Perfectly timed for I-Day. Poor Hope's been forced to play defense. I want to go on the offense: HRC's lies hurt DJT much more than the Russians could've ever helped."[53]

Those messages were being read by the law enforcement officials who had tapped my phones. Obama administration officials had further extended their corrupt spy operation by securing a second FISA warrant against me just a few weeks before the Trump inauguration. As the world would later learn, the illicit scheme extended far beyond the failed Clinton campaign. It included many public figures across the Democratic Party and the U.S. Intelligence Community establishment.

■ ■ ■

At long last, the FBI wanted to have a discussion with me. When I worked as an informant, they had called in advance for meetings; now they sprung on me unexpectedly on the afternoon of March 9, 2017, in the ornate, art deco lobby of the Empire Hotel in Manhattan. Two agents, both men, showed me their badges, and we walked around the corner near an empty conference room to have a slightly more discreet conversation. The agents asked me to meet them the next day.

I could have brought a lawyer, but I chose to stick with my plan—wagering that a spirit of openness would help them see what a sham this entire Witch Hunt had already become. I still had hope that the whole debacle might be written off by the FBI, which I imagined might have originally misunderstood what it was dealing with.

The next day, the FBI booked a suite at the Andaz Hotel across Fifth Avenue from the New York Public Library in Manhattan. I called them upon my arrival at the reception on East Forty-First Street. The two famous stone lions staring at me from across the busy thoroughfare had appropriate names for what would be required over the coming days and years. Legendary mayor Fiorello La Guardia nicknamed them "Patience" and "Fortitude" (though they were originally named Leo Astor and Leo Lenox, after major donors to the library).[54]

An agent came down to bring me up to the suite that afternoon. For only this first long meeting, there were three agents in attendance for my interrogation—the two men I'd met the day before and a woman. At first they spoke in friendly tones, but like gladiators in a ridiculous modern equivalent of the Forum Boarium from ancient Roman times, they came at me from every direction in a relentless onslaught. But I was by then adept at verbal sparring, with months of practice with TV conspiracy theorists under my belt. I had heard most of their questions many times before. And as had long been reported throughout those recent months and at the risk of stating the obvious, I immediately gave the agents extensive background information on the Democrats' role behind the Steele Dossier.[55] A day earlier, I had provided them with a letter that detailed the facts I had recently sent to Senators Richard Burr and Mark Warner of the Senate Intelligence Committee.[56]

If any of these larger investigations were to have any purpose at all, there should have been some shred of truth to the fraudulent accusation that I had met with the two Igors or some other sanctioned individuals. I also must have had conservations with these gentlemen or some other Russian operatives about some kind of a "quid pro quo" relationship between the Trump campaign and the Kremlin. When I honestly answered "no" to all of these outrageous preliminary questions, it seemed obvious that there wasn't much more to discuss.

After the frustrated agents ran out of relevant questions and started fishing further afield after various trivialities, I took the opportunity to fill them in on the "Dodgy Dossier" and its financiers, a dire warning sign of emerging scandals to come. I suggested that the purpose of using such a document would be to inject "false evidence" into a criminal or intelligence case. Essentially, it amounted to obstruction of justice.

The agents asked me about the Democrats' false allegations that I had received a stake in Rosneft. I replied that I obviously had not. I added that to the best of my knowledge, the only group other than the government of Qatar who had mixed politics with Rosneft was a commodity trading company named Glencore and its associates. In December 2016, Glencore had publicly announced the very same deal that I had been falsely accused of by the Democrats, the media, and the U.S. Intelligence Community.[57] Coincidentally, Glencore was founded by Marc Rich—the late donor to the Clinton Library and international fugitive pardoned by President Clinton on his last day in office.[58] Even the *New York Times* had called the decision "An Indefensible Pardon."[59]

When asked, I confirmed to the FBI that the New Economic School had not paid me a cent (or one Russian ruble) to speak at my engagement—unlike Bill Clinton who had received a half-million dollars for a Moscow speech while his wife served as U.S. secretary of state.[60] I did get an airline ticket for the trip, as I had countless times before for pro bono speaking engagements at other academic institutions worldwide. They asked for details about my schedule in Moscow. I walked them through it, including a meeting with a few executives I had long known at Tatneft, a vertically integrated oil and gas company I had done business with in the past. I confirmed that I had momentarily greeted Russian deputy prime minister Arkady Dvorkovich as he passed by me after walking off the stage of the NES graduation event. All complete irrelevancies.

They drilled down on Igor Divyekin. I reiterated that I was pretty sure I had never met him, even briefly or in passing.

Just like a lot of silly media reports, we talked through the events of the Republican National Convention in Cleveland and any possible contact I might have had with Russian ambassador Sergey Kislyak. In his Senate confirmation hearings after appointment as attorney general, Senator Jeff Sessions had been raked over the coals for not remembering his fleeting, irrelevant encounters with Kislyak. I drew them a diagram of the conference room in Cleveland where Sessions and Kislyak had sat. The senator and the ambassador were on the other side of the large banquet hall, far away from me, but I recalled the two men having a brief conversation amidst a large congregation of lollygaggers after Sessions finished his speech. Far from offering any kind of forum where one might engage in collusion negotiations, most of the audience at this Case Western Reserve University event were lazily hanging out to listen to some vaguely intellectual chit chat.

As our conversation began, I set up my MacBook laptop on the living room table of the Andaz suite and began to present a PowerPoint slide deck. Earlier that morning and throughout much of the previous night, I had composed a presentation that outlined the connections in the swamp between the Democrats, the media, and their bosses at Justice and FBI headquarters. I spoke with these FBI agents as Americans who would actually care about underlying issues of fairness and democracy. Little did I know that those principles continued to elude their government superiors and their political allies in Washington.

I also gave them a USB with a lot of my documents, not that I needed to bother. As I subsequently learned, the FISA warrants signed by their director, James Comey, and the former U.S. deputy attorney general Sally Yates had already given them the run of pretty much everything I had. I did not yet know that Perkins Coie was the law firm that had helped to orchestrate the financing of the Dodgy Dossier, but I informed the agents of what I had heard: that a law firm had acted as the intermediary between the Democrats and their opposition research team from London.

That wasn't the last that I'd hear from the FBI. Six days later, the same two agents interviewed me about a more recent trip that I'd made to Russia. I traveled to Moscow in December 2016 in a fruitless endeavor to restart my business and engage in dialogue with some of the academics I had previously met there. With the recent Trump election victory, I had incorrectly assumed that the world would return to normal. During a dinner at a Russian restaurant with Shlomo Weber and an associate, Deputy Prime Minister Dvorkovich briefly stopped by and expressed interest in the possibility of better bilateral relations between our two countries following Donald Trump's victory. Again, nothing of substance was discussed, as I informed him that the manufactured controversy was still upending my life. I was also asked about my earlier, fleeting contact with Viktor Podobnyy. I emphasized to the agents how young this man was. I told the FBI that I viewed my interactions with Podobnyy in much the same light as my NYU students. The only difference was that NYU students had a lot more interest in what I was saying and asked much better questions.

My third interrogation was on March 16, 2017, at the W Hotel in Midtown Manhattan, where I again met the same two primary agents. By this time, the death threats were coming in bulk. I complained that the FBI did not seem to be taking the mounting death threats seriously. They told me to call them if I had a "specific future threat."

This time, they wanted to talk about former Trump campaign official Paul Manafort. As with so many other topics, once I told them that I had never met Manafort and that he had never returned any of the several emails I had sent him, a hundred other questions fell to the floor. The conversation returned to Kislyak. I told them that in our brief conversation, I had handed the ambassador one of my business cards. He had not reciprocated and seemed entirely uninterested.

The agents asked me about the platform committee and the change in the Ukraine plank. All I knew was that J.D. Gordon had been involved in that process a week before the main events of the RNC convention. I didn't even find out about it until the decisions had been made.

Our fourth pre-scheduled meeting was at the Hilton Manhattan East Hotel on the afternoon of Thursday, March 30, 2017. They peppered me with questions about a Rosneft employee I had known for a decade, since his years as a junior capital markets staffer at Gazprom. I told the FBI that we had never discussed anything remotely secret or politically sensitive. I had seen this young man, Andrey Baranov, at a party held by one of the banks in Moscow on my July 2016 trip. Two longtime acquaintances briefly catching up, we did little more than exchange pleasantries. To give the agents an idea of what I was up against, I told them how Obama's former ambassador to Russia, Michael McFaul, had started live-tweeting during my NES speech. He became a key node of the network trying to make the false case against me.[61]

Every time the FBI agents asked a question, I would answer it and then try to remind the agents of the fraudulent sources behind these ridiculous allegations. That of course didn't break through. Unbeknownst to me, and as America would learn years later, I wasn't telling the agents anything they weren't already aware of.

The agents wanted to return to Kislyak again, and I detailed every conceivable moment in which we might have been in proximity to each other, such as walking with a group to a shuttle bus on our way to the next event. Always surrounded by countless others in large gatherings, I made the definitive statement that I had never met with Kislyak alone at any point in my life.

When asked about the campaign, I showed the agents my response to Don McGahn's letter spelling out that I had never advised the candidate. I discussed the texts I had exchanged with Steve Bannon, telling them that we talked about getting together but never got around to it.

My fifth and final interrogation was in a conference room at New York's Grand Hyatt, next to Grand Central Station. Called in at the last minute, I wondered the reason for the surprise rendezvous. I got a clue when I picked up a copy of that Friday's *Wall Street Journal* as I headed out the door. One of the headline stories of that morning's March 31, 2017, edition announced: "Flynn Offers Deal for Testimony."[62] As expected, this was the first question and the intended primary line of interrogation as our meeting began. They both seemed very disappointed to hear that I had never met or spoken with General Flynn at any point in my life. Yet another Russia collusion theory, quickly dashed.

It ended up being the shortest meeting we ever had, but when the Flynn allegation proved a dead end, the agents decided to have me go over a lot of the same old ground. Perhaps in an attempt to prevent the meeting from being a complete waste, they tried to see if I had left anything out. I answered almost every accusation with a flat denial that seemed to put a further kibosh on the unnecessary questioning. There really was very little for us to talk about. I did notice, however, a change in the agents. In the early meetings they were brisk and aggressive, telling me what they wanted to talk about and interrupting me when they felt I wasn't giving them the answer they wanted to hear. By our last talk, they often seemed more casual and for the first time began to refer to their questions as things their "bosses" wanted them to ask about.

Perhaps the agents had seen my appearance on Fox News the night before, including an insightful interview with Catherine Herridge.

Herridge and her colleagues reported: "For his part, Page argued that the attacks on the Trump administration by its political foes have harmed the U.S. political system more severely than the allegations that Russia meddled in the U.S. election."

I told Herridge: "Liars and leakers in Washington and more broadly the political class in the United States actually had a much more negative impact. All of the discussions about the influence that the Russian government had on the U.S. election would actually pale in comparison to the much heavier influence that the U.S. government actually had in trying to hurt then-candidate Trump. That negative impact based on these complete lies has continued to put a dark shadow over the United States in general."[63]

What I said on Fox News was essentially the same as what I had told the FBI. The main difference consisted of the additional details which I had given the intelligence agents within the confines of the hotel suites in Manhattan throughout the month of March 2017. As the world continued to slip further away from reality—despite my best efforts to acquaint these people with the truth—my saga was about to take another series of turns for the worse. Making matters worse throughout much of the rest of that year and exposing me to a few congressional de facto comedians, I was required to increase my interaction with the partisan showboat legislators on Capitol Hill. As the national narrative continued to veer off the tracks in 2017, I found myself stuck on a crazy runaway train.

CHAPTER FIVE

TERROR THREATS AND THE ADAM SCHIFF SHOW

"I genuinely hope, Carter, that you're innocent of every-thing, because you're doing a lot of talking. It's either admirably bold or reckless, but I guess we'll find out."

—Chris Hayes, MSNBC[1]

SPRING 2017

The conspiracy to overturn the legitimacy of President Donald J. Trump's first election victory had, as we've seen, many nodes. Surely one of the most important—a root node—was Congressman Adam Schiff. Not only has Schiff remained annoyingly in the media spotlight, but he has continued to stick to his lies.

Schiff's home district in California includes Burbank, self-proclaimed "media capital of the world," home to Walt Disney and Warner Brothers.[2] Adam Schiff follows an information-age version of the hallowed tradition of congressmen bringing home the bacon. For example, members from rural districts might fund agriculture subsidies, or those from districts with aerospace-defense plants win increases in defense spending. Instead, Schiff supplies liberal media constituents with endless conspiracy theories bolstered by "bombshell" revelations fired in rapid succession. For a media struggling for relevancy and credibility after the election of a candidate who correctly decried "fake news," Schiff has been a godsend, a one-man fake news factory for a few television networks that welcome him as a regular guest and newspapers that value him as a leaky source.

First as ranking member and then as chairman since January 2019, Schiff has transformed the House Permanent Select Committee on Intelligence (HPSCI). During his tenure, HPSCI has been malformed from a relatively quiet realm of earnest national security professionals to the toxic, partisan Adam Schiff Show. On March 20, 2017, the confrontational Schiff repeated the preposterous allegations from Steele's Dodgy Dossier into the congressional record and more to the point, on national television. He repeated the lies about my supposedly having accepted a brokerage fee from Igor Sechin for the sale of 19 percent of Rosneft.[3] For members of my family and myself, it was one of the darkest days in our lives. Schiff later released a report with the ironic title "Correcting the Record—The Russia Investigation." It asserted that "[f]ar from 'omitting' material facts about Steele, as the Majority claims, DOJ repeatedly informed the [FISA] Court about Steele's background, credibility, and potential bias."[4] This conclusion, as we shall see, would later be crushed by the Horowitz report as well as by Judge Rosemary M. Collyer's angry and rare public condemnation of the secret FISA court for the FBI's failure to inform it about "information in their possession which was detrimental to their case for believing that Mr. Page was acting as an agent of a foreign power."[5]

Yet to this day, Adam Schiff clings to most of his pet theories and apologizes for nothing.

A favored ally of House Speaker Nancy Pelosi, Schiff would later play the preeminent role in spearheading the impeachment of President Trump. Like the late slapstick duo Laurel and Hardy and with unintentional hilarity, the congressman from California paired with House Judiciary Chairman Jerry Nadler of Manhattan. In ways reminiscent of the bullying antics of the heavyset Oliver Hardy of yesteryear, Nadler's buffoonery included his own February 2018 rebuttal of the Nunes Memo.[6] The meritless scheme to remove the president collapsed in the end, not long after House Democrats failed to follow up on their sub-poenas of Trump officials by going to court.[7] Schiff's Democrats alleged bribery, then backed off from it.[8] To paraphrase my old boss Senator Daniel Patrick Moynihan, Schiff would lead the Democrats into defining impeachment downward.

The more Adam Schiff lies, the more aggressively he defends his lies. The more often he is proven wrong, the quicker he moves on to new attacks such as trying to find an impeachable offense in President Trump's call to Ukrainian president Volodymyr Zelensky. The more Adam Schiff manages to create a narrative that obscures the truth, the higher he rises in the esteem of his supporters from both parties, including the radical Democrats. Schiff is rumored to be either waiting to run for the House speakership when Nancy Pelosi retires, or to run for a U.S. Senate seat in California.[9]

I began to face a similar type of nonsense when HPSCI first contacted me in early May 2017. The Republicans were in the majority at that time, but that didn't stop Schiff. In fact, it seems to have inspired even greater animus and sneakiness in his partisan antics. As one *Politico* headline noted not long before: "Pelosi, Schiff Call on Nunes to Recuse Himself from Russia Probe." The article's subtitle foreshadowed the many miles of scorched earth that lay ahead for HPSCI: "The calls for recusal are a stunning breakdown for a committee that has traditionally operated in a bipartisan manner."[10]

After seeing what Schiff had recently done to Chairman Nunes, particularly as my FISA news about the Democrats' wrongdoing began to illegally leak out, I had little doubt that I would become one of the next contestants in yet another episode of the Adam Schiff Show.

■ ■ ■

Not long after President Trump's inauguration, I received a letter from Senators Richard Burr and Mark Warner of the Senate Select Committee on Intelligence in February 2017. In a sneak preview of things to come, they instructed me in particularly pompous prose to preserve my documents, emails, and other electronic communications and demanded that I not alter any of them. Of course, this was not necessary since America had learned that spring how the government already had access to every email and document I possessed. But after a lot of negotiation and fruitless attempts at gaining help with my quest for justice, I eventually compiled and handed over an extraordinary amount of material on a thumb-drive. Several months after that initial letter from the U.S. Senate, I received a similar request from the House Permanent Select Committee on Intelligence. Amidst some rivalry between the respective chambers of Congress, the two intelligence committees began a closely watched contest for relevance.

In addition to having to perform dozens of hours of free administrative work for the intelligence committees by scouring years of emails and messages, I faced the unenviable task of preparing myself for their ludicrous congressional gauntlet. I expected my every word to be scrutinized for a potential perjury trap between something I said in committee and what I'd told the FBI. And both would look for any flaw in my memory as compared to the countless documents which forces in Washington had already illegally hacked.

The price of such a mistake could, of course, be a lengthy trial, being branded as a criminal, and facing years in prison. I refused to be intimidated. It is said that good liars must have exceptional memories. But those who have done nothing wrong need only tell the same story over and over.

Later that year, after testifying in the House and Senate, I spent part of a day walking around New York City with Jason Zengerle of the *New York Times Magazine*. I should have known better, and Zengerle chose to write a hit piece. Portraying me as an oddball and filled with disparaging quotes from adversaries like Schiff, Zengerle's rendition left room for only one conclusion—I must be guilty of something. Nonetheless, and based on our long meeting on that November day, he realized that I had chosen to face this continued crisis as an open book.

"While others have lawyered up and disappeared behind a scrim of crisis-communications consultants and attorneys, Page has chosen to wage his battle almost entirely on his own, in the public spotlight," Zengerle wrote. He contrasted me to "Manafort tugging on his car's sun visor to shield his face from reporters."

Zengerle said that "people" have "begun to wonder about not just his competence but also his sanity. But as we walked through Manhattan that afternoon, Page assured me that he was playing a long game. 'How do I say this without sounding overly confident or arrogant?' he mused. 'No one is better prepared to have gone through this than me.' He flashed that familiar beatific smile. 'Not only am I ready for it,' he said, 'I savor it.'"[11]

And I did, even when many in the press behaved more like tabloids than investigatory reporters. Much comment was made of the bright red and blue "Gilligan's Island" bucket hats I wore outside while strolling to the Capitol to dutifully deliver my memory sticks full of documents to the Senate and House committees. Learning from the problems that Senator McCain and many others I knew had faced, I often wear hats to guard my head from the sun and skin cancer.[12] Though initially surprised by the media coverage of my headwear choices, I came to find the criticism funny.[13] In the middle of this dystopian situation, I found it helpful not to take the circus so seriously.

■ ■ ■

On my first trip to "Sissy"—the Senate Select Committee on Intelligence or SSCI—in early March 2017, I was approached by a young female reporter named Ali Watkins. She would later reveal me as Male-1 and discuss my involvement with the FBI on MSNBC's Rachel Maddow Show. She had been lurking nearby and seemed eager to turn this seemingly chance encounter into an ambush interview. As I walked away from SSCI's supposedly secure facility on the second floor of the Hart Senate Office Building, I wondered why Watkins just happened to be hanging around there. I've been to many intelligence-related offices worldwide, but never one where a reporter was within feet of the front door. It immediately seemed strange at the time.

It wasn't until much later in this saga that the public learned that Ms. Watkins had a special connection to the Senate Intelligence Committee. One of my main points of contact on the committee staff was James Wolfe. The first letter from Warner and Burr ended with a welcoming offer: "If you have any questions about this request, please contact either Christopher Joyner, Staff Director, or Mike Casey, Minority Staff Director, at (202) 224-...." As I would later tell the FBI that month, Christopher and Mike were all but completely unresponsive when I tried to reach out. I somehow got passed off to Mr. Wolfe instead.

As the so-called "Security Director," Wolfe then held one of the most sensitive intelligence posts in Congress. It gave him access to highly classified briefing materials. These types of documents were held within the committee's Sensitive Compartmentalized Information Facility, colloquially known as a "skiff."

As the person theoretically in charge of security for the Senate Intelligence Committee, Wolfe's official responsibilities presumably might have included catching leakers among Senate staff. In Washington's hypocrisy-laden swamp world, of course, this post was the perfect position from which Wolfe could become a prolific leaker himself.

A married man and a father, Wolfe had a reputation for socializing with female reporters. We later learned that this included giving several of those ladies tips on committee business, such as when I might be stopping by.[14] After Ali Watkins joined the *New York Times*, her new employer in a later, full disclosure piece, reported that Wolfe had previously been presented by Watkins as her boyfriend at Ali's backyard parties in Washington's Adams Morgan neighborhood.[15]

Wolfe had begun to cultivate Watkins when she was just a senior in college and had sent her a pearl bracelet as a graduation gift.[16] They commenced a long relationship that continued as Watkins racked up her scoops and became a rising star at BuzzFeed and *Politico*, leading to her current position at the *New York Times*. Her personal story broke into public view in 2018 when James Wolfe was arrested after lying to FBI agents about his links with Watkins. He denied it at first, only to be shown undeniable photographic evidence by FBI agents. He was convicted. After pleas to the federal court for leniency from Senators Burr, Warner, and Dianne Feinstein, Wolfe was sentenced to two months in prison.[17] He was not, however, charged with revealing any secrets to Watkins.

This seemed like yet another curious development, hard to explain given the facts of the case.

In the indictment of James Wolfe, the disclosure of the identity of Male-1 is purported to contain "classified information that had been provided to the SSCI by the Executive Branch for official purposes."[18] As we have thus far seen in countless instances, from Hillary Clinton to James Comey, mishandling of classified or confidential information is not treated as a crime for people with the right connections. Just make sure you don't try this at home, especially if you're not a well-connected Washington insider.

The pattern of Wolfe's sharing, at best, non-public information with journalists was palpable. In contacts with multiple reporters, Wolfe had used messaging apps like Signal and WhatsApp to communicate.[19] He met reporters in restaurants, bars, secluded areas of the Hart Senate Office Building, and their private residences.[20] According to his indictment, Wolfe exchanged tens of thousands of electronic communications, including daily texts and phone calls, as well as encrypted cell phone messages with Watkins.

After my auto-da-fé on MSNBC's Rachel Maddow Show, Wolfe texted Watkins: "I've watched your career take off even before you ever had a career in journalism…I always tried to give you as much information that I could and to do the right thing with it so you could get that scoop before anyone else…."[21]

■ ■ ■

During her time at BuzzFeed, Ali Watkins broke the story that I was "Male-1," interviewed by the FBI for my inconsequential contact with

Victor Podobnyy.[22] The DOJ's mishandling of this case had unnecessarily caused me immense problems since I had been so lightly "masked" in the government's misleading representations in the indictment. But until then, no reporter had managed to figure out that I was the energy finance executive who had been so recklessly described in that disingenuous federal court filing.

Then a resident of Washington, Watkins called me out of the blue and asked to meet in New York City on Monday, April 3, 2017. I was attending the Independent Petroleum Association of America's annual oil and gas investors conference at the Sheraton New York Times Square Hotel, so I told her that she could come meet me at the Starbucks there if she wanted to.

After some chit chat about a boyfriend of Ali's who used to serve in the U.S. Army, she proceeded to inform me of the leaks she had received. She told me she had learned that I was the FBI source referred to in the Russian spy indictment. At that point, I could lie (not an option for me), confirm that I was Male-1, or refuse to answer—which, given the exceptionally light masking by the Obama administration's Justice Department, would only serve to further confirm that I was, in fact, Male-1.

So, I confirmed that I was the guy who had helped the FBI with that case.

In what I then considered a strange coincidence, another journalist from ABC News had also gotten in touch to say that he wanted to meet. So I headed a few blocks down Seventh Avenue to the *Good Morning America* studio in Times Square to speak with producer Matthew Mosk in a conference room. Oddly enough, he also asked about my being the FBI's Male-1 source.[23] With ABC owned by the Walt Disney Company since a 1995 corporate merger, there were cartoons of Mickey Mouse and other Disney characters throughout the back hallways. One of Snow White's Seven Dwarfs, the little guy named Dopey, seemed like the perfect symbol for what the U.S. Intelligence Community had already become by that stage. The following week I'd again be back in that same studio for an interview with George Stephanopoulos about the latest government leaks, this time regarding my illegitimate FISA warrant.[24]

When Ali Watkins appeared with Rachel Maddow on Maddow's eponymous show a few hours after my meeting with her, it heightened the young journalist's profile exponentially. ABC News missed the scoop but reported soon afterwards the same spin as Maddow: "Trump Adviser Carter Page Targeted for Recruitment by Russian Spies."[25] That was a lot of freight for the media to load onto a story that was entirely disingenuous from the beginning. By the time BuzzFeed and ABC News contacted me, it had already long become clear that I was the target of unlawful disclosures of my identity from confidential government documents.

These pieces came on top of other recent headlines that March, like this one: "There's a Smell of Treason in the Air"[26], and "All the President's Traitors" in HuffPost.[27] After these stories appeared, the public's impression of myself and other Trump supporters as traitorous Russian agents only grew, while the death threats for "treason" left on my voicemail, in my inbox, and online multiplied. Building upon the Male-1 revelations, things only deteriorated in April 2017.

Often personal relationships carry many benefits in life. Perhaps only at the intersection of foreign intelligence, politics, and the media can malicious objectives that put the lives of innocent citizens at risk become their end game. It seems unthinkable, at least in a free country like America, that lovebirds would conspire to bring down their fellow citizens.

■ ■ ■

After a lot more back and forth correspondence with the various congressional committees throughout that summer, I finally had a chance to begin filling them in on reality later that year. I got up early on November 2, 2017, for a workout before my House Permanent Select Committee on Intelligence testimony.

In keeping with my open and transparent approach, I did not bring an attorney with me. I had consulted that year with some great lawyers on the Mueller Witch Hunt madness. The most professional and helpful was Tom Buchanan, a Winston & Strawn partner and former Justice Department official who specializes in complex civil and white-collar criminal litigation. I was eager to set the record straight with my government, though I was reluctant to confront the bum-rush of hysterical reporters that were always congregating in the underground of the Capitol, hopeful to catch wind of the next fairy tale that Adam Schiff and his brethren were getting ready to sprinkle in the air like basement stardust. So thinking ahead with HPSCI's chief clerk Nick Ciarlante, my default point of contact for administrative matters related to "Intelligence" on the House side, we planned to meet at the House security post in the Capitol building over an hour early. In contrast to James Wolfe, Nick was a consummate professional. His quiet and intense professionalism epitomized how congressional spy committees and indeed the U.S. Intelligence Community in general are supposed to comport themselves. He must be a figure from a bygone era.

Nick led me downstairs into the House Intel skiff. With a front entrance now famous from so many Adam Schiff made-for-TV moments, the inside is essentially just a bigger and fancier version of most other skiffs I've been in at various points in my life. It's a large, austere assortment of rooms encased in enough metal and baffling deep inside its walls to defeat any attempt at electronic espionage.

Devin Nunes, then chairman of the committee, did not attend my hearing. He had unfortunately been forced to temporarily step aside while he faced a nonsensical House Ethics Committee investigation for the alleged unauthorized disclosure of classified information. In the bitter partisan environment of that committee, Nunes was the Democrats' constant target. They had tried to sideline him over disclosures of the effort to criminalize General Michael Flynn's contacts with Russian officials while he was the president-elect's designated national security advisor. Essentially placed on the equivalent of the injured reserve list for a sports team until December 2017, Nunes was eventually cleared by the House Ethics Committee.[28]

As a result of these machinations, Mike Conaway, a tall Texan, chaired the hearing for the then-Republican majority. I tried to read the room. The Republicans looked bored, giving cold, skeptical looks at many of their Democratic colleagues, including Schiff, who even by that relatively early date had already wasted much of their time with his Russia Witch Hunt. Republicans were distracted by far more important real business that day, including work on H.R. 1. This substantive legislation which was enacted later that year "amends the Internal Revenue Code (IRC) to reduce tax rates and modify policies, credits, and deductions for individuals and businesses."[29] Nonetheless, the Republicans, mostly staffers, who hung around were eager to hear what I had to say and willing to give me a fair shake. Sitting on the Republicans' left wing were Democrats Adam Schiff, Eric Swalwell, and others. They mostly looked stone faced, and not as overconfident as I had originally expected. They would, of course, be looking to break open any inconsistency in my testimony in an effort to prove that Donald Trump had in fact been illegitimately elected with help from Russia.

I had a chance to start reading my short opening statement. Before I was cut off, I didn't hold back. I spoke of "the historic impact of the big-money opposition political research operations on the U.S. Intelligence Community." Echoing the many stories about the damage supposedly inflicted on the election by hundreds of thousands of dollars' worth of posts from Russian "trolls," I questioned who the real trolls were. The official definition of a social media troll is someone who uses social media or media outlets to sow discord. That is precisely what the legacy media did in the forty-five days leading up to the 2016 election after Yahoo published the Michael Isikoff hit piece against me in September.

I asked whether U.S. government agencies, state-funded media like NPR and the Voice of America, and paid media users or "trolls" had, in fact, been the real threat to the proper functioning of our democracy.

The false Russia collusion narrative, paid for by the Clinton campaign, had almost derailed a razor-thin victory in a presidential contest.

Then I cut to the chase, previewing my answers to specific questions that would be posed in various forms by the committee.

"I personally saw no active measures by the Russian government or other foreign entities to interfere in any political campaigns whatsoever—neither last year nor at any point throughout my life."

I quoted Adam Schiff's risible rhetorical question: "Is it a coincidence that the Russian gas company, Rosneft, sold a 19 percent share after former British intelligence officer Steele was told by Russian sources that I was offered fees on a deal of just that size?" I reminded Schiff and the Democrats that a month after the election, it was Swiss company Glencore that bought that stake in 2016.

Glencore, I further reminded Schiff and the Democrats, was founded by the late Marc Rich, the uber Clinton donor and beneficiary of an unusual presidential pardon while an international fugitive. So if there was any partisan connection to that transaction with Russia, I suggested, Adam Schiff might want to take a look closer to home. I referred to my letter to James Comey and contrasted my openness with Comey's declaration in March denying that any surveillance of the Trump campaign had taken place. I wondered if "the resources of the U.S. Government might be better allocated towards addressing real national security threats," particularly given the Boston Marathon bombing that had taken place around the time I was first being interviewed by the FBI in New York's Plaza Hotel in 2013 while helping them as Male-1.

My interrogation lasted the whole day. It alternated between the majority and minority, with Schiff and Swalwell taking most of the time for the minority. When Schiff pointedly reminded me that I was under oath, I told him: "I don't lie, Congressman Schiff. So everything I say, whether it's under oath or not under oath, is going to be equally accurate and to the best of my knowledge.... Again, just to be very clear, every meeting I ever had in Russia was completely benign. It was nothing, you know, nothing I would be ashamed of having broadcast on national television.... "

Schiff and Swalwell, prepared for my denials of ever having met Igor Sechin or Igor Divyekin, drilled down looking for any inconsistency they could find. When I said that I had no high-level meetings, Schiff focused on my cursory exchange of pleasantries with Arkady Dvorkovich, the head of the New Economic School. "You don't consider him to be a high-up official or someone in an official capacity?"

"I greeted him briefly as he was walking off the stage after his speech."

Thinking he had his 'gotcha' moment, Schiff turned to a memo I had dashed off from JFK airport between two back-to-back transatlantic flights. In that memo, I had written that "Dvorkovich expressed strong support for Mr. Trump and a desire to work together toward devising better solutions in response to the vast range of current international problems."

That benevolent platitude hardly seemed to me to be the language of a bag man. I told Schiff that Dvorkovich had expressed that sentiment in our short greeting, measured in seconds. I had also gathered a strong sense of this message from listening to his speech, which Dvorkovich had finished a few minutes before.

Schiff turned to what he hoped would be his next 'gotcha.' He cited an email I wrote to campaign aides on July 8 about "incredible insights and outreach I've received from a few Russian legislators and senior members of the presidential administration here."[30]

I told Adam Schiff that I had never met Donald J. Trump, but that I got some great insight from watching him at rallies and on TV. I explained the excellent feedback and positive feelings expressed mostly by academics and other average Russians in the New Economic School's intellectual discussions and from reading Russian newspapers.

In one of his constant refrains, Schiff asked if I had contradicted myself. It seemed pretty ironic, coming from one of the most dishonest and unethical members of Congress. "What you have related privately to the Trump campaign, that you had met with Russian legislators and senior members of the presidential administration?" It was all meant as another one of Schiff's showboat moments to try and catch someone out on minutiae.[31] I tried hard not to laugh at him, but sometimes couldn't control myself.

I replied: "I do not see the word 'meeting' in this sentence, Congressman Schiff."

Former federal prosecutor Trey Gowdy saw my point.

"You seem to draw a distinction between a meeting, a greeting, a conversation, and you hearing a speech," he said. I was grateful to Gowdy for recognizing the difference. I noted that in the reception hall of the New Economic School event were parents of graduates, many whom were legislators. I had exchanged pleasantries with several of them.

The questioning turned to WikiLeaks and the alleged hack of the Democratic National Committee. I told the committee that the only Russian I had ever heard reference that event was an employee of RT, the Russian international news station, when I was being interviewed. All this newsman said was that there was so much information coming out on WikiLeaks, he didn't know how to keep track of it all. That was the full extent of my only conversation with anyone associated with Russia about WikiLeaks. But more essentially, I didn't even have that conversation with him until long after the WikiLeaks files had already been released to the public. I had learned about those leaks at the same time as everyone else, or maybe even later given the amount of time I was spending on airplanes. I obviously didn't have anything to do with it.

Gowdy bore on a little about my skepticism that Russian interference in the election had taken place. I appreciated what he did given the historic impact of subsequent stages of the investigations, but suffice it to say that we didn't always see eye to eye on things. He eventually admitted years later in May 2020, "My mistake was relying on the word of the FBI and the DOJ and not insisting on the documents."[32]

Adam Schiff sought to learn about the lavish stay that he seemed to imagine I had in Moscow. My original economy class ticket only got a complimentary upgrade due to my Delta Sky Miles Medallion status. I had stayed at a decent but not extraordinary hotel. It certainly did not add up to the treatment of someone who was about to be rewarded with a multibillion dollar sale of a large stake in the oil giant Rosneft.

I did have to admit one thing—at my hotel, breakfast was included.

Consistent with his characteristic form, Adam Schiff tried to twist my New Economic Speech into a call to lift sanctions on Russia over Ukraine. I corrected him. I also reminded him that my use of the word "hypocritical" regarded general interactions between Central Asia, the United States, Europe, China, the Middle East, and Russia. It was, I said, misconstrued as a statement exclusive to Russia.

I swatted away all kinds of minutiae like this throughout the day.

One line of questioning sought to discover how well I knew George Papadopoulos. Hardly at all. We walked through our negligible history. Another line concerned my brief interaction with the Russian ambassador Kislyak in Cleveland and his distinct lack of interest in my business card. I was asked about General Flynn and surprised Adam Schiff when I told him that we had never met. I was, of course, asked about Victor Podobnyy. I told Congressman Mike Quigley, a product of Cook County, Illinois, that nothing corrupt had transpired between us.

"So you two talked about Gazprom?"

We certainly did, though hardly in any detail. At that time I had a relationship with Chesapeake Energy, then the second largest gas producer in the United States. Chesapeake had experienced some of the same market, technology issues as many in the Russian gas industry.

Quigley wanted to know if Podobnyy had asked me if I wanted a stake in Gazprom. I told him that not only did Podobnyy not ask me that, but I had to explain that he was a junior diplomat. At the time, I had known many senior people at Gazprom headquarters for a decade. If any nefarious act had been my goal, a twenty-something working back in New York would certainly have made an odd point of contact.

At Congressman Swalwell's insistence, I then had to detail for the committee the funds that I owned. Despite the unnecessary invasion of privacy, nothing unusual there either.

Predictably, Swalwell turned to the trip I had made to Russia in December 2016. The more the interrogation session tried to catch me in some misstatement, the more the facts helped to expose where the real crimes and national security threats had taken place. Unfortunately for the Democrats and the media, it all came back to the scam that they had been pulling for over a year already since the blockbuster reports stemming from the DNC's Steele Dossier.

MR. SWALWELL: Who was protecting you in Russia that made you feel safe?"

MR. PAGE: No one is protecting me. There's just—I've never been threatened in Russia. I've been threatened on multiple occasions in the United States following in the wake of the Dodgy Dossier and the trolls that sort of spun up this false story about me.

The facts and the immense related damages would come full circle, most especially for the Democratic questioners whose party had been at the epicenter of these misdeeds.

■■■

To help dispel all the Democrats' lies, I had asked for my House testimony to be shown on C-SPAN. It was far more advantageous, however, to Schiff to be able to selectively highlight whatever he wanted. After all I had been through, I should have expected that the media portrayal of my testimony would take kernels of answers and turn them into shocking reports.

Into...BOMBSHELLS!!!!

"Carter Page's Testimony Is Filled with Bombshells—and Supports Key Portions of the Steele Dossier" screamed one headline from *Business Insider* by Natasha Bertrand.[33] Among the many innocuous greetings I made on my trip was one with an old friend who, as I also noted in my FBI interviews, had risen to become the head of investor relations at Rosneft. That and a few cherry-picked details, such as my ex post facto memo applauding the change in the Republican platform, was enough to validate the Steele report and all related Democratic-government transgressions in the eyes of *Business Insider.*

On the afternoon of my testimony, I walked out of the Capitol building towards Independence Avenue and saw Trey Gowdy on the grounds across from the Library of Congress. As I explained to him, among my main motivations for wanting to clear the record before the committee were memories of a dear friend I had lost overseas. I told Gowdy I had first become friends with Chris Stevens, the diplomat killed in the 2012 Benghazi embassy attack, while I was an international affairs fellow at the Council on Foreign Relations. At the time, Chris had been the Iran desk officer at the U.S. Department of State in Washington, a sadly ironic job title given that he was prevented from traveling to Iran. Just as I provided briefings to the CIA on my travels and observations around the world, I debriefed Chris on multiple occasions following business trips to Tehran.

I mentioned this to Congressman Gowdy and told him I remembered and appreciated everything that he had done to try to achieve some semblance of justice after Chris Stevens lost his life on September 11, 2012, when the Benghazi Embassy was overrun by terrorists.

The congressman undoubtedly already knew that if the Obama administration had spent a tenth of the energy protecting our embassy that they had put into posterior-covering fairy tales they would later tell their friends in the media, Chris and his defenders would most likely be alive today. I wanted to make sure Gowdy understood that we were dealing with a culture of deceit and an expertly rehearsed pattern of deception in the highest rungs of government. Now it was returning with a vengeance to overturn the results of an American election, putting many other lives at risk.

■ ■ ■

Back in April 2017, one of my lawyers had spoken to an FBI attorney named Kevin Clinesmith and requested that the Bureau allow a "proffer letter." This procedure gives a witness the chance to provide evidence about an alleged incident with limited ability of the prosecutor to use that evidence against the person.

Among the many fine attorneys who volunteered their services to me was Adam Burke, an experienced criminal defense lawyer in Columbus, Ohio.

Though we were not fully aware of it at the time, Clinesmith was one of the people involved in crafting the secret applications for my FISA surveillance warrants before the secret FISA court.[34]

Adam spoke with Kevin Clinesmith, who said the FBI considered me to be only a witness at this stage. I had heard rumors that there had been FISA warrants secretly granted that would give the FBI the ability to spy on the Trump campaign. This meant the FBI had already convinced the secret FISA court that it had probable cause to believe I was an agent of a foreign power.

If they believed that I was just a witness, then why were there so many contradictions? Nothing seemed to make sense, and the lies by the government and their Democratic allies in Washington just continued to pile up. I was coming to terms with the fact that the government didn't seem to accept my attempts to clarify matters. The agencies that I had long served were now treating me as an adversary due to my personal opinions and support for President Trump.

General Michael Flynn in late March of 2017 had allegedly offered to testify to Congress about the Trump campaign's ties to Russia in exchange for immunity.[35] Again, lots of crazy stories blasted on the news all across the country. But no one seemed to have any idea what was really going on yet.

Both Adam and I noted to Clinesmith that every flurry of publicity about my purported treason often led to another round of abusive calls and death threats. As if I weren't already concerned enough about becoming the apparent target of several investigations, I now had perpetual worries about my own safety.

Despite the Democrats' antics, led by people such as Schiff, Warner, and Pelosi, I never feared that their crazy conspiracy theories would lead to my imprisonment (one of their favorite fantasies). They often publicly fantasied about hobbling President Trump and setting him up to be impeached, convicted, and run out of office.

Peter Strzok, Lisa Page, James Wolfe, Ali Watkins, and Kevin Clinesmith. This group included: a highly partisan FBI official charged with investigating both the Clinton email scandal and the Trump campaign, a highly partisan lawyer for the deputy director of the FBI, one of the Senate's top protectors of classified information, a young journalist who had a meteoric rise partly fueled by disclosures from her lover, and an FBI lawyer crafting FISA warrants with an agenda. And yet all of them, even if they didn't all know each other, were effectively working together to portray me as a criminal. It was all part of a broader campaign by the Democratic Party and their allies to set me up for prosecution and prison. The first majestic paragraph from H. G. Wells's *War of the Worlds* came to mind: "Intellects vast and cool and unsympathetic... slowly and surely drew their plans against me."[36] The only difference was that one would be hard-pressed to find much intellect among the sorry cast of characters that helped advance this plot.

■ ■ ■

One of my last material interactions with the Congressional Intelligence Committee circus came when I finally surrendered all of my personal documents on USB sticks the day before I testified in front of the similarly ridiculous Mueller Witch Hunt. Completely disgusted with them all, I decided that the appropriate headwear to don that day was a big, floppy red bucket hat. It seemed like the perfect fit for the big clown shows that I had been subjected to in the wake of all the Democrat-funded lies about me that had continued to that day.

As I headed to Capitol Hill that day, I didn't realize that then-Senator Al Franken had become the center of his own media firestorm.[37] Unfortunately for him, it was due to a situation that he had himself in fact created. That morning, journalist Leeann Tweeden posted an article with a photo on Twitter alleging that Franken had kissed and groped her without consent.[38] Franken had pompously harassed Attorney General Jeff Sessions earlier that year during his confirmation hearing about Russia conspiracy theories; now it was his time to feel the heat from the media. Another boomerang, coming right at the Minnesota senator.[39]

On that fall day in November, the journalists had unexpectedly camped outside of Franken's office in the Hart Building with hopes of asking about the scandal that would end his Senate career. While he remained in hiding amidst the controversy, the journalists started to get bored. After one of them noticed my big red hat, I became the focus of their attention. Slightly out of season in the late fall, the hat nevertheless seemed appropriate for the three-ring extravaganza that the Democrats had succeeded in creating with the Russia investigation and other travesties on Capitol Hill.

Reporter Natasha Bertrand who had written the "bombshell" *Business Insider* piece about my testimony a week prior sent me a text as I got into a taxi outside the Hart building. She asked about my hat. As I wrote to her, there was a more basic reason for my big red brim: "I've learned a lot from the past mistakes of my fellow Annapolis grad, Senator McCain. Sunny day in DC and skin cancer is one of them. Substance over style."

Natasha texted me again later: "Ok. Another q: were you copied on any emails with Sergei Millian? During the campaign" I informed her that I didn't think so.[40]

Just moments after surrendering to Congress much of my personal information from way back when I was a private person and before all of the Democrat-funded drama began, the incessant inquiry nevertheless continued. I thought it would all come to a halt after I cleared my name in public, but the harassment only accelerated as the stakes continued to rise for the perpetrators who had worked to unseat President Trump. Like anyone in my situation, I started to worry that my time in the hot seat might never end. But I determined to keep pushing forward and not to allow the circumstances various bad actors had put me in break my resolve. I knew that my background and training had prepared me well to get through it. Just like my high school coach had said, I could take pain. Unfortunately, I would be asked to endure a lot more before I could hope to find any semblance of justice.

CHAPTER SIX

WHAT'S IN MY POCKET? A DAY IN MUELLER'S WITCH HUNT DUNGEON

*"I am unable to address questions about the opening of
the FBI's Russia investigation, which occurred months
before my appointment, or matters related to the so-called
'Steele Dossier.' These matters are the subject of ongoing
review by the Department."*

—Robert Mueller, July 24, 2019[1]

NOVEMBER 2017

The morning after I mockingly wore a big red bucket hat for my visit to the Senate Intelligence Committee clown show, I wore somewhat more subdued attire for my appearance before the grand jury assembled by Special Counsel Robert Mueller. I had good reason to believe that the U.S. Department of Justice's Special Counsel Office (SCO) operated with the same bag of politically-minded tricks that Senators Mark Warner, Richard Burr, and their "Security Director" James Wolfe had recently relied on. There was one key difference: Mueller's SCO, without question, had infinitely more prosecutorial power than those lollygaggers in Congress. Perhaps realizing that they still had nothing on me, my FBI handler chose to make my red bucket hat a topic of conversation when we met. The agent brought it up that morning as I prepared for my short ride in the Bureau's unmarked squad car into the E. Barrett Prettyman FISA Courthouse on Friday, November 17, 2017.

I had last seen this agent over seven months earlier, throughout March in New York City. It had the awkward feel of a mutually uncomfortable reunion. The complete mockery of the entire situation turned out to be a perfectly apt start to the day. My final illegitimate FISA affidavit had been approved by another broken-down legal forum in that very same building less than five months prior, a result of the outrageously false court filing of June 2017 by Mueller's appointer Rod Rosenstein and his colleagues.[2]

This investigation targeted not just myself, but the entire Trump movement and indeed the president of the United States, Donald J. Trump, all of whom had been swept up in this outlandish fictional drama concocted by the Democrats. It was still tearing America's legal system asunder. But the month and a half that led up to my one grand jury appearance followed an old, familiar pattern: the more preposterous the partisan operatives could make these prolonged experiences, the better they seemed to feel about themselves. After months of getting slammed, often on national television, I waited to be submerged in the darkness of the underground tunnel to the courthouse on C Street Northwest. I was about to receive a thorough dunking in the filthy murk of the Swamp.

■ ■ ■

I had growing reasons to be skeptical of this special counsel grand jury process. A month earlier in October 2017, I had received a surprise call from my accountant. As the national news surrounding privacy invasions grew more preposterous, an FBI agent had barged into the office of my accounting firm demanding my personal financial information. After everything I had been through during the past year, nothing really surprised me anymore. I had developed a thick skin throughout my many years of service, so on a personal level it didn't bother me too much. What annoyed me was when other innocent people, like my accountant, were pulled into the Witch Hunt dragnet.

It had already been a long time since the Democrats had succeeded in turning me into a social pariah and an infamous public figure, beginning with the strategic leaks that created the first, false news reports about the DNC Dossier in September 2016. After a year of continued defamation, any return to normalcy remained effectively on hold. I tried in fits and starts to reestablish some sort of routine in my life. Every time I did, acts like this unnecessary, even thuggish, harassment of my accountant certainly didn't help give my friends and associates the sense that I could still be considered a functioning member of society. The FBI could barge into the office of anyone I knew without any semblance of legitimately justified due cause.

I remained a pariah.

The same week as the FBI's visit to my accountant, I received a few subpoenas to testify before the grand jury in November 2017. In total, the Mueller Witch Hunt would tally over 2,800 subpoenas, or an average of at least four per day.[3] Like ballplayers trying to jack up their statistics, this waste of taxpayer dollars often served as little more than an ego boost for the bureaucratic harassment squad.

Earlier that year, I had spent many hours with my lawyer Tom Buchanan at Winston & Strawn. After looking at most aspects of my life, both before and during my limited volunteer work with the Trump campaign in 2016, it became clear to him, as it would to any reasonable individual, that I had never done anything even remotely wrong, unethical, illegal, or otherwise questionable in Russia.

A few weeks before the FBI came knocking again, on September 22, 2017, my final secret surveillance warrant expired.[4] But hope springs eternal, and the Rosenstein–Sessions DOJ continued to try any last step to dig up dirt. Like Custer's Last Stand, my testimony before the Mueller grand jury could offer a last ditch restoration of credibility to their ill-fated endeavor in this media disinformation war. Having tried constant harassment and unprecedented civil liberties violations, the Justice Department focused their efforts on snaring me in small procedural errors or minor mix-ups in my recollection. They needed to catch me in some—any—wrongdoing after digging themselves into a deep hole with their corrupt FISA bargain.

There was more than a whiff of authoritarianism in their approach. As Harvard Law School Professor Alan Dershowitz has similarly noted, it reminded me of the famous boast Stalin's sidekick Lavrentiy Beria once made: "Show me the man and I'll find you the crime."[5] I wondered what these people would be like unconstrained.

For the sake of all Americans, not just myself, I wanted to do everything I could to end this madness as quickly as possible. That's precisely why I had spent over ten hours talking with the FBI during my long series of meetings in March, over half a year earlier. I had been an open book to them in the interest of putting an end to the illegitimate Russia Witch Hunt. I had done so without an attorney present and had provided the agents with countless documents. All of this exculpatory evidence should have made the allegations against me seem preposterous to any official without a political agenda. On the face of it, I had already shown each of the allegations from opposition research consultant Christopher Steele to be demonstrably false.

And yet, the central danger I faced still remained. Amidst this grand miscarriage of justice, my eagerness to talk could have put me at even greater legal risk. The special counsel and Congress had requested tens of thousands of additional documents via their subpoenas. While trying my best to fulfill these demands, I soon realized that it would be impossible for me to provide a comprehensive record that could match the enormous data collection, processing, and storage capacity of the National Security Agency (NSA). Although full details of the spy scandal had still not been confirmed at the time, I started to learn that the NSA and FBI had already wiretapped and hacked me for at least a year. Nearly five months had passed since I submitted my Privacy Act and FOIA requests for the FISA warrants on May 21, 2017. But the powers that be still dragged their feet. The authorities were equally defiant of Senators Grassley and Graham and other senior members of Congress who had continued strenuously to demand the truth.[6] Other than Rod Rosenstein and Jeff Sessions, some of the people I really needed help from were burrowed deep in the bowels of government. The Office of Information Policy and Freedom of Information Act (FOIA) team over at DOJ had blocked disclosure, essentially daring me to spend a fortune on more assertive legal tactics. It became a game of chicken—a lone advocate against a behemoth with unlimited resources. Basically wiped out, I continued to fight for my life.

I had no experience in anything like this. With few personal sources of insight, I assumed at the time that what the *Washington Post*, *New York Times*, CNN, and other news outlets had reported since April 2017 was mostly correct. If, as reports said, I was the target of FISA collection expeditions, then data I provided to the special counsel, FBI, or Congress could never conceivably match all of the more detailed information that the U.S. Intelligence Community had already hacked from my email and wiretapped from my phones. This made it clear to me that I faced thousands of opportunities to step into a perjury or false evidence trap. Given this preceding year of government surveillance, testifying before the Mueller grand jury carried the risk of inadvertently stepping in one of those traps.

■ ■ ■

Meeting my subpoenas' demands was challenging enough without the threat of perjury hanging over my head. Few people know how grueling compliance with the demands of a full-fledged political investigation can be. In many ways, as the saying goes, the process is the punishment. In my case, that punishment was wholly undeserved and a result of my support for a presidential candidate I believed in. As the investigation made more and more demands of me, causing me to direct years of efforts towards defending myself, I couldn't help but feel betrayed by the permanent federal bureaucracy. Is this how our country treats some of its most dedicated servants and military veterans?

When I first received my subpoenas, little did I know what a young lawyer on the Mueller investigation, Lawrence Rush Atkinson, and his colleagues had in store for me.[7] Weeks later found me bunkered away in hiding at my laptop, sorting thousands of personal data files. Having already hacked these documents amidst the FISA abuse of the past year, the government was unnecessarily prying them away from me once again. These latest excruciating administrative challenges persisted throughout much of the month leading up to my interrogation in their dark dungeon.

Many people in the legal arena told me that such colossal document production exercises often cost millions of dollars. The process of combing through all of one's countless personal documents and sorting through them in a way that complies with the precise requirements requires a platoon of lawyers. To comply with the precise terms of the subpoena, in such a high-priced scenario, each of these attorneys would keep billing away as they defused countless potential land mines. Rather than go bankrupt, I decided to just do the work myself. In doing so, I erred on the side of caution while further relinquishing my civil rights in the process. Rather than going through and sorting every file, I just gave them close to everything I had in this massive data dump.

Though they had already finished wiretapping, hacking, and otherwise recording about a year's worth of my personal communications, the Witch Hunt nevertheless included many specific new demands in its twelve categories of information. On the face of it, several of their requests reflected the unmistakable political nature of this foolhardy process: "Any and all records and documents (such as e-mail messages, text messages, and chats) reflecting communications or correspondences with employees, representatives, advisors, or volunteers of the Trump Campaign."[8]

After spying on my communications and correspondence with volunteers and other associates of the Trump Campaign since 2016, what conceivably could be the purpose of this exercise? I believed then, as many Americans increasingly realize now, that it was nothing more than political harassment.

■ ■ ■

As I prepared to testify before Robert Mueller's grand jury, I thought back to how my perceptions of Mueller had changed over the weeks and months since his investigation launched. Way back when Mueller was originally appointed special counsel by Rod Rosenstein on May 17, 2017, I had had a fleeting glimmer of hope.[9] Still on the run following many months of threats, I was hiding out that week at the Hyatt Regency Greenwich in Connecticut. Big parties for the rich and famous were happening in the hotel's ground floor event space, but I stayed bunkered down in my room doing research on my laptop throughout most hours of the day. With the door of room 3116 latched tight and the shades drawn for security purposes, I continued to try to make sense of what was happening to me. When I read the initial headlines, I thought Mueller might offer an unexpected source of civility and help. After so many misdeeds by the Democrats over the past year, the latest news stories such as "Republicans Jump on Special Prosecutor Bandwagon" made me think that the partisan circus might finally be over.[10] Sanity might soon be restored, I told myself, and Mueller could help me get my life back.

Reading into Mueller's background, the career he led at an earlier stage in his life gave me some initial reasons for hope. First, Mueller had served in the U.S. Marine Corps. As an Annapolis graduate myself, somewhere around a quarter of my classmates had joined the Marine Corps following graduation. I had served with Marines in various capacities for many years. I depended on them and knew them almost to a man or woman as officers of high integrity. A decade after resigning from the Navy, one of my closest friends was a U.S. Marine Corps intelligence officer on assignment in Moscow whom I spent a lot of time with while we both worked in Russia.

I expressed similar optimism to CBS News, when they asked for my reaction to the news the next day: "A good Marine, Robert Mueller learned principles on the battlefield, which represent the polar opposite of the corrupt Clinton/Obama regime which instigated his latest assignment: 'Putting others before yourself.' As with that regime's earlier weak failures worldwide, Mueller's lifelong commitment to truth and justice should put an end to their latest unsuccessful coup attempt."[11]

Back then, I still thought that the campaign against me was the product of Hillary Clinton and the DNC's operatives in the media. I thought that once these new professionals stepped up to the plate, my name would be cleared. But as we would all soon learn, the rot had taken hold much deeper than I or anyone else could have originally believed. I hadn't the faintest idea of Rosenstein's illicit scheme against President Trump's administration, in which Mueller had agreed to play a central role. It wasn't until the following year that America would see news reports claiming that Rosenstein had allegedly suggested "that he secretly record President Trump" and "discussed recruiting cabinet members to invoke the 25th Amendment to remove Mr. Trump from office."[12] Like most Americans, I still knew relatively little about what exactly the secret government forces were doing in the shadows. With media reports continuing to drip out, the information warfare then being waged against the American system of government and the White House continued unabated. Day in and day out, all of my quixotic early attempts to expose the truth became a race against the clock. The more I tried to reason with Rosenstein, Mueller, and so many other operatives in Washington in person and in writing, the more my goal of restoring normalcy and sanity seemed increasingly irrational.

As I had optimistically suggested to the media back then, Mueller appeared to be a man with common decency. I believed he might also have some semblance of consideration for other people. In a graduation speech Mueller once gave at the University of Virginia School of Law, he pontificated about "putting others before yourself."[13] Unfortunately, Mueller's team of Witch Hunt partisans didn't reflect that philosophy.

Instead, the Special Counsel Office's real ethos seemed to be, "push others under the bus before yourself."

The other reason for my original optimism was more personal. Long before Comey and McCabe's FBI had turned my prior assistance of the Bureau into an ill-conceived indictment with a highly misleading 2015 court filing in the Southern District of New York, I had also helped the FBI during the Bush administration while Mueller was still the Bureau's director. The Mueller Report would later claim in April 2017: "In 2008, Page met Alexander Bulatov, a Russian government official who worked at the Russian Consulate in New York. Page later learned that Bulatov was a Russian intelligence officer, ███████████████████████ ███████████████████."14

As usual for the many partisan anti-Trump operatives who had burrowed into the Washington bureaucracy by that point, this despicable misrepresentation by Mueller's team of Democratic donors left out many of the story's most essential details. Characteristic of the rest of their dossiers—be they collected by Steele or Mueller—they once again twisted the facts to advance their vindictive political agenda.

During those early years, as the world had already learned about my "Male-1" work, I often gave the FBI information about contacts of mine that they expressed interest in. Bulatov was a senior expert with the Trade Representation of the Russian Federation in the U.S.A. and was based in their New York office on Lexington Avenue. Around the time of my meetings with Bulatov in 2008, the then-FBI director Mueller's agents asked me to provide them with extensive information about our conversations. Having long served my country throughout the decades, I was more than happy to assist in their operations.

But during this prior age of perceived U.S. Intelligence Community sanity and partial discretion, there was one key distinction. Apparently no federal authority ever indicted Mr. Bulatov during Mr. Mueller's tenure at the FBI. And why would they? Like Podobnyy, my conversations with Bulatov had been entirely benign and largely uninspiring. During the Obama administration, when Attorney General Eric Holder and U.S. Attorney Preet Bharara announced the case against an alleged Russian intelligence officer in 2015, they and their subordinates were disingenuous at best about my role.[15] In contrast, Mueller and the FBI remained mum while he was FBI director, during the time I met with the agents about this matter in 2013. Since Mueller had never personally damaged me with false information before, I had initially assumed he might be a voice of reason. Based on both my firsthand experience as well as the countless show trials that the Mueller team led in Washington over those dark years, my confidence in the integrity of this increasingly political process continued to sink over the years.

■ ■ ■

Amidst the waves of death threats inspired by Democrats, their allies in the media, and their associates within the Justice Department, I remained on the run throughout May 2017. Many months before I ever heard from any of the partisan operatives on Mueller's staff, and soon after the new "special counsel" was appointed, I sent Mueller and Rosenstein a series of requests that sought their help in fixing the U.S. government spying agencies' domestic political intelligence operation against me and other Trump supporters.

It was, of course, wishful thinking on my part, but I had to start by finding the truth about what had happened during the Democrat-led government spying operation against the Trump campaign. I initially focused on getting access to the documents that could help expose all the wrongdoing against President Trump, myself, and other innocent Americans during the Democrats' disinformation exercise related to so-called Russia collusion. Unfortunately, I learned the hard way that I had had far too much faith in the integrity of the justice system. Passed by Congress many years earlier, the Privacy Act of 1974 as well as the Freedom of Information Act offers ways by which people can get access to any system of records that the government maintains about them. These laws like so many others on the U.S.

statute book were effectively demolished by the highly unethical undertakings of the Rosenstein–Sessions Justice Department.

The world would learn the next year that in June 2017, Rod Rosenstein signed what was allegedly the most invalid and illegitimate FISA warrant affidavit of them all, the last of them, when the supporting evidence for probable cause in my case was demonstrably non-existent.[16] Rather than reward my efforts with Privacy Act disclosures, Rosenstein only helped to further mislead the Foreign Intelligence Surveillance Court again. Underscoring the severity of the Rosenstein affidavit and an outcry for details from House Republicans,[17] the White House originally noted that "pages 10–12 and 17–34 of the June 2017 application to the FISA court" would be made available for declassification.[18] Eventually revealed as more DNC-funded lies, that information disclosure was long postponed after British intelligence services applied great pressure to cover for Steele in an effort to protect their own reputation and block the release.[19]

Increasingly desperate to find a crime, Mueller's team's best bet seemed to be a perjury trap. It might mark yet another political scalp that their allies in the Democratic Party could hoist on dramatic, larger-than-life signs with my photograph and "GUILTY" written in big red letters. These types of indictments eventually became regular features on television, later hoisted as banners at Congressional hearings in the U.S. House of Representatives.[20] Another Trump supporter effectively neutralized, lifted up in front of a national audience solely for political retribution and propaganda purposes.

■ ■ ■

My opinion of the Mueller team had already begun to decline by the time the media started fawning over the special counsel's office. Like a modern-day version of Robin Leach's *Lifestyles of the Rich and Famous*, the pro-Mueller *New York Times* ran a profile piece about the taxpayer-funded celebrity lifestyles of the special counsel team at the glamorous

Westin on Courthouse Square in historic Alexandria, Virginia. The *Times* saw humor in a New York Jets football player lounging at the hotel bar, wondering who was so important that they would attract so many cameras.[21] Too privileged to be bothered to drive in to work from their nearby homes, the members of Mueller's special counsel team prosecuting Paul Manafort were given these luxurious accommodations at taxpayer expense. The sky was the limit when it came to the Mueller squad.

After it was all said and done, the cost of the Mueller-led segments of the long Witch Hunt rang up to well over $32 million.[22] To put that figure in perspective, the price tag of the 448-page creative writing project cost U.S. taxpayers over $70,000 per page. On average, the print on any one of those sheets of paper cost more than the highest average annual salary for journalists in any state across America.[23] A largely fictional writing project, that's not bad work if you can get it.

While furnishing themselves with luxury accommodations which they booked for themselves as a Swamp "staycation," Mueller's Witch Hunt team made it clear that no travel assistance would be provided to me. Making matters worse, they didn't even give me the courtesy of committing to a firm date for a meeting. I had originally been ordered to travel to Washington for a grand jury scheduled for Friday, November 3, 2017. I booked my travel arrangements for those dates, only to be told that it had been pushed back two weeks. As I later came to realize, the shifting dates didn't just show a lack of professional courtesy. Mueller and the Democrats changed the timing in order to gain more ammunition from my Congressional testimony due to take place in early November. They could then use it to try and trip me up on an 18 U.S. Code § 1001 false statement charge, for the rarely cited "matter within the jurisdiction of the...legislative...branch of the Government of the United States."[24]

■ ■ ■

The more I saw, the more concern I felt for the rule of law in our country. Among the conservative organizations that Democrats tend to demonstrate the most hatred for is the Federalist Society. "FedSoc" has frequently found itself in the crosshairs of illegitimate investigations being used as a tool for harassing political adversaries.[25] A 2020 *New York Times* profile of conservative judges in the U.S. courts caustically noted: "All but eight had ties to the Federalist Society, a legal group with views once considered on 'the fringe.'"[26] I signed up as a member of the Federalist Society and optimistically planned to attend their 2017 National Lawyers Convention at the Mayflower Hotel in Washington on Thursday, November 16, 2017. With my Mueller grand jury a few miles away the next day, I hoped to be done in time to make it back to the convention by 2:15 p.m. for an address by Attorney General Jeff Sessions. It would be nice to get a measure of the man whose failure to stem the Witch Hunt had caused me and many other Trump supporters so much grief.[27] I was also banking on the Mueller grand jury interrogation's maybe even being over in time for me to make it back to the noon international and national security law session on comparative counterterrorism surveillance and cooperation.[28] This session was of particular interest since one of the scheduled speakers was the United Kingdom's former Government Communications Headquarters chief Robert Hannigan. His resignation earlier that year, *The Guardian* reported, had "prompted speculation that it might be related to British concerns over shared intelligence with the US in the wake of Donald Trump becoming president."[29] Given my own creeping suspicion that GCHQ had most likely been involved in the unjustified surveillance of the Trump campaign and myself during my time in London, I saw the event as a rare opportunity to confront an accuser. Certainly the illegal activities indirectly referred to in that discussion would cover far more relevant ground than anything I could possibly touch on during my grand jury appearance.

Mueller's office ended up calling to say that my reporting time wouldn't be until about an hour later than initially scheduled that Friday morning, November 17, 2017. So I decided to go to the Federalist Society breakfast at the Mayflower instead that morning. Little did I know that the Democrat interrogation routine would run for the entire day and I would never make it back for any of the substantive material after all. Instead, I faced a barrage of attacks and trash talking from Mueller's attorneys.

■ ■ ■

Rather than run the media gauntlet into the Prettyman FISA Courthouse, I had been instructed to show up for an 8:45 a.m. pick-up by that same old agent contact from the FBI, up the block—in front of one of the office buildings used by the U.S. Attorney for the District of Columbia.

Still hoping that I could finish up with my grand jury in time to return to their National Lawyer's convention before Sessions's speech, I optimistically kept my Federalist Society conference name badge and lanyard around my neck the whole day. The FBI special agent warned me that it would probably be best if I took it off while I was in their forum. Wise advice perhaps, but I nonetheless threw caution to the wind and left it on throughout my inquisition, further exacerbating the bad blood with the three Democrat donors in the process. (By political donors, of course, I mean my official government interrogators.)

The first time I ever met Jeannie Rhee, I saw her in the courthouse hallway outside my grand jury room. I politely introduced myself, "Hello, I'm Carter Page." Rather than identify herself, she angrily scowled and pointed a finger towards my holding pen area. Like a cold prison warden she barked orders and indicated that I would be summoned when they were ready. I was starting to get the picture of how the day was likely to go down.

I had got a sense of her lieutenant Rush Atkinson's place in the pecking order by watching him shadow Rhee. Given no advance warning of whom I was dealing with, I looked up stories about the Mueller team during one of my breaks that day. The reason for Rhee's aggressive stance quickly became quite clear. The essence was later encapsulated in a *Business Insider* profile of Mueller's "all star team": "Rhee represented Hillary Clinton in a 2015 lawsuit that sought access to her private emails. She also represented the Clinton Foundation in a 2015 racketeering lawsuit."

Worse, the profile continued: "Rhee is also one of the members of Mueller's team under scrutiny for her political donations, and has doled out more than $16,000 to Democrats since 2008, CNN reported. She maxed out her donations both in 2015 and 2016 to Clinton's presidential campaign, giving a total of $5,400."[30]

I struggled to comprehend: one of the financial funders who contributed cash to the Democratic organizations which launched this whole domestic political-intelligence operation is also among the same people now effectively leading this official U.S. government interrogation against me?

Adding further insult to injury and more specifically, such Democrat campaign donations were the same fuel that paid for the DNC-funded consultant Christopher Steele's infamous Dodgy Dossier. The fact that such individuals had now found a way to perpetrate this vindictive harassment against their political adversaries in their official roles as U.S. government prosecutors seemed to defy common sense and common decency.[31]

As I put two and two together, I was almost in a state of shock. In just a few minutes, my break would end, and I would have to face Rhee again. Like walking back to my seat from the concessions area at a circus, I began to fully understand the frivolous game that I had been forced to play. Though I was hardly comforted, things were starting to make sense.

In a defining moment in his term as attorney general, Jeff Sessions famously recused himself from the Trump–Russia investigation based on an encounter with the Russian ambassador that was so incidental that he struggled to remember it, as well as his political support for candidate Trump.[32] In my group dinner with the senator in June 2016, Sessions had said that he had given his endorsement to candidate Trump during the campaign simply because one of his former staffers had suggested that he do so. Certainly any such perceived conflict of interest did not extend to anything like a maximum campaign contribution or serving as his personal attorney in highly contentious legal cases, as Jeannie Rhee had done for Mrs. Clinton.

By comparison, Lawrence Rush Atkinson reportedly only gave a paltry $200 donation to the 2016 Clinton campaign.[33] A token sum to be sure, but that was enough to reveal his loyalties. Clearly Rush had not yet graduated to the big leagues of political prosecutions.

I faced about twenty grand jurors—each of them studying my face as I spoke, looking for any sign of intimidation or deception. The relatively junior lawyer Rush Atkinson took up much of the grunt work in the interrogation. It immediately became clear who was driving the train. Atkinson would ask me a question, and Rhee would furiously write her next question on a yellow sticky note, her choice of communication medium, and slap it in front of Atkinson for him to verbalize. He would get something wrong in her eyes, and she would wrathfully scribble a correction and slap it down even harder.

I started to wonder: If there's something she wants to know, why doesn't she just go ahead and ask all of these foolish questions herself?

Having had no advance warning that this prominent Democratic lawyer would be there that day, I eventually figured out the likely reason for her methods. Similar to many courthouse forums, the three Democrat prosecutors were sitting next to a court reporter who kept record of who said what throughout the day. Certainly it would be a bad look if some independent-minded attorney sitting somewhere in the Rosenstein–Sessions Justice Department noted that the stenographer had transcribed records showing Jeannie Rhee was the one asking all the highly aggressive and blatantly political gotcha questions. She clearly intended to trip me up but didn't want to be the one doing so on the official record.

Atkinson humbly complied with the yellow stickies and recited, as best he could, the questions that Rhee demanded. After going through an additional stack of stickies, the junior prosecutor meekly noted how prolific her requests were. As the day wore on and Jeannie grew increasingly irritable, she would slap the yellow stickies down even harder next to Rush's photocopies of my personal documents. Perhaps the rising mound of stickies was becoming an all-too-symbolic reminder that she could not manage to succeed in her quest to ensnare another Trump supporter.

The show trial format of the day had all the trappings of a quiz bowl–styled game show. Instead of the more amusing brain-teaser competitions such as Trivial Pursuit, the game cards for this contest consisted of big stacks of paper that the partisan special counsel team had printed out. For some reason, one of the quirks of the grand jury game prevented contestants such as me from bringing even one sheet of paper into the arena. I felt as if I were being asked to participate in a game of "What's in my pocket?"

Though it was over two years ago, my memory of the day's events is as vivid as ever. Rhee, working through Atkinson, impatiently demanded to know things like: In January 2016, you wrote an email referring to someone without mentioning their name. Who exactly did you have in mind then?

As I tried explaining the details of what really happened, one of the grand jurors sitting right before me slightly nodded his head in agreement before I got rudely cut off by my questioners. At least one member of the jury wasn't buying this political charade.

■ ■ ■

Around the time the Mueller Dossier was released to the public, the report's official lead author was videotaped looking befuddled as he was approached by a journalist. As Robert Mueller was about to enter his vehicle, he handed the car keys to his wife, and she went around to the passenger side to let him in.[34] The moment carried particular irony for me. As a result of unofficial leaks portraying me as a traitor, I had been subjected to countless terrorist death threats. But Robert Mueller's being mildly harassed by journalists actually doing their job was portrayed by many in the media as a dangerous attack on the public order.

Meanwhile, no one was being held accountable among the Democrats and government operatives who instigated this unnecessary process based on false evidence. But it wasn't until I read his bestselling Mueller Report in spring 2019 that I learned that giving Robert Mueller the benefit of the doubt had been the wrong move.[35] It was then that I realized, if anything, the Mueller Report had become another Dodgy Dossier.

The Mueller Report was released to the public on April 18, 2019. Similar to the DNC-funded Dodgy Dossier, it was hard to find a single sentence in the "Mueller Dossier" that didn't mislead the public in some way. Now that the document has increasingly been rendered moot with subsequent revelations that show the true intentions of these political prosecution perpetrators, I'll spare you the point-by-point refutation. But the day did mark many important milestones and turning points.

Over a year earlier in February 2018, Adam Schiff had told reporters at a *Christian Science Monitor* breakfast, "there is already, in my view, ample evidence in the public domain on the issue of collusion if you're willing to see it."[36] For three years, the media barrage on the Trump–Russia collusion narrative had plowed through all barriers like a runaway train. The arrival of the Mueller Report in the spring of 2019 started to siphon the steam from that train.

No American was charged with any crime related to the suborning of the U.S. election in a conspiracy with Russians. Several were hit with process crimes like charges of lying about relatively minor aspects of the investigation. Unrelated to his work on the Trump campaign, Paul Manafort went to prison for bank fraud and tax evasion. After hitting Roger Stone's home with a dawn raid by a SWAT team, prosecutors could only get him for crimes related to the investigation.

Not a single crime related to the campaign or related to Russia in any significant way was identified. Given my position as the one Trump supporter who probably spent the most time in Moscow in 2016, this recognition held special significance to me. All the partisan Democratic challengers who tried prosecuting this series of show trials started to limp back to their old jobs without anything material to show for their expensive efforts.

■ ■ ■

Robert Mueller testified on Wednesday, July 24, 2019. With control of the U.S. House of Representatives now held by the party that paid for the introduction of the Dodgy Dossier into the American justice system and Intelligence Community, their loyalists were in charge of managing the information flow. The complete mockery continued, broadcast across many of the same television stations that had followed every move of the largely-Democratic team throughout the past few years. The seventy-four-year-old Mueller spent much of the day looking lost as he provided answers. Even Dana Milbank of the *Washington Post* had to report: "He looked dazed and confused as he listened, mouth agape."[37] Mueller couldn't even identify which president had appointed him to be a United States Attorney, much less identify a coherent conspiracy theory from his report.

Though my time in the barrel was now over, I still didn't feel that I had seen justice. In fact, Mueller's testimony only deepened the sense that so many Americans had been betrayed. I had eagerly supported Robert Mueller's appointment, believing that his record of military service and his prior reputation would help clear my name. But by the time his investigation came to a close, with no evidence of any wrongdoing, the Mueller Report still let suspicions hang around President Trump, myself, and countless other innocent souls. Watching Mueller on television showed me how deep the decay ran in our justice system. The man I had thought would exonerate me was evidently not the person running the show. And after all this time, justice still hadn't been served.

With so many questions still left unanswered, the dark but enigmatic innuendos of the Mueller Report festered like an open wound. It wasn't until the following year that a few more of the questions started getting addressed by other offices within the Justice Department.

CHAPTER SEVEN

A HEIGHTENED DUTY OF CANDOR

*"Unfortunately, DOJ/FBI's intransigence with respect to the
August 24 subpoenas is part of a broader pattern of behavior that can no longer be tolerated.... at this point it seems
the DOJ and FBI need to be investigating themselves."*

—*Congressman Devin Nunes*[1]

O ver recent years, we've become accustomed to seeing former leaders
of the Intelligence Community as either paid contributors or frequent guest commentators on highly partisan cable news shows. Among
the many examples are former director of National Intelligence James
Clapper, former CIA director John Brennan, and prior FBI officials
Andrew McCabe and James Comey.[2] While each has a constitutional
right to be as partisan and as outspoken as he wants to be, the recent
directors from top U.S. Intelligence Community agencies' attacking the
sitting president on a regular basis marks a new turn in our culture. The
spectacle of the past several years has brought them out from the shadows, and the culture of this Community has increasingly been revealed.

After three years of pushing their false narratives on the American
public, the Obama-era leadership of the FBI, CIA, and other intelligence agencies have gradually been exposed as partisan operatives.
They created the Russia collusion hoax to preserve their power and to

silence their opposition. My case and the FISA abuse surrounding the 2016 presidential campaign showcased their tactics, but I was hardly the real target of their attacks. This was an attack on Donald J. Trump and the movement that he has led from the campaign trail and the Oval Office. The people charged with protecting our rights launched an assault on American democracy and the core principles of justice enshrined in the U.S. Constitution.

Against this dangerous backdrop, will real facts actually matter anymore? The battle for the narrative has become a battle for survival. So who and what will survive? More lies or the truth?

■ ■ ■

For all their hysteria, especially Comey's unctuous and preening appearances on television, I have never forgotten the many hard-working agents in the FBI, CIA, and other agencies I have come to know over the years. These are men and women who are not involved in headquarters's intrigues or media gamesmanship. Instead, a vast majority of them are true professionals who never looked to become talking heads after they left government service. I think of the agents who regularly miss their children's school plays, musical recitals, and soccer games to work over-time to keep us safe. I have met many of these people over the years, and I was at one point proud to serve with them as an informant.

Most of the agents I've met with seemed to be true patriots, just try-ing to do their job. When they asked me to do something for my country, I never hesitated. I was always happy to meet American intelligence officers in Moscow and did so on a regular basis. And, though it has never before been reported, I was also happy to meet with CIA agents to discuss what I've learned about China and my insight into other countries as well.

On January 18, 2013, one of my firm's international advisory board members invited me to the Asia Society's symposium on Sino-American Energy Diplomacy at which he was presenting.[3] Throughout many years of work in the energy finance sector, my travels often took me to China to consider a number of oil and gas transactions, as well as financing alternatives. Similar to myself, my colleague had long balanced a career working in both the energy sector and foreign policy academia. For many years, he helped China National Petroleum Corporation (CNPC) with their investments around the world. He was a member of the Chinese Academy of Social Sciences, affiliated with the State Council of the People's Republic of China, considered among the most respected think tanks in Asia. On the energy side, he frequently put me in contact with exceptionally well-positioned finance and energy industry contacts in China.

After many of my trips overseas, I was asked to sit down with CIA debriefers. I talked with them about essential strategic observations as well as some of the more mundane details of my interactions worldwide. I trusted the U.S. Intelligence Community at the time. So I left it up to them to sort out what might prove operationally helpful, both for the agency and for the U.S. government as a whole.

The person who originally introduced me to my Chinese colleague once mentioned that his contact in Beijing might have similar ties to the intelligence services of China. From my perspective and analogous to what I would later explain to my FBI interrogators during the March 2017 inquisition, it's only natural that true patriots around the world share their insight with their own country's government. Little did I know that people like Comey, Brennan, and McCabe were starting to advance a new career path. That transition would turn the traditional arrangement of trust between the IC and private American citizens on its head.

In my interactions with U.S. government intelligence officials, I never did anything but tell the truth, the whole truth, and nothing but the truth. Unlike what transpired more recently with the personal attacks against President Trump and me, I never served my country with any political or personal agenda in mind. I simply saw it as patriotic service in which some of the accurate information I shared might help to fill in

a fuller picture of world affairs. I considered that service a moral impera-
tive, and in some instances a national security necessity. I am sure many
of the people I discussed with the agents were, themselves, giving similar
debriefings directly on their end.

But most importantly, I believe the flow of reliable and accurate
information is the best chance for the avoidance of conflict on both sides
of any relationship. The more I told the CIA and other federal agencies
about Russia, China, the Middle East, or other strategic hot spots worldwide, the more basic knowledge that might lead to better cooperation
was at their disposal. At the end of the day, contributions from American
businesspeople like me might help to improve prospects for international
security and peace—not just for the United States, but worldwide.

■ ■ ■

Once Devin Nunes, Chuck Grassley, Lindsey Graham, and Michael
Horowitz started to complete their various eponymous memos and
investigative reports in 2018 and 2019, most of the world began to grasp
just how well organized and immensely powerful the Russia collusion
conspiracy theory had been. I would use the word "vast" to describe it,
but only Mrs. Bill Clinton can use that adjective for a conspiracy without
being portrayed as a lunatic.[4] When it came to vast conspiracies, however,
members of her team would have a lot to do with this one.

After some of the investigations were completed, I could look back
and see that while I was focused on my modest work in the summer of
2016, others were focused on personally destroying me with a Democrat-
funded dossier. It wasn't really about me. It was all just a way to beat
Donald Trump and subvert American democracy. For example, a "field
memorandum" from Christopher Steele in July detailed the substance of
my purported meetings with the two Igors. According to an "anonymous" source, Igor Sechin mentioned the dropping of Ukraine-related
sanctions by a future Trump administration with an associated "bilateral
energy co-operation" deal.[5]

Steele also alleged a sweetener in this deal for me personally. According to an "associate" of Rosneft, Sechin offered me the contract to broker up to 19 percent of the privatization of Rosneft. Steele had reported my being offered fees for arranging such a deal, which on a percentage basis might still easily be counted in the hundreds of millions of dollars, if not more.[6]

Such a bribe, even at the brokerage level, would be a James Bond–villain level of compensation that would surely be noticed by financial reporting and intelligence agencies around the world. Again, it became increasingly clear that there were a lot of frustrated novelists in the intelligence, journalistic, and political consulting communities.

After Steele was fired as a confidential informant by the FBI for leaking to the media, Assistant Deputy Attorney General Bruce Ohr maintained the flow of information from Steele to the DOJ. Here is where we find a node in the conspiracy that connects partisanship, officialdom, front-line investigators, and, through a variety of twists and turns, the media. To begin with, Bruce Ohr did not have to leave home to find assistance with this endeavor. His wife, Nellie, while working for Fusion GPS, served as a conduit to help funnel Steele's anti-Trump information to her husband.[7]

"Hi Honey," began a typical email from Nellie Ohr to her husband at the Department of Justice, now made public thanks to a Freedom of Information Act request from Judicial Watch. "If Putin wanted to concoct the ideal candidate to service his purpose, his laboratory creation would be Donald Trump." She singled me out as someone who "continues to work with Russian investments." In 339 pages of emails to the Justice Department, Nellie Ohr also benefited from her husband's direct conduit to other high-ranking Justice officials. Nellie, who knew Christopher Steele from past work, had smoothed the way for her husband to meet with him. Bruce explained to Congress that it was Nellie who gave him a thumb-drive full of partisan opposition research to share with FBI officials assigned to various investigations.[8]

Ohr later testified that he had met with FBI agents at least a dozen times, providing a back door for the FBI to continue receiving information from a political consultant it had already fired. James Baker, the former FBI general counsel who later became a CNN legal analyst, would later admit that he was also a conduit for opposition research dirt from a Democratic National Committee lawyer to agents investigating the campaign.[9]

As John Solomon wrote in *The Hill*: "So, Bruce Ohr became a conduit of information not only for intelligence from Clinton's British opposition-researcher but also from his wife's curation of evidence from a Clinton foreign ally and Manafort enemy inside Ukraine. Talk about foreign influence in a U.S. election!"[10]

Part of Ohr's freelancing on the political aspects of this project involved a July 30, 2016, breakfast with Steele, and it continued for close to a year, including online and video conferences with the ex-spy.[11] He had learned, and would later testify, that this foreign intelligence source was "desperate" to sink Donald Trump's candidacy.[12] Ohr nevertheless pitched the Dodgy Dossier to Andrew McCabe, then deputy director of the FBI, and Lisa Page, his counsel.[13] He also reached out to Peter Strzok, lead investigator of the melodramatically named Crossfire Hurricane, which included the pursuit of FISA warrants against me.[14] It was Glenn Simpson, head of Fusion GPS, who had allegedly overseen the transfer of the Steele Dossier to John McCain's aide David Kramer. Kramer gave a copy to Senator McCain, who hand-delivered it to James Comey.[15] Not everyone who was fed the Dodgy Dossier swallowed the poisonous concoction entirely. Deputy Assistant Secretary of State Kathleen Kavalec listened in agreement to Ohr when he let it slip that the dossier was "kind of crazy... kind of wild... quite a tale."[16]

Later that year, Deputy Attorney General Rod Rosenstein expressed shock when he learned that Ohr had been spreading Steele's dirt around Washington. Tellingly, Rosenstein demoted Ohr but did not fire him.[17] As Ohr and Co. spread the Dodgy Dossier far and wide, it fell into the hands of helpful people like David Kramer, who made sure to keep the Washington media in the loop.

The skein of personal contacts in this conspiracy to deceive the public and harm the president crossed all boundaries, from foreign ex-intelligence agents to senior levels of the DOJ, the FBI, elected politicians, journalists, and even federal judges like the four who signed off on my false warrants. After short-lived national security advisor General Michael Flynn issued a guilty plea, another U.S. district court judge, Rudolph Contreras, was recused from his case. The likely reason can be found in the text messages between Strzok and Page when Judge Contreras was appointed to serve part-time on the Foreign Intelligence Surveillance Court, the secret court that issued the four FISA warrants to surveil me as a suspected agent of a foreign power.

"Rudy is on the FISC! Did you know that? Just appointed two months ago," Lisa Page texted her colleague and lover, Peter Strzok.

"I did," he texted back. "We talked about it before and after. I need to get together with him."[18]

Strzok mentioned "a graduation party" at which he and Judge Contreras had talked.[19] This is a prime example of the kind of backstage, familiar relationships that prompt so many to see Washington, D.C., as a swamp where elites from all walks of life socialize and blur the lines that traditionally define the proper boundaries of their professions.

The world did not learn much of what was going on until late 2019, but like so many people across America, I increasingly saw an unmistakable pattern: a hidden network of people in the Intelligence Community, law enforcement, and the media were cooperating to try to damage and put me in prison as part of their post-election campaign against the president.

■ ■ ■

The runaway train that was the Trump–Russia collusion conspiracy theory had continued to plow its way through 2017, with James Comey often serving as one of the lead conductors. Before the inauguration, Comey had ventured to Trump Tower to brief the president-elect on the

Steele dossier and to tell him that there were allegations that the Russians had a video of him with prostitutes in a Moscow hotel room during his visit for the 2013 Miss Universe pageant. "I did not go into the business about people peeing on each other, I just thought it was a weird enough experience for me to be talking to the incoming president of the United States about prostitutes in a hotel in Moscow," he later told a reporter.[20]

Comey noted that for some reason, the president elect—just told by his FBI director that he consorted with prostitutes—was "defensive."[21] There can be little doubt as to why: Donald Trump thought the whole experience was weird, too.

After another discussion with the new president in February about leniency for fired national security advisor General Michael Flynn, Comey wrote up what essentially seemed to be the equivalent of an FBI 302 form on the president, something he would only tend to do if he considered Trump the target of an investigation. He later passed on one of those memos based on conversations with president-elect Trump to a Columbia law professor and close friend, who dutifully leaked it to the *New York Times*.[22] The search for possible predicates to launch an obstruction of justice investigation continued; these stood as early attempts to prepare a case to remove the president from office.

By early May, President Trump had had enough of these shenanigans and rightly fired Comey.[23] Some of President Trump's closest advisors, including former White House chief strategist Steve Bannon, criticized the Comey decision, claiming in September 2017 that it might be the biggest mistake in "modern political history."[24] But as I had said the week Comey was fired, I knew right from the start that the president had done the right thing. The evidence of the Comey FBI's FISA abuse, revealed over the years that followed, only confirmed my belief.

At the time this book was being completed, the investigations have continued regarding an infamous White House meeting on

January 5, 2017.[25] As time goes on, these inquiries have rightfully only seemed to escalate.

■ ■ ■

Before the truth came out, however, the machinery of secret surveillance and public leaks that had been set in motion to smear me—and by implication, to portray Trump's surprise victory as the result of Russian interference—remained in high gear behind the scenes. The process of filing FISA applications to spy on me ran from 2016 to the fourth and final filing in June 2017.[26] Director James Comey signed three FISA applications and Deputy Director Andrew McCabe signed one. At DOJ, FISA warrants were signed by Deputy Attorneys General Sally Yates, Dana Boente, and Rod Rosenstein.[27]

By law, each FISA order on an American citizen must be renewed every ninety days, and each renewal requires a separate finding of probable cause.[28] The FISA process is an anomaly in our constitutional system—an *ex parte* proceeding in which the target has no representation in court, and is almost always unaware that he is being targeted. Judge Rosemary Collyer noted in 2019 that it is precisely because the proceedings are secret that the court must provide "an external check on executive branch decisions to conduct surveillance" in order "to protect fourth amendment rights of U.S. persons." This only works, she wrote, if the government adheres to "a heightened duty of candor."[29]

Originally, the upper echelons of the FBI fiercely rejected any suggestions they had been anything less than rigorous and candid in my FISA application. In December, 2018, ex-FBI director James Comey ventured to Capitol Hill, where he said he had "total confidence that the FISA process was followed and that the entire case was handled in a thoughtful, responsible way by DOJ and FBI."[30] Such assertions, however, were already contested. Ten months before Comey's spirited defense of the FBI and the FISA process, HPSCI Chairman Devin Nunes, aided

by Congressman Trey Gowdy, released a memo from the majority that
zeroed in on the origins of the Steele Dossier.

"Steele was a long-time FBI source who was paid over $160,000 by
the DNC and Clinton campaign, via the law firm Perkins Coie and
research firm Fusion GPS, to obtain derogatory information on Donald
Trump's ties to Russia," Nunes wrote. His memo also noted that the
citation of the Isikoff Yahoo article "does not corroborate the Steele dossier because it is derived from information leaked by Steele himself to
Yahoo! News."[31]

The Nunes Memo also reported on what the Department of Justice
was learning about Steele: "[I]n September 2016, Steele admitted to Ohr
his feelings against then-candidate Trump when Steele said he 'was desperate that Donald Trump not get elected and was passionate about him
not being president.' This clear evidence of Steele's bias was recorded by
Ohr at the time and subsequently in official FBI files—but not reflected
in any of the Page FISA applications."

As I continued to learn more about the way political actors had
abused the justice system, these results closely matched many of my
personal experiences over these years. Many supporters of Donald
Trump were exposed to severe injustices, enabled by a nearly constant
flow of outright lies sprinkled with half-truths.

Making matters worse, the Nunes Memo also found that: "The
Ohrs' relationship with Steele and Fusion GPS was inexplicably concealed from the FISC."[32]

The Nunes Memo later came under intense criticism from the same
media which had pushed the lies for over a year, and always willing to take
a shot at President Trump, Adam Schiff validated those critiques by journalists.[33] With more information coming to light, it's clear that Nunes
came much closer to the truth than many were willing to believe, despite
having to overcome scores of administrative obstacles set by the Rosenstein–Sessions DOJ. Nunes was right that Steele's Dodgy Dossier played
an "essential" role in my FISA applications, presaging DOJ Inspector
General Michael Horowitz's similar conclusion.[34] After chipping away at

the brick wall that had helped to cover many misdeeds, Nunes correctly reported what he found and helped to break open the scandal of my FISA applications. Profoundly grateful for what he did to help restore justice in America and integrity in the U.S. Intelligence Community, I was excited to see then-Chairman Nunes receive a well-deserved "Defender of Freedom" award at CPAC in 2018.[35]

While Nunes was being honored, Adam Schiff and his partisan allies on the committee, then in the minority, hit back with a memo of their own titled "Correcting the Record—The Russia Investigation." Schiff described Bruce Ohr as "a well-respected career professional," despite the fact that Rod Rosenstein and others at higher levels of the Justice Department reported that they had felt blindsided and betrayed by Ohr before demoting him.[36] Schiff and his partisans on the committee reported: "DOJ cited multiple sources to support the case for surveilling Page—but made only narrow use of information from Steele's sources about Page's specific activities in 2016, chiefly his suspected July 2016 meetings in Moscow with Russian officials."[37]

The conclusion of Schiff and friends was that "DOJ met the rigor, transparency and evidentiary basis needed to meet FISA's probable cause requirement."[38]

A third memo, written by Senators Chuck Grassley and Lindsey Graham of the Senate Judiciary Committee, was declassified soon after the release of the Nunes Memo. Grassley–Graham carefully peeled away much of the protective coverage and bland assertions of the Schiff–Comey narrative. The two senators reviewed classified documents against sworn statements by Christopher Steele in British litigation, and concluded "it appears that either Mr. Steele lied to the FBI or the British court, or that classified documents reviewed by the committee contain materially false statements."[39] Grassley–Graham reported that Steele had testified that he had conducted two rounds of interviews that included the *New York Times*, the *Washington Post*, Yahoo! News, *The New Yorker*, and CNN at the direction of Fusion GPS.[40] Far from making narrow use of the Steele report, the FBI based their application on it.

In short, the senators found that in this episode of *l'affaire Page*, all roads led back to Steele and his paymasters in the DNC and Clinton campaign. As Steele spread his muck far and wide, his investigation became increasingly an open source venture.

"Simply put, the more people who contemporaneously knew that Mr. Steele was compiling his dossier, the more likely it was vulnerable to manipulation," Grassley and Graham wrote. "In fact, in the British litigation, which involves a post-election dossier memorandum, Mr. Steele admitted that he received and included in it unsolicited—and unverified—allegations. That filing implies that he similarly received unsolicited intelligence on these matters prior to the election as well, stating that Mr. Steele 'continued to receive unsolicited intelligence on the matters covered by the pre-election memoranda after the US Presidential election.'"[41]

Much later, during the hearings on the president's call with Ukrainian president Volodymyr Zelensky, Adam Schiff would hear Fiona Hill, President Trump's former NSC senior director for European and Russian affairs, reportedly testify that the Steele report itself could well have been disinformation, and that Steele himself might have been "played" by the Russians.[42]

Ms. Hill, now back at the Brookings Institution and no fond admirer of her former boss, said of Russia: "Their goal was to discredit the presidency. Whoever was elected president, they wanted to weaken them. So, if Secretary Clinton had won, there would have been a cloud over her at this time if she was President Clinton. There's been a cloud over President Trump since the beginning of his presidency, and I think that's exactly what the Russians intended."[43]

■ ■ ■

Despite the fact that Steele was the primary impetus for the Russia collusion conspiracy theory, Comey continued to maintain that the Steele Dossier was "part of a broader mosaic of facts that were laid before the

FISA judge."[44] Somehow Comey could maintain this collusion narrative in public; in June 2017, before congressional investigators, former director of National Intelligence Dan Coats testified that Comey had told him "there is smoke but no fire" on collusion. The DNI went on to say that he was targeting me, but "there is no evidence to indicate at this point that the president had collusion with the Russians."[45] The public contentions of collusion would not be torn down for good until they were examined by a holdover appointee of the Obama administration, Michael Horowitz.

Given his political ties to the prior administration that nominated him, I did not have high expectations for Horowitz's investigation or his report on the FISA abuse against President Trump and me. Whether from an institutional desire to save the deep state patient by cauterizing a festering wound, or some level of commitment to finding the legitimate truth, Horowitz issued a 476-page report that refuted the contentions of Adam Schiff and James Comey and leveled an initial condemnation of the FBI.

Days after its release, Chris Wallace's interview of James Comey on Fox News put the impact of the report in context. Every time Comey tried to softly walk back Horowitz's findings, Wallace rebutted him by turning to a clip of Horowitz directly contradicting the former FBI chief.[46]

The results of Horowitz's official investigation and the blithe characterizations of Comey and Schiff could not be more at odds. Horowitz reported that the FBI "did not aggressively seek to obtain certain potentially important information from Steele. For example, the FBI did not press Steele for information about the actual funding source for his election reporting work."[47] Nor did agents question Steele about his role behind the Isikoff/Yahoo! News article, which was often cited as an independent source.[48]

The inspector general (IG) reported that "the FBI assessed in the Carter Page FISA applications, without any support, that Steele had not 'directly provided' the information to Yahoo! News."[49] The FBI is required to conduct a process known as the Woods Procedure to pains-takingly verify facts about a target for surveillance. "We found," Horowitz reported, "that the team had speculated that Steele's prior reporting had been corroborated and used in criminal proceedings without clearing the representation with Steele's handling agent, as required by the Woods Procedures." Contrary to his Democratic sponsors' attempts and despite their best efforts, Steele's information was never used in criminal proceedings against me.[50]

Horowitz's office reported that among the FBI's transgressions was the omission of assessments from people who had previous professional contacts with Steele. The inspector general report included statements that Steele "[d]emonstrates lack of self-awareness, poor judgment," and that he "pursued people with political risk but no intelligence value," and "didn't always exercise great judgment...."[51] The FBI knew that Steele's so-called "intelligence" was questionable from the get-go, but decided to hide their concerns from a FISA court that relied on their good faith. They were motivated by the power of Steele's false assumptions as a driving force for their shady investigation, rather than protecting my constitutional rights as a loyal American citizen and U.S. military veteran.

The FBI agents involved in the FISA application didn't just misrepresent their main source's integrity; they repeatedly omitted exonerating evidence that the sources they ran against me had collected. The Horowitz investigation found that the FBI's FISA applications had not informed the court that the FBI, in surveilling my conversations with Stefan Halper, had heard me specifically deny knowing Paul Manafort and deny having met with Igor Sechin and Igor Divyekin—I had not even known who the latter was. These failures were repeated in all three of my renewal applications, including the final one signed by Rosenstein and McCabe.[52]

The IG found that the FBI omitted information indicating that I "played no role in the Republican platform change on Russia's annexation of Ukraine...inconsistent with a factual assertion relied upon to support probable cause in all four FISA applications."[53] But they left out so many more details, like the fact that I wasn't even in Cleveland when those Republican platform deliberations were happening and that I hadn't even heard about it until the decision was already made.

Perhaps worst of all was the deliberate hiding of my relationship with the CIA and the service I had performed for my country. One government attorney had specifically asked my case agent in late September 2016, whether I had a current or prior relationship with the CIA. The case agent had replied that I had such a relationship, but that it was "dated," going back to my time in Moscow in 2004–2007 and was therefore "outside [the] scope" of the current investigation.

The IG report reads like a real dud, despite containing some of the most explosive political news in recent memory. It's like an intentionally boring novel that waters down the true drama behind the story. The Obama-appointee Horowitz continues: "This representation, however, was contrary to information that the other agency had provided to the FBI in August 2016, which stated that Page was approved as an 'operational contact' of the other agency from 2008 to 2013 (after Page had left Moscow). Moreover, rather than being 'outside scope,' Page's status with the other agency overlapped in time with some of the interactions between Page and known Russian intelligence officers that were relied upon in the FISA applications to establish probable cause."[54] Like the saying goes, this was just the tip of the iceberg. Each of these fleeting allusions represents only a small part of the story. Despite sensitive intelligence information being involved, further steps must be taken expeditiously now to finally reveal the full truth surrounding these details.

As the Horowitz report started to expose, the FBI should have informed the FISA court about all of the help that I had given to that "other agency." They likely avoided doing so because it might have shown how incompetent and deceitful the Obama administration had been throughout this historic moment. Buried beneath the rock are tons of essential specifics. Future books still need to be written on this. But for the time being, I agree with many members of Congress including Devin Nunes who believe the FBI tried to cover up as much as it could.[55]

Given the lengths that the Bureau went to to portray me as a villain on behalf of their political benefactors, it is unsurprising that the FBI hid that the CIA had given me a "positive assessment" for my candor. But the FBI didn't just hide exonerating evidence in their attack against me. The agency went even further. Perhaps most astonishing of all are the half-truths that have been exposed thus far. As an example, an FBI attorney altered evidence to present to the FISA court to say exactly the opposite of what an e-mail contained. The email from the CIA affirmed my service and record as an informant but was doctored to say that I was *not* a source for that agency.

So who was the FBI attorney behind this fabrication submitted as sworn testimony to the court? It was allegedly Kevin Clinesmith, the same attorney who had earlier denied my offer to continue helping with the ongoing investigation in early April 2017. It all occurred while he and his colleagues at the Bureau refused to address the terror threats I was experiencing while criminal leaks continued to make their way to the press. One week after these discussions with Clinesmith, the *Washington Post* became the first news outlet to disclose more preliminary details about my FISA warrant.[56]

Despite the incomplete nature of Obama-appointee Horowitz's analysis and his team's complete blocking of any input from the falsely accused (such as myself), he has done a fairly good job of keeping pace with the record he criticizes. In late 2017, Congressman Nunes famously wrote to Rod Rosenstein that, "at this point it seems the DOJ and FBI need to be investigating themselves."[57] So far, DOJ's self-investigation has not yet achieved a full solution to the underlying problems, nor has it given a full account of the truth.

■ ■ ■

Despite Mr. Horowitz's own shortcomings, the inspector general's FISA abuse report did unearth those seventeen significant errors or omissions. It made mincemeat of Schiff's assertion that "FBI and DOJ officials did not 'abuse'" the FISA process, "omit material information, or subvert this vital tool to spy on the Trump campaign...."[58] And to Nunes's oft-criticized claim that the Steele report was "essential" to my FISA applications, Horowitz added that Steele was "central and essential" to the FBI's and Justice Department's *decision* to seek the FISA order.[59] Many have tried to parse some of my FISA applications as legitimate, some as not. If anything, this observation validates what most of us have known for a long time: all four FISA warrants were illegitimate because the predicate was illegitimate.

The Horowitz report blew through Washington like a tornado through a swamp, roiling the waters, throwing a few alligators on the bank, and purging, if only for a time, some of the murk. The misdeeds of the FBI and DOJ were, for once, exposed. It is up to us, however, to expose the larger ecosystem that perpetuates such lies and transforms them into cable-news commodities. The fact is, my story doesn't just implicate the crooked cops at the FBI who lied to the FISA courts. Instead, it's a severe warning about the way our entire political system works. The Intelligence Community didn't just restrict the information they gave FISA judges tasked with protecting the rights of American citizens, they manipulated the media narrative and used it as a key instrument in their fictitious presentations to the court. In that light, the judiciary could stand some examination of the way their process has failed as well.

In her blistering rebuke of the FBI, Judge Rosemary Collyer sanctioned FBI agents but never answered the question of how four FISA judges decide to surveil people involved in a campaign for the presidency of the United States without thoroughly questioning what they were told by the FBI. Not one judge thought to invoke his or her ability under current law to consult with independent legal scholars with high security clearances, known as *amicus curiae*, to inspect cases that present "novel or significant" interpretations of the law.

Consider this: the FISA court had been asked to investigate officials in one of the two major party campaigns for president, and it saw nothing novel or significant worthy of a higher threshold of scrutiny.

The scrutiny should also be turned on a press corps that has become too habituated to the dog treats of the IC, and people like Adam Schiff, who have turned their access to secret material into a ticket to deceive. Though they had access to the same documents and sources as Nunes, Grassley, and Graham, people like Schiff received very little negative coverage from the mainstream media for papering over the truth, while Nunes was regularly reviled and denounced by the media. There was a time when journalists, if so severely burned, would turn from a source like Schiff. Today, officialdom and the media continue to work behind the scenes with Schiff to craft the narratives that shape the perceptions of millions of Americans. Many journalists who purport to "speak truth to power" continue to celebrate lies as a way of protecting their own power.

■ ■ ■

I firmly believe there is much more to be learned about how the Russia collusion investigation began, and how the campaign behind it operated. We will probably never know the whole truth, but until we do, the rule of law will not be re-established. The system of secret surveillance will remain a threat to our liberties and constitutional principles.

We must never forget that at bottom, this was not about harming one guy like me. It was about invalidating the legitimacy of the election of the forty-fifth president of the United States and setting the basis for the effort by people like House Speaker Nancy Pelosi and Adam Schiff to remove him by impeachment.

It can be frustrating to think what partisans have done to our democracy. It disturbs me to think of all the people this episode has damaged. Even at the periphery of an attack like the Russia-collusion conspiracy theory, there are many people whose lives have been damaged, who've had to take out second mortgages or bust retirement plans or college funds to pay lawyers. Many have developed health issues and perhaps had their lives shortened.

Someone who seems to have weathered the storm relatively well was Steven Schrage, the Cambridge Ph.D. who had invited me to the seminar where I was introduced to Stefan Halper. Despite Schrage's prior career in the White House, the State Department, and academia, he was sometimes mentioned in the media and the dark corners of the blogosphere as a sinister enabler. While I was being pummeled in the media, Steven was the subject of rumors about being in league with his one-time professor Stefan Halper. Was Steven Schrage part of an anti-Trump conspiracy? Was he some kind of "cutout" for Halper? Did he exploit his friendship with me?

Steven told me that he was, in fact, blissfully ignorant of Halper's spying. As one of the leaders the program, he had merely extended an invitation to the Cambridge event. For this tangential connection to Halper, his life was added to the list of those turned upside down by years of personal attacks and investigations too.

It is often said that the fear of being investigated, and ruined, by a special counsel or zealous prosecutor keeps quality people from considering public service. A snippet of conversation, a chance meeting is enough to land any American in a cauldron of controversy and attacks that can go on for years. From J.D. Gordon, whom I got to know during the campaign, to Michael Caputo, whom I would only meet years later, and General Michael Flynn whom I've never met, many people continue to endure the consequences of connections to the Trump–Russia scandal.[60] It remains an unresolved fictional story that had real-world consequences for these and so many others. The narrative's only potential flicker of legitimacy seemed to come in the procedural vagaries of long, drawn-out federal litigation that has paralleled these other high-drama investigations.

CHAPTER EIGHT

A LEGACY OF LAWSUITS

"To some lawyers, all facts are created equal."
—*Justice Felix Frankfurter*

SEPTEMBER 2017

Other than my faith in God, country, and family, the law has permanently stood among the defining principles in my life. From my upbringing and my youthful admiration of my grandparents, I always held our country's legal principles in the highest regard. Beginning with the U.S. Constitution, I viewed the law as the foundation upon which much of America had been built. I took obeyance of the law as a given. Perhaps it was naïve, but I had always assumed that if you simply do the right thing and act honestly then you run little risk of incurring the wrath of the legal authorities. The law isn't just meant to punish wrongdoers. It is a guardrail that makes it easy for law-abiding citizens to stay on the road.

Later as I peered out over the ledge at the wreckage created by the U.S. Intelligence Community following the election of President Donald J. Trump, all of my assumptions about how America's legal system functions came crashing down. As we eventually learned, so-called legal experts across both the private and public sectors had helped crooked politicians smash through nearly every guardrail. By creating false Foreign Intelligence Surveillance Court documents, lawyers didn't treat our legal code like the bedrock of American life. Instead, they turned the law into a weapon to use against their political opponents. As I and others who supported Donald Trump were pummeled by years of legal processes, the "experts" were chipping away at the very foundations of American life.

The exceptionally aggressive tactics displayed by legal practitioners' abuses in the U.S. Foreign Intelligence Surveillance Court embodied a whole new approach to judicial proceedings. Where there weren't enough facts, government officials used their media contacts to create new fictions. I had worked with top legal practitioners throughout my career, but I had never encountered this class of lawyer. From the campaign onward, I would get a practical education in how the other side of the law is widely practiced today.

■ ■ ■

For more than two centuries, the U.S. Constitution established the core doctrines upon which our country is based and the law is practiced. But the unmooring of the practice of law from constitutional constraints has left fundamental aspects of our legal system and our country in shambles. The damage goes beyond the self-inflicted wounds of the FBI, Intelligence Community, and justice system. The underlying source of this deterioration stretches back deep into prestigious law schools. Within most of the legal ivory tower, the Constitution and its guarantee of equal treatment is often considered flawed guidance at best. Instead left-wing ideologies abound, treating the law as a tool with which to perfect society from the top down.

Many of our leaders who oversaw various aspects of the FISA debacle had credentials from the country's preeminent legal institutions. They included Harvard Law School graduate Barack Obama, Yale Law School alumna Hillary Clinton, and University of Chicago Law School graduate James Comey.[1] Other prominent lawyers directly involved in the fiasco included former "acting" U.S. Attorneys General Sally Yates and Dana Boente, graduates of strong, regional law schools.[2]

Rod Rosenstein had signed what was allegedly the most flawed FISA warrant affidavit of them all, extending my surveillance when it should have been clear that the Steele accusations were the complete "garbage" that I had warned Comey of nine months earlier.[3] Rosenstein's former section mates from Harvard Law School included prominent Trump one-time communications chief, now critic, Anthony Scaramucci.[4] While Rosenstein was still at the Justice Department, Scaramucci told ABC's George Stephanopoulos that he was "a great guy" and that he shouldn't be fired.[5] At the end of the day, such a collaborative sentiment epitomizes the inherently incestuous nature of American legal circles. Under the surface, those who have joined the elite clubs like Harvard Law School protect their networks. The term "EQUAL JUSTICE UNDER LAW" is engraved in capital letters atop the U.S. Supreme Court. But as a practical matter and as my experiences have shown, who you know in the right legal circles often carries far more weight than any commitment to justice among the powerful establishment elite. Perhaps to my personal detriment, I have always followed my grandfathers' example and stuck to what I knew was right. Amidst such an incessant tipping of the scales, I have consistently refused to surrender to this broken system.

■ ■ ■

My obligatory isolation from the world left me with extra time, a lot of energy, and increasingly high motivation as I came to realize what was really going on. Rather than wait forever for a decrepit legal system to eventually fix itself, I decided that there must be some better way to address the breakdown in the law that I was witnessing in real time. Like a person watching structures designed and built by top professional architects collapse into rubble, I chose to take the Home Depot approach,

DIY-style. I came to realize that I was in the middle of an unprece-dented legal firestorm, very few so-called experts would be in a posi-tion to help me. I had the full force of government, the media, and the general public against me. But since I knew most of the inside facts regarding how I was being framed, I was in a unique position to cut right to the core of the problem. In the middle of the crisis, I saw an opportunity to address the national legal problems that urgently needed to be confronted. These dilemmas had to be fixed, so instead of waiting for someone to come to my rescue, I immediately got to work.

Whether on Capitol Hill, in the federal courts, or in the monolithic bureaucracy of the central government, I came to learn that many law-yers had ceded control to other attorneys with more intense political motivations and less accountability. I was particularly disappointed by the actions of then-Attorney General Jeff Sessions. To be fair, he is a gentleman to the core, and I was happy when I learned that I might have the opportunity to work with then-Senator Sessions on candidate Trump's foreign policy advisory team. On the other hand, Attorney General Sessions could never muster the courage necessary to constrain the partisan operatives who freely functioned under him in the Depart-ment of Justice with little to no accountability. President Trump's antago-nists interpreted Mr. Sessions's gentlemanly demeanor as a blank check to exercise nearly limitless power. Only about forty days into the new administration, in early March 2017, Sessions recused himself from anything having to do with the investigation of Donald Trump and his associates. Sessions did this after the media manufactured a scandal out of his incidental contact with the Russian ambassador. The senator's interactions had been entirely appropriate given the role under our Con-stitution of the U.S. Senate in foreign policy.[6] The recusal initially struck most as a minor note of administrative trivia. Or in pompous legal par-lance, many viewed it as simply "procedural" in nature. But the recusal quickly allowed the Department of Justice to become the epicenter of misdeeds. Into this space stepped Deputy Attorney General Rod

Rosenstein. Not far behind him, Rosenstein introduced another partner into this power vacuum. Inspiring a bit more confidence and bringing more name recognition to the whole endeavor, former FBI director Robert Mueller joined the drama onstage.

Just like most people who think through the economics of a do-it-yourself home improvement project, the calculus of personally hiring a big team of lawyers didn't seem to add up. Contributing millions of dollars to support an insider law firm didn't seem very attractive either, especially when I knew that I was falsely accused and had done nothing wrong in the first place. I had already learned the hard way that if lawyers dared to speak the complete truth about how corrupt the entire system had become, it would denigrate their whole clubby profession. As a branding exercise and after investing in many years of training, all legal practitioners could risk losing immensely if the word got out. Plus, the swamp lawyers in Washington, D.C., had the most to lose by uncovering the dirty game that was at play. When so many of the fundamental rules of the game are built upon deception, is it worth jeopardizing a job that pays up to $1,000 an hour (or even more in the private sector) to break this professional code of silence? Would it be worth clashing with another lawyer at DOJ who once worked at a friendly law firm with whom you might someday be reunited as equity partners?

For most, the answer is a resounding "No." In any adversarial system of justice, practitioners are trained to directly focus their attention on the precise target in their crosshairs. Targeting the entire tainted system by fully explaining all the corrupt inner workings of this monolithic enterprise would be a bridge too far and would involve undue risks to the professional ambitions of the lawyers I hired on my cases. I worried that some would bill me for millions of dollars, while mailing in my case so as to maintain credibility in their elite law professional circles. Given all that I had learned about the manipulation of the law, I knew that I couldn't trust most of them. The shady scheme that I had come to learn about the hard way seemed like a challenge that only an outsider, effectively a legal vigilante, might take on.

■ ■ ■

The fact that many of our laws had become empty shells was already perfectly clear to me in April 2017. Until then, I had clung to the hope that this legal hell was the product of some grave misunderstanding rather than an essentially corrupt system. No one can now question the illegality of the FBI's secretly surveilling myself and many members of the Trump team via my FISA warrants. They illegally leaked the existence of those applications to smear me, and by implication, the Trump administration. As the months went on, it grew increasingly clear to me, long before others could see it, that fundamental legal frameworks had been broken by the Intelligence Community and certain political actors. Some members of Congress were starting to wake up and began at least making calls for more information. The fact that lawmakers were taking initial action encouraged me to keep going forward, despite the fact that their calls often went unanswered.

By April 2017, I already realized that I would need to undertake the Herculean labor of getting myself out of the legal morass I was in by myself. I quickly got the sense that there were very few lawyers I could trust with my case. They might take my money, but would they really fight on my behalf when most of the world stood against me?

I had never been trained as a lawyer. I had limited background in the law, aside from my experience working alongside lawyers in the military and private sector. But as I had learned from experience in all sorts of different occupations, I knew that I could begin to find my feet if I put my head down and tried to figure out what was going on for myself. I began voraciously consuming legal references pursuant to my case, reading as much as possible about the bind the corrupt cops in the Intelligence Community and their political allies had put me in. I was learning how the law worked at the highest levels back then, with my own life and the lives of many others stuck in this opressive predicament.

If I was going to be forced to take a crash course in the law, then I wanted to find ways to challenge the corrupt system firsthand. Diving deep into the facts and the law surrounding my situation, I filed *pro se* lawsuits against the government and private sector perpetrators. "*Pro se*," in keeping with the translation from the original Latin, is legalese for "someone does his own legal work" in court cases. According to *Black's Law Dictionary*, the definition is: "For himself; in his own behalf."[7]

From my research, I knew that I could file a case against the government based on the Privacy Act of 1974 statute. The Privacy Act proclaims that: "No agency shall disclose any record which is contained in a system of records...except pursuant to a written request by, or with the prior written consent of, the individual to whom the record pertains."[8] On May 21, 2017, I sent the Justice Department an official request for all of my fraudulent FISA documents. I mailed similar requests to the FBI and the NSA that same day. My letter asked for, "All information gathered pursuant to the warrant issued by the Foreign Intelligence Surveillance Court authorizing the electronic surveillance of Carter Page."[9] I also sent the FBI and DOJ similar Privacy Act requests related to the Male-1 case in the Southern District of New York. Rather than sending me this information to help them correct the record in 2017, each of those tainted organizations was preparing new false information regarding other times I had helped the U.S. Intelligence Community in the past.[10]

My quest for information wasn't motivated by a desire for vengeance. I just wanted more evidence that could help me prove my innocence and win back my good name. I hoped to dispel the clouds of suspicion that had formed over my head and spread across many Trump supporters and the president himself. But lo and behold, the DOJ started to slow walk and block my requests at every turn throughout the initial years of the Trump administration. While they had previously expedited fraudulent FISA proceedings against me, DOJ officials simultaneously blocked my legal right to documents the government had in their possession. Interacting with the DOJ on this issue showed me just how deep the rot had sunk into our legal institutions.

With Sessions having recused himself already, I would have to battle with Rosenstein, Mueller, and a large assortment of Justice Department attorneys instead. Though they are now infamous for their inaccuracies, at least according to their website, these DOJ lawyers had no lack of help: "With more than 9,500 attorneys, the Department of Justice is the largest legal employer in the world."[11] After I'd waited patiently for over a month, DOJ's Office of Information Policy finally got back to me in late June 2017. I was told that various aspects of my records fell into their category of "unusual circumstances," which meant that they were going to require more time. Unusual, all right. That seemed to be a major understatement. Without going to court yet, I began a series of appeals internally with the Justice Department.

In an early introduction to the lengths that government lawyers will go in order to avoid doing any work or afford any help that they're legally required to provide to their political opponents, my series of follow-up correspondence over the summer of 2017 made it clear that my claim was going nowhere. After various emails, letters, and phone calls to the Justice Department hit roadblocks, I pointedly noted what former Deputy Attorney General Sally Yates had written for the *New York Times* then. It was posted a half a year before the Nunes Memo, which exposed her own involvement in the FISA abuse earlier that year: "The president is attempting to dismantle the rule of law, destroy the time-honored independence of the Justice Department, and undermine the career men and women who are devoted to seeking justice day in and day out, regardless of which political party is in power …. It's almost impossible to take all of this in. And while we risk becoming numb to the daily barrage of alarming news, we can't lose sight of the fact that this is beyond abnormal. It's dangerous."[12]

Interacting with a Justice Department that was out to destroy me taught me many things about the tiered justice system we have established in this country. Donald Trump and his supporters were constantly accused of crimes that could only be considered laughable if there weren't real lives at stake. And yet, the Trump supporters unfairly targeted by the establishment powers saw significant damage to their livelihoods and wellbeing, while the same people who grandstanded with high profile disinformation about the importance of the rule of law did much more to undermine the authority of law in this country. Yates herself was the one who had worked to undermine the rule of law. Hardly a neutral career Justice Department official, Yates had used her privileged position in the DOJ to submit the first false FISA warrant with Comey in October 2016, which effectively began to dismantle the rule of law. The time-honored independence of the Justice Department was destroyed on Yates's watch, when DNC consultants found willing participants inside the government to conduct unprecedented abuse of the once-revered FISA court.

Seeing the way Yates and her collaborators walked out of government and into the highest echelons of elite law firms was exasperating. After ruining my business and portraying me in a way that elicited frequent death threats, Yates and her colleagues would comfortably roll through the revolving door back into a partnership in the Atlanta office of King & Spalding. This is the same firm that previously gave current FBI director Christopher Wray a generous flow of $14 million payouts.[13] Having helped set things motion with the first two false affidavits, Yates left behind a train wreck for her successor as deputy attorney general, Rod Rosenstein, to preside over.

How bad was the reign of Rosenstein? Just a few days after the declassification of my FISA warrants in July 2018, then-Congressman Mark Meadows introduced House Resolution 1028 of the 115th Congress. It boldly proposed: "Impeaching Rod Rosenstein, the Deputy Attorney General of the United States, for high crimes and misdemeanors ... "[14] Amidst countless layers of secrecy maintained years after these abuses, we may never know the full extent of the damage done during Rosenstein's term at the Justice Department. Putting aside the monumental cost of the unnecessary Mueller Report he commissioned, the incalculable damage that Rosenstein oversaw to the Foreign Intelligence Surveillance Court is truly enormous. Working in conjunction with related spy institutions across the federal intelligence bureaucracy that contributed to this scam, Rosenstein and his subordinates' misdeeds vastly exceed the frivolous accusations hurled at President Trump during his own subsequent impeachment.

But never fear. The Washington legal industry gave Rod Rosenstein a comfy gig not too long after his big going-away party at Main Justice.[15] Just weeks after the FISA abuse report came out, Rosenstein became a partner at—unbelievably—King & Spalding, in their Washington office.[16] Rosenstein still has the audacity to throw around more of the same propaganda and lies that helped him damage America and innocent Americans like me in the first place. To help Rosenstein celebrate his birthday in January 2020, *Politico* asked him: "What's a trend going on in the U.S. or abroad that doesn't get enough attention?" His response echoed the party line that the Democrats have been pushing for years: "Russian intelligence officers did not stumble onto the idea of hacking American computers, dumping embarrassing email messages and promoting disinformation because they had a free afternoon. Every day, foreign adversaries plan cyberattacks on government agencies, private companies and individuals. The cyber threat is persistent and growing. Combating it was a big part of my job."[17]

Like Adam Schiff and others, Rosenstein shows a stunning lack of self-awareness every time he crawls back into the public eye. After the deflation of the Mueller Report and the exposure of the damning facts of the FISA process and FBI misbehavior, Rosenstein sees every kind of disinformation but his own.

Harry Reid, another one of my former accusers and a prior chairman of the Senate Democratic Caucus for over a decade, was Senate minority leader for the last two years of the Obama administration.[18] A further reflection of the damaged state of America's legal academy, the University of Nevada, Las Vegas's William S. Boyd School of Law subsequently bestowed upon Reid the title of "Distinguished Fellow in Law and Policy."[19] Reid is also the advisory board co-chair of the MGM Resorts Public Policy Institute at UNLV.[20] His co-chair at the MGM Institute is John Boehner, who previously served as a Republican speaker of the House during the administration of Barack Obama, with whom, allegedly, he is said once to have developed a "bromance."[21] From coast to coast, the elites of Washington go through the revolving door to partner with their former colleagues and adversaries. And ordinary folk like you and I get crushed under the immense weight of the government machinery.

Now that the Band-Aid of the FISA abuse has started to get ripped off, the Latin words "pro se" meaning "for himself" or "acting on his own behalf," should actually be updated to reflect the new reality that this recent affair has exposed. As basic U.S. constitutional principles have been largely abandoned for the self-centered motivations of government attorneys and their civilian political legal allies, it has grown exceptionally rare to find attorneys who are not primarily "for himself" or "acting on his own behalf." That was certainly the case in the election interference against Donald J. Trump which began during the first political campaign of his life.

At least in theory and according to U.S. Supreme Court precedent, pro se court submissions must be held to "less stringent standards than formal pleadings drafted by lawyers."[22] Unfortunately, the history of the past several years has resulted in precisely the opposite. Perhaps no symbol of the dual standards of justice could be more telling than the difference between the harsh treatment I have been submitted to as a pro se law student compared to the relatively clean bill of health received by the bad-actor lawyers within the FBI and across much of the DOJ.

■ ■ ■

By the end of 2017, my legal fight had captured my full attention. As I strategized, I had spent most of the past year responding to the damage created by the Obama administration and the Democratic Party. Between all the Congressional investigations, the Mueller charade, and the lies in the media stemming from the FISA abuse and other false allegations, it had already become more than a full-time job anyway. My personal legal problems had national implications, not just for President Trump and his administration, but for Americans of all political persuasions.

These recent tribulations with lawyers could not have stood in starker contrast to almost all of my prior experience with professional attorneys in America and worldwide. I now found myself entrapped in a much uglier realm and an infinitely bigger game. I had previously seen lawyers act competently and honorably when billions of dollars in business deals were on the line. But it is often the lure of government power, not money, that has a corrupting influence on lawyers. With the stakes raised to national and international politics, they chose to play with people's lives as a means to advance their political objectives. I refused to surrender in the wake of these historic and life-changing abuses.

Almost two decade earlier, and as I neared the completion of my term of service in the U.S. Navy, like many junior officers I saw graduate school as part of my transition to the civilian world. Always a bit of a bookworm and enjoying the prospect of entering a new field, I decided the the two most attractive options were either an M.B.A. from a business school or a J.D. from a law school. I was eager to get started with my civilian career back then, so I decided on business school for a very practical reason: it was a two-year program, not a three-year one. But in 2017, the new intellectual challenges of my continued legal battles made it necessary to sharpen my pencils once again, this time for the law. Since the legal arena has been a longtime intellectual interest of mine anyway, jumping into the law from both a practical and academic perspective made sense.

A lifelong student, I frequently sustained academic work through part-time studies. This new legal endeavor would be no exception. At night and on the weekends, I burned the midnight oil trying to put together the pieces of my case. Like a lot of U.S. military veterans, continuous learning is in my DNA. While I worked in the Pentagon, I remembered hearing stories about Major General Bernard "Burn" Loeffke. A West Point class of 1957 graduate, General Loeffke decided to pursue a medical career after retiring from the U.S. Army. Like me, General Loeffke already had a Ph.D. in an international relations field and spoke Russian too. After his thirty-five years of service, rather than kicking back on the porch in retirement, General Loeffke started his medical studies and after five years became a physician's assistant in 1997.[23]

Deciding to try my hand at something in the mold of General Loeffke, I got in touch with Professor Philip Alston at NYU Law School about attending his classes and was granted special permission to sit in on his Strategic Human Rights Litigation course. I had taught for many years as an adjunct faculty member at New York University and previously completed my MBA there at the Stern School of Business, so in some ways it felt like I was just resuming my grad student days, but this time as a colleague as well as a student.

Just five days before my final FISA warrant expired on September 22, 2017, I emailed Professor Alston as the Fall 2017 semester was starting.[24] In an electronic communication that we now know was inevitably hacked by the U.S. government and applying the name of his class, I explained that I was "getting ready to embark upon a Strategic Human Rights Litigation project of my own...related to prior human rights abuses committed against myself and others by the U.S. Government last year."[25] Much of the course description seemed like a perfect fit for exactly what President Trump and I had been dealing with in the wake of the Obama administration and the Democrats' election interference campaign: "At its best, strategic litigation in defense of human rights both tests and advances a society's commitment to the rule of law. In its relatively short life, such litigation has freed political prisoners, given dissidents a voice, compelled far-reaching changes in education policy..."[26]

I stand by what I wrote Professor Alston. If anything, I hardly knew the half of it back in the autumn of 2017. So many members of the Trump movement had become political targets of the partisans who had managed to burrow themselves into the U.S. government's bureaucracy. Like roots on a large weed, the network we were up against spread across an extraordinarily vast array of Justice Department legal positions. To violate someone's fundamental political and civil rights is to abuse their human rights. These human rights abusers worked in conjunction with other power centers in Washington, most especially the media. As the DOJ's inspector general report on recent FISA exploitation subsequently made clear, the laws protecting against such human rights abuses had effectively been demolished by incompetent and deceitful attorneys. Professor Alston replied: "Dear Carter, You're absolutely welcome to sit in on any of our sessions. Good to hear that you're mixing it up with the Russians! Best, Philip"[27]

I was excited by the unusual juxtaposition of subjective controversies with the objective rigors of tactical litigation we would take up in Professor Alston's course. As I learned about the superstructure of our law and rights, it became hard for me to understand why so many lawyers in DOJ were willing to damage our democracy. The more I learned, the more their creative writing project for the Democrats, which they had submitted to the U.S. Foreign Intelligence Surveillance Court, became increasingly incomprehensible and unconscionable.

I did not get the chance to continue sitting in on that class. Just a few weeks after agreeing to let me participate in his course, Professor Alston emailed again under the heading, "Bad News."[28] He had previously explained that since I was joining, he would need to "seek the approval of those who are going to be making guest appearances in the classes."[29] For a class related to human rights, in a country like the United States with the First Amendment, that seemed odd to me. But I couldn't imagine why any human rights expert worth his salt would possibly object to my presence.

Unfortunately and contrary to his prior generous invitation, Professor Alston told me the following week that plans had changed. I was now officially banned from the class for the foreseeable future. "As you know,

I have no problem but I do have to respect their preferences. I trust you will understand."[30]

You can imagine my indignation at being told that I was barred from a class that I had hoped would help me restore my civil rights. I wonder how legal scholars can fail to see the true abuse of power that has developed in our own country's legal systems. The Democrat-led political organizations that assisted in manipulating the U.S. court system helped achieve precisely that, using the law to punish political movements and speech.

In the years since, then-Chairman Devin Nunes and other Republicans have fought hard to get the precise details of the specific funding arrangements behind the Democrats' Russia dossier which Steele and Fusion GPS compiled.[31] More information is still coming out. As conservatives like me were increasingly blacklisted from even the most casual associations, the NYU law school became a faculty lounge full of former DOJ operatives, including some linked to abuses of power against a legally elected administration. Other former Obama administration officials on NYU Law faculty include their "Distinguished Scholar in Residence" Bob Bauer, who was "General Counsel to Obama for America, the President's campaign organization, in 2008 and 2012." In between those political operations and before coming to NYU Law, he was also Obama's White House counsel.[32]

Some NYU lawyers had links to the people engaged in abuses of power against a legitimately elected administration. For example, NYU Law was also the new home of Mueller's former deputy chief of staff and Obama's assistant to the president for Homeland Security and Counterterrorism Lisa Monaco. Following the Democrats' election interference in 2016, Monaco was the only senior member of the Obama administration that I ever directly challenged about the severe abuses I was then being subjected to. Three weeks before NYU Law officially appointed Monaco as a distinguished senior fellow at their Center for Cybersecurity, I confronted her about the cyberhacking that the administration she was about to depart had recently been engaged in.[33] On the morning of

January 10, 2017, just hours before the DNC-funded Dodgy Dossier was published by BuzzFeed, I attended a breakfast meeting at the Council on Foreign Relations in New York City, at which Monaco gave a talk.[34]

After her speech, a question and answer period began, and I patiently waited my turn. When I was called on, I began to ask my question, which I had written out early that morning. Unsurprisingly given the substance of my inquiry and my having become a public enemy to left-leaning journalists, I was pressured by a pro–Obama administration journalist-moderator who impatiently encouraged me to end my question promptly. Just like at NYU, I was frozen out of an institution I had once been welcomed at with open arms.

At the time, I thought that asking Monaco about the details of my case was a good opportunity to get some insight into what had gone on. Monaco had a lot of prior experience in the FISA arena and might have been the perfect person to address these still-unconfirmed accusations. She was a former University of Chicago Law School graduate where Obama had previously taught. Monaco had also previously worked as Obama's former assistant attorney general in charge of the Justice Department's National Security Division (NSD) during his first term in office. Among the various tasks involved in overseeing the NSD, she and her staff were "responsible for preparing and filing all applications for Court orders pursuant to FISA."[35] During Obama's second term, Monaco moved over to the White House. Ironically, given the question I was now asking his counterterrorism advisor, election law stood among the subjects the outgoing president used to teach students at Ms. Monaco's alma mater according to the *New York Times*: "Mr. Obama marched students through the thickets of campaign finance law."[36]

Though I didn't fully realize it at the time I put my questions to her, Ms. Monaco's associates might have known a lot more about my particular FISA application than I could have even suspected. I was in effect asking Ms. Monaco about her colleagues' own actions that morning.[37] As I later learned, the Obama administration submitted its next inaccurate FISA warrant against me just two days later, on January 12.[38] So it is not a surprise that Monaco's reply was a complete dodge. She answered curtly, "My experience with the FISA process is that the—it's a group of Article III judges who've been confirmed by the Senate and who conduct rigorous oversight of government applications for surveillance authority. And it is an extremely rigorous process. And so that's my experience with the FISA process."[39]

Later in October 2019, Senator Chuck Grassley complained about essentially the same questions I had for Monaco on that January morning when he famously observed: "All of the delays and excuses why the Horowitz IG FISA report isn't public yet after several months of anticipation of its issues leads me to the suspicion it's going to be 'deep six' by the deep state."[40] Indeed, it would take nearly three years to overcome internal resistance from Monaco's former DOJ colleagues and Democrat lawyers for the world to learn how much of an "extremely rigorous process" their former administration's FISA abuse had been. The seventeen significant errors or omissions ultimately exposed with the release of the Horowitz report in December 2019 started making all the niceties of that "extremely rigorous process" pretty clear.[41]

In the wake of the FBI's legal incompetence and political belligerence towards myself as well as so many other members of the Trump movement, Yale Law School graduate Christopher Wray eventually submitted his own *mea culpa* letter to DOJ. Starting to see the light that had already been glaring in his face for years, even this beleaguered government bureaucrat was forced to recognize precisely the opposite of an "extremely rigorous process." Among the piecemeal token responses planned by the director of the FBI and his fellow government lawyers was included: "Developing and requiring new training focused on FISA process rigor .... " I guess their brethren didn't have such an "extremely rigorous process" after all.

Though many other Obama administration attorneys had come to lurk at NYU Law, the real icing on the cake came when Mueller's so-called "pit bull" prosecutor Andrew Weissmann eventually returned there following his term on the Witch Hunt. He is now the "Distinguished Senior

Fellow at the Reiss Center on Law and Security" at NYU Law.[42] When I first started teaching as an adjunct faculty at NYU myself in 2008, the exploits of Weissmann were already particularly infamous to some of my colleagues. I was then working with the investment banking division at Merrill Lynch. As Sidney Powell, a former federal prosecutor, wrote in *The Hill* following Weissman's appointment to the Mueller team: "Weissmann creatively criminalized a business transaction between Merrill Lynch and Enron. Four Merrill executives went to prison for as long as a year.... Weissmann's prosecution devastated the lives and families of the Merrill executives, causing enormous defense costs, unimaginable stress and torturous prison time. The 5th Circuit Court of Appeals reversed the mass of the case."[43]

Then there is the reckless clip of lies and innuendo from NYU Law's Faculty Director of the Reiss Center on Law and Security, Professor Ryan Goodman. A representative sample: "...there is an avalanche of information, in the public record alone, of Page's involvement with the Kremlin and Russian spies, plus his highly suspicious denials of meetings with Russians. Several of those denials have since been disproven, even by Page himself. He is not exactly the poster child you want on your side of a political or legal argument."[44]

Over the last two years and unlike the false evidence fabricated by Steele, unaltered factual evidence has continued to be released. Contrary to the true story, the fictitious narrative of Russia collusion continues to find an intellectual oasis in places like NYU Law. After the U.S. Senate Committee on the Judiciary blocked me from testifying for more than a year,[45] they invited none other than Professor Goodman to testify in June 2018 about election interference.[46]

But perhaps I am being unfair. The Obama DOJ crowd and their like-minded cohort that now typify NYU Law and other preeminent institutions of the legal academy clearly have a great deal of expertise in interfering in elections.

CHAPTER NINE

OVERCOMING THE ABUSES AGAINST AMERICAN DEMOCRACY

"Change not the law but the attitude of the mind."
—*Calvin Coolidge, 1920*[1]

Many Americans are working hard to emerge from recent ordeals with the knowledge we are stronger and more resilient than we realized. We continue to maintain that there is hope for America. Many core principles of the American way of life remain intact. We are also incrementally returning to innovation, cooperation and, one hopes, treating each other with a little more kindness and respect.

While the recent COVID-19 coronavirus emergency brought unprecedented health and economic ramifications, much important work to address the historic spy scandal has continued behind the scenes. As the nation shifted its focus to this global pandemic, the senior Department of Justice lawyer Michael Horowitz revealed that the breakdown in the surveillance state has been much worse than we originally realized—of twenty-nine FISA applications surveyed, all twenty-nine had serious deficiencies. In several cases, the inspector general could not even find the document that shows that the FBI's mandatory procedures were followed.[2]

The inspector general revealed something that has been apparent to many for a long time; the whole system of secret surveillance is broken.

One example of this break-down was the call detail records program. It allowed the NSA to collect "metadata" on millions of calls made by Americans.[3] Metadata does not record the contents of a call, just who called whom and for how long. This may not sound like much, but metadata allows the government to make inferences that amount to a handy X-ray of our most intimate secrets. A Stanford University study of the metadata records of 546 volunteers revealed that from that information access, you could tell who was diagnosed with multiple sclerosis, who had bought a gun, who needed Alcoholics Anonymous, and who took certain disease tests at a clinic.[4] It also tracked a woman who called her sister repeatedly, then her doctor, and then an abortion clinic, leading to the obvious conclusion that she had had an abortion. It's not just personal secrets that can be gleaned from metadata. If the government takes "two hops" from the original subject (anyone the subject calls, and anyone that person calls), a single point of interest can reveal much about the personal lives of tens of thousands of Americans.

Last year, NSA announced that it had purged all the data from this call details records program because of technical problems. It had to be suspended because the program could not be made to operate within the law, while it failed to stop a single terrorist plot.[5] And yet the Intelligence Community fought hard to try to retain the authority to restart this program whenever it chooses.

This is just one sign of a national security establishment that is divorced from the values and freedoms of the people it is charged with protecting. Yes, we need a robust ability to track terrorists and spies, but it will be futile to protect ourselves against external enemies if we succumb to internal monitoring and the inevitable political suppression that such monitoring inevitably encourages and promotes.

As we face our own government, it is important, as never before, for Americans to understand how this system of national security surveillance actually works. Only then can we ask what it says about the state of our country and how we can do better.

■ ■ ■

You probably have a friend who, if you pressed him or her, could not tell you much about the contents of the United States Constitution. But I suspect that if you questioned that friend further, you would find that he or she has an intuitive sense that one's home, conversations with family and friends, and personal items—such as a diary or a Google search—are protected under our laws from casual surveillance. Most Americans appreciate, even if they can't always locate them, the two most essential clusters of our rights found in the First and Fourth Amendments to the United States Constitution.

The First Amendment enumerates an expansive list of natural rights we possess simply by being human: "Congress shall make no law respecting an establishment of religion, or prohibiting the free exercise thereof; or abridging the freedom of speech, or of the press; or the right of the people peaceably to assemble, and to petition the government for a redress of grievances."

Another vital cluster of rights are found in the Fourth Amendment, which prohibits "unreasonable searches and seizures." The history of this issue goes back to England, to a case called *Entick v. Carrington* in which a king's messenger named Nathan Carrington and several helpers invaded the home of a hack writer, John Entick, to break locks and rifle through Entick's papers for four hours. The jurist Lord Camden ruled in 1765 that the messengers, acting on the orders of a powerful politician, had no legal authority to turn Entick's home upside down. "By the laws of England, every invasion of private property, be it ever so minute, is a trespass. No man can set his foot upon my ground without my license ... "[6]

These principles were not established in the American colonies, where warehouses and homes were frequently ransacked by customs officials looking for contraband. These inspections were carried out as "general warrants" authorized by the king's "writs of assistance." No specific crime needed to be alleged. No particular target needed to be identified. With such a writ in hand, any colonial official had a free hand to go into any home to look for any item that might incriminate the owner. James Otis, a prominent Boston attorney, said that the writs put "the liberty of every man in the hands of every petty officer."[7]

It was colonial Americans' white-hot outrage over writs and general warrants that provided much of the fuel for the American Revolution. Afterwards, when it came time to craft a national constitution of their own, Americans realized there were legitimate reasons for searches and seizures. But this was also an awesome and dangerous responsibility that had to be regulated by law. James Madison made it clear that general warrants would not be allowed in our system—and that probable cause had to be established against a named person before a court could issue a warrant.

The Fourth Amendment reads: "The right of the people to be secure in their persons, houses, papers, and effects, against unreasonable searches and seizures, shall not be violated, and no Warrants shall issue, but upon probable cause, supported by Oath or affirmation, and particularly describing the place to be searched, and the persons or things to be seized."

The Founders were not unreasonable. A warrant based on probable cause for, say, suspicion of murder, gives homicide detectives ample opportunity to scour the home of a suspect looking for suspicious fibers or spots of blood. But to obtain a warrant, law enforcement must present a court with an application directed at a specific person, at a specific place, and the reason for believing that he or she may be guilty of a specified crime. The Founders added these restrictions because they realized that a broad power of surveillance enabled by a general warrant would give the government unlimited power.

In a digital age, our "effects" extend to our private emails, texts and phone calls. And yet for many of these modern modalities of electronic communications, general warrants are back in action. How exactly did America get from the principles of James Madison to those of James Comey?

■ ■ ■

The United States has allowed the surveillance state to grow in various foreign policy crises. External threats inspired internal oppression. During the First World War, the United States briefly became a police state under President Woodrow Wilson. Fearing any criticism of the government's war effort, the Wilson administration used the Espionage and Sedition Acts to throw prominent people who spoke out against the war into prison (that included Eugene V. Debs, socialist candidate for president). It would be as if the government had imprisoned Bernie Sanders for speaking out against the foreign policies of George W. Bush or Donald Trump. Postal officials were given the power to forbid the mailing of disapproved magazines and newspapers, limiting reporting and the national debate to approved publications.

The tendencies toward control and secrecy returned with World War Two and the Cold War, the latter of which only accelerated a secret intelligence bureaucracy within our government. With the new threat to the nation from nuclear war and the discovery of spy networks from powerful state-controlled intelligence agencies like the Soviet GRU and the KGB, the United States obviously needed some system to protect secrets from malevolent powers. Thus, the elaborate system of classifying millions of documents and of security clearances being issued to employees backed by investigations of personal lives became the institutional norm.

The practices of secrecy and the surveillance of foreign threats may be needed for our survival as a nation. In the twenty-first century outside threats to our way of life have, if anything, increased. In an age of WMDs, master terrorists and the discovery of Russian "sleeper" agents and Chinese scientists stealing every American patent they can find, most people agree we need to continue to allow the government to use surveillance to spot potential terrorists and people (including American citizens) acting as agents of a foreign power. Somehow along the way, however, we wound up with a secret government that is as absurd in its scale as it is often weak in its product, that is, intelligence. There are no fewer than seventeen intelligence agencies with over $60 billion in black budgets,[8] employing 854,000 Americans with top secret clearances.[9] How can effective oversight, coordination, and direction be provided for almost one million human beings operating under a cloak of secrecy? As we learned in the lead up to the impeachment of President Trump, such oversight cannot be effectively provided by Congress or the presumed watchdogs of the media. Not surprisingly, with all this budget authority, power and political heft, these agencies are effectively taking us right back to the era of general warrants.

■ ■ ■

"There is something addictive about secrets," the founding FBI director J. Edgar Hoover once said. As the Moynihan Commission on Government Secrecy established, outside the realm of nuclear secrets governed by the Atomic Energy Act, secrets in the government are whatever anyone in the government decides to stamp secret. A mindset which Moynihan called a "culture of secrecy" was emerging that was increasingly at odds with the outlook of James Madison and his band of brothers, as well as the average American's common sense understanding of how our country works.

A large subset of our government was becoming, as J. Edgar Hoover so memorably put it, addicted to secrets.

This led to official contempt for the strictures of the United States Constitution, which can be seen in how several administrations used the FBI, and to a lesser extent, the CIA, to monitor mostly left-wing domestic groups. Through COINTELPRO, the FBI not only surveilled organizations, it also infiltrated them with double agents and used covert action to disrupt and discredit them. With the approval of

Attorney General Robert F. Kennedy, Director Hoover monitored the Reverend Dr. Martin Luther King Jr. In a separate incident, Hoover's FBI sent a letter full of blackmail to King in an effort to prompt the civil rights leader to commit suicide.[10]

Similar to what would happen under Barack Obama's White House, it all broke open when Richard Nixon turned these powers on his enemies, even bugging the offices of his political opponents. Some of Obama's and Nixon's unfortunate mistakes have continued to be repeated by at least one other contemporary politician, Adam Schiff, who leaned on telecom companies to show him the metadata of his Republican colleagues.[11] After the Watergate scandal and President Nixon's resignation, Frank Church, a liberal senator from Idaho, conducted a wide-ranging investigation into the activities of the Intelligence Community. The Church Committee was a traumatic experience for the Intelligence Community. Many felt that Senator Church went too far and was indiscriminate in how he threw the IC's dirty laundry into the public domain. But few who care about civil liberties can dispute that the Church Committee exposed serious abuses. While the media's focus was on sensational stories, such as the CIA's mind-control experiments with hapless subjects using LSD, there were deeper issues that affected the rights of all Americans.

Declassification since the Church Committee, for example, reveals that the NSA maintained a "watch list" of thousands of Americans citizens (including Senator Church himself and actors Gregory Peck and Joanne Woodward), fed by data from Operation SHAMROCK, information on calls supplied by major telecommunications companies.

On *Meet the Press* in 1975, Senator Frank Church made a prescient statement about the evolving potential of technology to serve the national security state. He said:

> In the need to develop a capacity to know what potential
> enemies are doing, the United States government has perfected
> a technological capability that enables us to monitor the

messages that go through the air...that capability at any time could be turned around on the American people, and no American would have privacy left...there would be no place to hide...

The senator went on to explain:

If this government ever became a tyranny, if a dictator ever took charge in this country, the technological capacity that the intelligence community has given the government could enable it to impose total tyranny, and there would be no way to fight back because the most careful effort to combine together in resistance to the government, no matter how privately it was done, is within the reach of the government to know.[12]

Congress grappled with the need to give the government the power to surveil our enemies without the government's itself becoming our enemy. The result was the passage of a bill sponsored by another liberal, Senator Edward Kennedy, the Foreign Intelligence Surveillance Act, which in 1978 set up the system of secret surveillance applications before secret courts. It was at best a compromise. Until my case, most of the past precedent of the court was itself secret. It is under Title I of FISA that I was spied upon as a suspected agent of a foreign power. "In an entirely one-sided process," writes Neema Singh Guliani of the ACLU, "judges on this court sign off on classified government surveillance requests impacting countless Americans a year who are never suspected of committing a crime. Typically, no one outside the government— including defense attorneys in cases involving FISA surveillance—sees these requests, let alone has an opportunity to meaningfully challenge them."[13]

The Foreign Intelligence Surveillance Courts hold *ex parte* hearings that the targets almost never know occurred. In 1980, President Ronald

Reagan signed Executive Order 12333, which defined the hierarchy of intelligence agencies and the rules by which intelligence could be collected. Many apologists for the deep state regard 12333 as their ace-in-the-hole. In a recent Senate debate in which portions of FISA were up for reauthorization, Republican Senator Richard Burr of North Carolina startled his colleagues when he said the president can do whatever he wants under 12333, "without Congress's permission, without guardrails...."[14] Another power the federal government has is its ability to deploy an administrative subpoena, National Security Letters, forcing banks, Internet service providers and other companies to provide personal transactional information, along with a gag order to the company not to let you know your information has been compromised.

The surveillance state, already robust at the turn of the century, went into overdrive after September 11, 2001. Congress reacted to the trauma by doing what it usually does after a crisis—hurriedly pass legislation without carefully reviewing its consequences. In this case, Congress passed the Patriot Act, which provided the government with sweeping new powers to conduct surveillance on a larger and more robust scale. In a March 2013 hearing, Senator Ron Wyden asked James Clapper, then the director of the Office of National Intelligence, about how this authority was used in practice. Clapper unequivocally denied that the NSA intentionally collects data of American citizens in bulk. As we would soon learn, that was a bold-faced lie.

At the time Clapper spoke, the NSA was collecting metadata on Americans' calls by the millions. Watching this at home, NSA contractor Edward Snowden was so disturbed by Clapper's actions that he decided, he later claimed, at that very moment to break the law. Snowden would subsequently steal and leak some of the government's most sensitive secrets, before fleeing to Moscow. In June, Snowden leaked to *The Guardian* that NSA had collected 120 million phone records from American subscribers of just one telecom, Verizon.[15]

Exposed, Director Clapper pleaded forgetfulness and confusion, though Senator Wyden had provided him with the question in advance.[16]

With the exposure of Clapper's lack of candor to Congress about the mass collection of Americans' phone calls, it was clear that our country had returned to a system of general warrants. But unlike the colonial era, when one could see the king's customs official barging in with red coats to break locks and collect papers, most of us never see or feel these actions being taken against us by our own government.

■ ■ ■

The illegitimate case against me reveals several other forms of dysfunction. When I was targeted with four applications for FISA surveillance, the applications were filed under Title I, which defined me as a possible "agent of a foreign power." But I wasn't the only target. With my surveillance, as I noted, the federal government could make "two hops" from me. So the FBI could have reviewed private data on my contact, Steve Bannon, and from Steve Bannon to his contact, Donald Trump. In this respect, the "Carter Page" warrants were a direct assault on the First and Fourth Amendment rights of all Americans. This isn't a partisan issue. People from across the ideological spectrum see it as an American issue.

Is this, as James Comey put it, just a matter of "sloppiness" at the FBI?[17] Or was something more malevolent at work? Was my case a one off, or was it business as usual under the surveillance regime?

To guard against "sloppiness," the FBI has put into place a process known as "Woods Procedures," which is meant to ensure credible documentation to support each assertion of fact. But recent disturbing investigations prompted by my case have put those measures into question. In his subsequent investigation of a sampling of FISA warrants out of thousands filed, Horowitz found negligence in the FBI's adherence to its own process at alarming rates. Horowitz's sample size to determine the prevalence of errors in FISA filings was twenty-nine. Sure enough, he found that all were flawed. In at least three cases, investigators could not determine if the Woods File ever existed. They found an average of about twenty problems per FISA application.[18]

It is clear, at the very least, that the FBI under James Comey had a deeply flawed culture in which management looked the other way. This was a culture in which "sloppiness" was not an occasional issue, but the standard practice, perhaps even the expected practice. Is that as far as it goes, a sloppy culture? Were the well-documented political biases of James Comey, Lisa Page, Peter Strzok and Kevin Clinesmith a factor in how this investigation against me and the Trump campaign was conducted, or did the sloppy factor just happen to go against the Trump campaign adviser seventeen times? Was my work in Russia and my being socially friendly with some Russians really enough to strip me of my basic human rights and constitutional protections? Or was political bias in the DOJ and FBI necessary to conflate my career choice with a crime?

IG Horowitz was cagey on this question. After refusing to talk to me, he purported to find no documentary or testimonial evidence of political bias. But Horowitz didn't exonerate the FBI agents in question, either. Under questioning by the Senate Judiciary Committee, Horowitz added that he could not rule out political bias.

But what else besides bias could explain why FBI lawyer Kevin Clinesmith, whose anti-Trump bias is apparent in his texts ("viva la resistance"), doctored a document, and submitted his forgery as sworn testimony?[19] Why did so many connected to the investigation labor night and day to get as much of the Steele report into the media during the campaign? Why did so many connected to the Department of Justice and the FBI sandbag a newly elected president by getting the lurid parts of the Dodgy Dossier into the public arena? How else to explain Comey's later leaking of a Form 302 on the president?

Of all the things that were done to me, the most despicable was the leaking. People in official positions of power broke a law that they would send others to prison for breaking. However, the rare leaking of the existence of my FISA warrants raises a productive line of inquiry. Had I never known that my rights had been abused in a secret application before a secret court, I would have suffered no apparent harm. But

I believe we all suffer harm, apparent or not, when our rights are secretly violated.

The deepest personal harm came when the FBI and Intelligence Community relied on the media and ambitious politicians to mount a public pressure campaign against a suspect. On April 10, 2017, the day before the story about my FISA warrants appeared in the media, Lisa Page sent this text to Peter Strzok: "I had literally just gone to find this phone to tell you I want to talk to you about media leak strategy with DOJ before you go."[20]

While Strzok has subsequently denied culpability for the media leaks against President Trump and his supporters, whoever disclosed the story of my FISA warrants had to have been someone on the inside.[21] I have subsequently learned that when government collusion occurs with the media, officials are no longer just investigating a suspect. They are already inflicting a harsh punishment on someone who has not been, and might never be, charged with any of the preposterous crimes that have been falsely alleged. Instead of playing fair and square, the government tries to shape public perception in their favor. They can't rely on the strength of the evidence, so they have to build a narrative instead.

The FBI, concerned with the law, and the CIA, which is concerned for the safety of the public and forbidden from domestic operations, find that when they engage in leaks, their agendas get mixed up with the ambitions of journalists like Michael Isikoff. The scheme quickly extends to overpaid opposition researchers like Isikoff's "old friend" Glenn Simpson, or the hired subcontractor Christopher Steele.[22] Grandstanding politicians like Adam Schiff are more than happy to join this fanciful dance.[23] Such tactics become an exploding cigar that the FBI simply cannot keep itself from lighting, time and again. Think of the times the FBI not only falsely accused someone but publicly persecuted them in the media:

Richard Jewell for being the Olympic Park bomber...[24]

Steven Hatfill for being the anthrax terrorist...[25]

Now the crazy "Russian agent" and "useful idiot" stories about President Trump and his supporters like me...[26]

This happened, incredibly, despite being under the brightest spotlight imaginable.

Time after time, the strategy of pressure through publicity has not ended well for the FBI. The FBI/DOJ should have been doubly careful about leaking information that was overspun to such a highly partisan degree against a sitting president. Above all, the FBI and the Justice Department should not treat suspects as if their guilt were predetermined and their public punishment already well deserved.

Had my name never surfaced, my company and business relationships worldwide would not have been destroyed. I would not have had to waste time in the Star Chambers on Capitol Hill, trying not to make some immaterial verbal error that could land me in prison. Had none of this happened, I would never have had to endure a barrage of death threats after some of the most powerful members of Congress and the political class publicly accused me of being a traitor. As George Orwell's antagonist O'Brien once correctly warned in the novel *1984*: "If you want a picture of the future, imagine a boot stamping on a human face —forever."[27] For a long time, it seemed like this could have been my destiny too if I had not taken proactive action.

In the next chapter, I'll discuss how I weathered this relentless attack, how I kept my health and happiness. But I worry for people who lack my military training, calm nature and limited personal resources saved by my many years of conservative living. Thanks to a lifetime of habits, the public pressure campaign waged against me couldn't drive me to despair. Though I often felt frustrated, confused, and betrayed, I was at relatively less risk of the greatest psychological dangers these pressure campaigns often pose. As we have seen time and time again, people often feel helpless when society and the government target them unjustly. My story proves that in those moments of weakness, there is always a way to find hope. Perseverance can defeat despair.

■ ■ ■

Attorney General Barr has correctly noted of the investigation into Trump: "What happened to him was one of the greatest travesties in American history. Without any basis, they started this investigation of his campaign, and even more concerning actually is what happened after the campaign—a whole pattern of events while he was president...to sabotage the presidency—or at least have the effect of sabotaging the presidency."[28] But bureaucrats like FBI Director Christopher Wray have argued that government agencies can clean up this act on their own, through piecemeal steps like internal rule-making and better training.[29] In other dark chapters of American history, we've heard this line from the federal bureaucracy before. After being burned many times by the false promises of the Intelligence Community, Congress must continue to debate—and perhaps this time pass—further much-needed reforms.

At this writing, the Senate continues to deliberate whether to expand the *amicus curiae* program in the FISA courts. An *amicus* is an outside legal expert, in practice often a professor of law, who has a high security clearance to read classified material. In theory, they might bring some degree of independent analysis to a FISA application. At best, *amici* might occasionally function as internal advocates for civil liberties and the rights of the targeted person.

FISA judges already have the authority to request *amici* for cases that raise "novel or significant" interpretation of law.[30] Since they were given this authority, judges have resorted to it in fewer than 1 percent of the thousands of proceedings the court has heard. Most remarkable of all, four judges reviewed applications to surveil people inside the general election campaign of a major party candidate in the last presidential election without *amici*. Throwing caution to the wind, by all indications they saw no need for outside advice or counsel.

Some reform-minded senators, like conservative Mike Lee of Utah and liberal Patrick Leahy of Vermont, have suggested stiffening these requirements.[31] This might include the use of *amici* in cases that touch on our political, religious and First Amendment rights, with special protections for political candidates, religious or political organizations and domestic news media. These senators want to see these independent legal experts involved whenever the government requests court approval for new programs and technologies.[32]

Meanwhile, various House bills under consideration have sought to limit the use of these so-called *amici* and would also be highly restrictive in the sharing of exculpatory evidence with the court. Senators Lee and Leahy want to make sure the *amicus* advisor has access to exculpatory evidence. Other members of Congress have proposed that criminal defendants be informed when information gleaned from FISA is used against them. As Senator Lee has argued: "The amicus should advocate for the privacy and civil liberties of the person targeted. This provision would ensure that what happened to Carter Page can never happen again."[33]

Luckily, a few glimmers of common sense have arisen as some of the most expansive government spy capabilities have been reined in. For example, Section 215 or the business records provision, might allow the federal government to review your private information held by businesses from Google to 23andme, so long as it supposedly finds the information "relevant" for an investigation. As former U.S. Attorney Brett Tolman has bluntly noted: "There is no basis for reauthorizing Section 215 without meaningful changes."[34]

At this writing, it is unclear how many, if any, of the various conceptual ideas for reforming the system will survive the political disarray of Congress. Count me as skeptical. In a culture of secrecy, even with the most far reaching of reforms, outcomes can always be creatively re-engineered behind the scenes. For example, when the FBI, in response to Judge Rosemary Collier's rebuke, proposed a series of internal reforms to fix its approach to FISA, the secret court's presiding judge, James Boasberg, selected a former Obama DOJ national security lawyer named David Kris to oversee it.

Who is David Kris?

During the whole Spygate ordeal, Kris was a tireless critic of Devin Nunes and defender of the FBI, the FISA process and the dependability of Christopher Steele. He appeared on *The Rachel Maddow Show* to predict that the disclosure of the FISA warrants would be a disaster. After the partial declassification of my FISA warrants, he told Maddow: "[W]e're going to be in a posture of asymmetric political warfare with the president free to make up whatever facts suit him and the FBI limited in what it can say in response because of its obligation to protect its sources and methods."[35]

Throughout the entire charade, Kris tended to see little that was wrong with the process. And yet he was named as the outside advisor or *amicus* that Judge Boasberg brought in to fix the system. We have seen time after time that the forces in favor of more secrecy and surveillance are not only relentless, they are shameless in their pursuit of power and astonishingly lacking in self-awareness.[36]

But even if all of these insiders were fair-minded, the problem of surveillance would still be critical. The evolving nature of technology, the stickiness with which our devices and the information we send to the cloud cling to us and our every action have already created even more challenges. Looking ahead to the future, facial recognition technology and tracking is emerging as an entirely new way to infringe on what is left of the privacy outside our homes. And when we're inside our homes, we are subject to being overheard and recorded by our personal digital assistants. With only a matter of tweaks, robust technological capabilities originally designed to sell us ads could transform America in the surveillance state model perfected by the People's Republic of China.

The dangers of these technologies are still new and we are only beginning to grapple with them in a serious way. Consider: In 1984—the year, not the novel—information technology in the form of international phone calls, faxes and cable TV began to erode communism. It seemed as if George Orwell had gotten it exactly wrong. Technology would be a powerful force for social liberty and individual empowerment.

From our vantage point in 2020, however, it turns out that Orwell was wrong in only two respects. First, he was off in his prediction by thirty-six years. Second, the Orwellian vision was wrong to assume that it required an army of watchers to monitor society. Today, with artificial intelligence and pattern recognition, nearly infinite storage and retrieval, a surveillance army is not needed. Our own devices record us quite well without any need for human involvement. We already know this; we just don't want to think about it. We routinely exchange our privacy for convenience every time we click "accept" for terms of service agreements with the companies that track our every move and record our searches, emails and texts.

The increasing proliferation of information technology may ensure that every corner of our lives will be kept in a permanent, digital record. This is sure to rise to even greater levels of intrusion when all our devices are integrated into an "Internet of Things."[37]

While Congress gropes at fixes, we must all come to grips with the cold truth that as much as we dislike it, privacy as we have known it is dead, and without proactive leadership, likely dead for good.

In this environment, some still trot out the hoary old saying that "if you have nothing to hide, you have nothing to fear." This bromide has been a longstanding matter of debate in the privacy rights community. As the saying implies, government surveillance supporters often claim that there's no reason for innocent people to worry about state intelligence agencies snooping in every area of one's life. If you have nothing to hide, why should you be afraid to be seen naked in public?

In contrast, privacy advocates often point out that the "nothing to hide/something to hide" gambit is a false choice that gives nearly unlimited power to a swollen government bureaucracy. As my personal experiences and the wrongdoing that arose from it make clear, the possibilities for abuse enabled by surveillance remain real. Modest limitations may prove hard to devise, even with the best of intentions from officials.

The only reason I made it through this ordeal is because the basic "nothing to hide, have nothing to fear" dictum fit me. I am not an alcoholic and I've never used an illegal drug. There is nothing in my personal life and conduct that I am ashamed of. I don't cheat on my taxes. Because I still, at heart, maintain the same principles I developed as an Eagle Scout, a Catholic altar boy, and a graduate of the U.S. Naval Academy, the FBI could not defeat my personal strategy of full transparency. But imagine the fun that people like Comey, Clinesmith, Schiff, and Maddow would have had with someone who was as innocent as I was, but had some colorful private vice or professional failing to add a bit of spice to the story?

It should not be this way. But with the death of privacy, the only way to stay safe from a legal and security perspective is to remain absolutely above reproach in your personal life. This should not be essential for survival. We don't live in a theocracy and the FBI should not be in a position to monitor our personal morality. Even so, when you say something confidential to family, or you tell your beloved an endearing secret, understand that you need to do it in a whisper since you may well be recorded. If you are on the wrong side of the political fence, your words might be recorded and made accessible at the convenience of Big Brother.

■ ■ ■

If legal reform is at best a long shot, and technology is only going to make any remaining shreds of privacy disappear, where then should we focus our energy? If a culture of secrecy tends toward corruption—and secrecy is, as J. Edgar Hoover said, "addicting"—then perhaps our best efforts should be aimed at reforming our culture.

We should not forget that in dealing with surveillance issues, we're dealing fundamentally with people. What they believe shapes their behavior. After all, it is often said in Washington, D.C., that people are policy.

Tug at any thread, and the skein begins to unravel and reveal how personnel drives the uses and misuses of policy. For example, consider when President Trump fired Michael Atkinson, the inspector general for the entire Intelligence Community. Some partisans assumed it was payback for having brought forward the "whistleblower" complaint about the president's Ukraine call, which the Democrats used to justify their vote for impeachment in the House of Representatives.[38] Before becoming the Intelligence Community's IG, Atkinson joined DOJ's National Security Division (NSD) in 2016.[39] His boss at the time John Carlin has described Atkinson to CNN as, "someone who is very deliberate, thoughtful and tries to carefully review facts ... not someone who seeks attention."[40] Carlin served as the assistant attorney general for the NSD until just days before the first of my fraudulent FISA applications was approved.[41] Did Atkinson's care and thoughtfulness extend to my Spygate-era FISA warrants? Judge Collyer of the FISA court subsequently called out the ease with which NSD's surveillance system was manipulated.[42] Like ripples in a murky sea of classified information, the Intelligence Community has subsequently referred to this situation as "compliance incidents" related to other aspects of FISA.[43] Many such bureaucrats portray themselves as a conscientious group who protect society, especially when they work prestigious national security jobs. But from the outside and amidst significant limitations on disclosure surrounding these abuses to this day, such insiders often seem like nothing more than an egotistical, self-serving cabal. Like their colleagues and supporters in Washington, they seek protection of their own personal interests at the expense of the rights of average citizens.

How is it, for example, that Robert Mueller could assemble an "all-star" team composed almost exclusively of outspoken partisans who supported the opposing candidate? Are there not any lawyers in the Department of Justice who maintain, as many officers of the United States military do, a non-partisan identity, not contributing to candidates for office and not revealing to anyone how they vote? Who do these people think they work for? Political operatives in London and Washington, or the American taxpayers who pay their salaries? Would equal justice and accountability not be a good ethos to instill in Justice

Department lawyers who might be tasked with investigating candidates or incumbents of either party?

If it is true that "people are policy" in government, then policy is often swayed by the narrative in the media, just as people are. When journalists, expected to be the watchdogs of the Intelligence Community instead act as the IC's guard dogs, the narrative will always be against the accused. But along the way, there were a relatively small handful of other good people in the media who listened to me.

Sean Hannity, Maria Bartiromo, and Tucker Carlson of Fox News have been generous in offering precious airtime and the microphone to allow me to refute Christopher Steele's Dodgy Dossier and other false allegations. These journalists and a handful of others stayed committed to the truth through the intensity of many tough national battles. Even as they were mocked by some colleagues for considering the evidence that I brought to their newsrooms in New York and Washington, they listened with open minds.

Early on, when I was being attacked from all directions for my purported conspiracy with the two Igors, Josh Rogin at the *Washington Post* interviewed me. The piece Rogin produced was a detailed overview of some of my initial denials, without a trace of snark or innuendo.[44] Josh understood that I was being pummeled and he was more than willing to let me address the charges without an overlay of tendentious analysis that other journalists would have felt compelled to add. While they called it "speaking truth to power," it was really kicking a man when he was down.

For journalists to stand against the crowd takes courage. In the case of Rogin, I am told that after the *Washington Post* posted his article about my interview, he received angry calls from the Clinton campaign and others. At that time, many considered the election of President Hillary Clinton as a *fait accompli*. Rogin's very job depends on access to power, based on a relationship of trust with powerful people and preeminent institutions. His willingness to listen to the accuracy of my side of the story was nothing less than an act of bravery.

We need more journalists who are willing to at least consider the unofficial narrative, especially within media outlets that have traditionally represented the party line of consensus. We need journalists who will not buy-in to a given narrative and the constant requirement for "breaking news" because of which "side" it comes from or which "side" it afflicts. And we need journalists who can swim in the pool with other elites yet maintain their distance when it comes to reporting on stories in the public interest. If well-heeled journalists in Washington are going to socialize with judges, politicians and intelligence officials, they should take pains to maintain their skepticism, independence and degree of distance, even from their friends.

In short, the system would work better if everyone stayed in their lanes.

FBI directors shouldn't entrap presidents and then leak their memos.

High-level Justice officials shouldn't freelance the distribution of "oppo" dirt provided to them by their spouses.

Journalists shouldn't uncritically tout false stories just because they are juicy.

And high-level intelligence officials who created a phony scandal and retired to become paid commentators should not be allowed by television networks to present their biased side of their own case as if they were impartial and independent experts. Would you hire a Watergate figure to inform the American people about Watergate?

The hardest cultures to reform are those of the prosecutor and the intelligence official. Prosecutors routinely lie to suspects and create perjury traps. They are taught to adopt a scalp-hunting mentality, where an investment in a target must be justified, no matter how much the subsequent investigation proves the target's innocence (see Richard Jewell *et al.*).

Counterintelligence officials have a similar cultural challenge. They are steeped in a culture of duplicity, a necessary evil to navigate the wilderness of mirrors that spies often work inside. Big problems emerge when these two cultures are mixed, as they have been in the Department of Justice recently. Duplicity and double-dealing have become a point of pride for many prosecutors. The world of the spy has infected some law enforcement officers.

It may sound quaint, but we need to get back to a system where the FBI only has an investment in the truth—and agents are not unduly pressured from above if they decide the evidence does not validate the investment in a given investigation.

A final point. Cultural reform begins when our hectoring, lecturing, arguing, and sometimes rioting culture learns to listen.

It is often noted that the online world of news, blogs, and streaming commentary allows us to avoid opposing points of view. The old model of three national news shows had its problems, especially with bias. But that model did serve to force the nation to look at uncomfortable truths. Today, every consumer of news provides his or her own filter—whether it is The Daily Caller and Sean Hannity for me, or BuzzFeed and Rachel Maddow for someone else.

I have found that it is good to get out a little, ideologically speaking. Even when faced with threats of violence, I have always enjoyed engaging with people with very different political perspectives. I don't often argue with them; instead, I try to see the world through their eyes. Even though no one has managed to bully me off my stand, I usually learn a thing or two when I have an in-depth conversation with a thoughtful person. It also helps you to see that outside of Washington, D.C., most people have good intentions. Most people yearn to see many of the same goals fulfilled. More Americans lifted out of poverty, a cleaner environment, a good meal, healthier children better prepared for the future. Outside the halls of power, most people think this way. At least most *normal people*. The constant vitriol and "gotcha" game of Washington is irrelevant and it disgusts most Americans.

This may sound simplistic to some, but for many in Washington, it would be a revelation.

As we recover from recent trials while looking ahead to the 2020 election and the next presidential term, it is essential that we do a better job of listening to one another.

As most Americans try to come together to continue rebuilding our economy and great nation, I believe that we can only do better by being better. I have tried to do my part. I am happy to highlight a few of the abuses by those who have tried to frame me and put me in prison for something I did not do. But I did not come out of my ordeal a cynic about America or about human nature. I still see America as a glass that is much more than half full, of promise still being fulfilled—as I think most of us do.

CHAPTER TEN

WINNING IN
TROUBLED TIMES

*"Arise, shine, for your light has come, and the glory of
the Lord rises upon you."*

—*Isaiah 60:1*[1]

My personal story has seemed to many like a journey on the long road of bad luck. This increasingly became the case as more twisted subplots have since come to light. Millions of Americans including some reluctant members of Congress have progressively come to appreciate just how dishonestly the U.S. Intelligence Community operates, and how partisan its upper ranks have become. I've had countless people come up to me to offer their words of support.

"I can't believe what happened to you."

"It's an absolute disgrace what the Obama administration, the Democrats, and the intelligence agencies did to you."

"How did you survive?"

While I am grateful for the kindness so many have shown me, there are two insights that we should all understand from this experience. First and most importantly, the efforts to surveil me were part of a grand political strategy to use intelligence to interfere with an election, and when that failed, to help set the predicate to remove a duly elected president. I have never forgotten that despite my name being emblazoned on the top secret FISA warrants, the real victims here were President Trump and indeed all of us—our collective stake in a fair democratic process.

I realized this in the early hours of the Wednesday morning immediately after the 2016 election. Along with millions of others, I watched Donald Trump stride onto the stage to tell the crowd at the New York Hilton Midtown Hotel: "I've just received a call from Secretary Clinton. She congratulated us. It's about us. On our victory..."[2] But we now know that behind this veneer of gracious defeat was a determination by our president-elect's adversaries to use any means necessary to get even.

Because the aftermath of this operation continued well after the election, a dark cloud still hangs over our democracy. Despite the many accomplishments of the Trump administration, this president—and Democrats in Congress—could have achieved considerably more if he had enjoyed a traditional political honeymoon. Instead, he was forced to advance straight into a game of all-out partisan, scorched-earth political warfare while fighting off allegations that he and senior members of his team had committed treason. That's not fair to the millions of Americans who voted for Trump and sent him to the White House to fulfill his agenda.

The national media was a lead actor in this destructive drama. The mainstream press would go from one breaking-news Russia story to another, each time publicly fantasizing about dealing the death blow to this presidency. They could not stand the fact that Donald J. Trump was elected to change a swamp that had long provided a comfortable habitat for political journalists, not only in Washington but from coast to coast, nationwide. With their own self-interest in mind, the media cynically exploited First Amendment portections with their dishonest tactics. For those who could maintain a grip on reality while watching, a vast array of prominent news outlets became outright comical. Many primetime hosts on respected television networks were detached from reality, entertaining the most ludicrous theories on air on a nightly basis. But it wasn't a joke, and those narratives convinced hundreds of people to take drastic action against their fellow citizens. While these frequent falsehoods and misleading storylines may sometimes inspire the occasional chuckle, the impact was not at all funny.

The second insight, in some ways also related to the media, is more personal. I have found that we can endure almost anything if we simply trust our own common sense and maintain basic principles of decency. This requires disregarding the narrative of the media and much of the Washington consensus as an essential prerequisite. While my reputation had been largely destroyed and much of my life savings wiped out, I still had my principles, my eyes, and my brain. In most cases, the crucible I underwent only further reinforced values I had developed throughout my life and career.

Both before and after my short stint as a Trump campaign volunteer, I've sometimes learned these lessons the hard way. After the FBI showed no interest in my death threats, and it seemed like I had been cut off from personal security protection, some thought I might lose hope. But I never even came close. My core values based in my faith have helped me get through these challenges, time and time again.

Encouraged by my faith, I steadfastly denied the narrative that was being sold by powerful politicians and national media outlets. But I can now understand why many subjects of political investigations, after hours of being berated by partisan interrogators, might get flustered or consider giving up entirely. At one point, you can be tempted to agree to anything that could finally make their excruciating interrogation end, even if that means admitting guilt to a charge you know to be false. At times, it can become hard to continue believing in yourself. Accepting whatever you are told by overpriced attorneys or government prosecutors starts to look like a much easier option than continuing to fight for justice. I can easily understand why after someone reads accounts of his or her misbehavior in the media, they might be tempted to accept an accusation that something happened. Even when it had not happened at all.

My primary defense from this danger came from my commitment to common sense and an orientation towards my core values.

■ ■ ■

Over that three-year period, every time I went out in public, I ran the risk of being assaulted or spat upon. Old friends, like my colleague in London, suddenly had no time for me. Organizations that I had long worked for no longer sought my assistance or, as we saw in at least one case, wanted to prevent me from getting involved with them at all.

Before social distancing and personal security became necessary precautions for health and safety reasons, I learned to effectively do so when I was turned into a political leper. I became a fugitive, isolated as I worked on my correspondence with the government and lawsuits in federal courts to help clear my name. Based on this philosophy, I have so far survived and have continued to grow in the process. At the Trump inauguration, the new president's and our first lady's first dance was Frank Sinatra's "My Way."[3] The famous words of that late singer from Hoboken, New Jersey, reflect a potent approach to life: "I did what I had to do, and saw it through without exemption."

Everyone deals with existential challenges and threats in different ways. Finding a flexible and strong strategy that allows you to effectively overcome unexpected personal trials might seem like it requires some kind of true grit or extraordinary skills. Instead, it's often just a matter of staying true to our ability to search for solutions and recognize the truth. Dangerous challenges often seem daunting at first. I consider myself immensely fortunate to have spent so much of my earlier life in military war zones and perilous emerging market settings, which taught me a great deal about how to handle stressful situations. But most aspects of my approach are exceptionally straightforward, effective and a lot easier than one might assume. In many ways, it comes down to simple principles of common sense. By maintaining a common sense approach, I was able to maintain an upbeat attitude as I went through my dangerous, isolating and sometimes devastating experience.[4]

Throughout this long journey, I lived by five life principles that became my secret weapons. In different ways, I've often watched these principles work for others too. In the heat of recent battles, I really didn't have a choice but to fight and trust my instinct. At times, defending my name and innocence felt like a matter of life and death. So it is, ultimately, for us all: a fundamental matter of life for ourselves and our families, as we proactively choose to live without fear.

Amidst my many eccentricities, I tell my own personal story not to put myself forward as a model, a life coach or to write some sort of self-help book. The moral I suggest from this history is to encourage you to have no fear in thinking for yourself. Or in the words of Sinatra, in doing it your way. Don't always believe what the consensus and self-appointed subject-matter experts tell you. My experiences help to underscore reasons why people often need to use their own capabilities, day in and day out.

As my story shows, we have become too dependent upon the wisdom of others and not reliant enough on our own good sense. Like we saw with many of the lawyers in preceding chapters, experts often advise the public in ways that strangely coincide with their self-interest. And in the public health crisis, we all learned that when push comes to shove, you need to answer tough questions for yourself. What happens when grocery stores are out of supplies that we find necessary? What happens when you cannot get into a hospital because it's said to be overcrowded? What happens when you cannot leave your home due to a violent revolt in the streets? Should we look up to people for advice because they are movie stars, on TV, on a basketball court, or have large amounts of money in the bank? In times like those, we especially need to be able to find and follow our internal compass. But we also need to take our lives into our own hands in more mundane situations, like when considering our political positions or the society we want to live in. We don't need always to defer to the so-called experts. We know more than we think we know. We are wiser than we realize.

Looking into the future and throughout my recent past, proven approaches can help you navigate the kinds of trials and tribulations that we all face. Five core values of my life have helped me survive the challenges that adversaries threw at me.

1. A LIFETIME OF LEARNING

People have traditionally considered going to school as the standard model of education. But as the global coronavirus pandemic eventually forced schools and universities to shut across America and worldwide, people around the globe are beginning to develop a new perspective on how they can learn.

Throughout my career, learning has never been confined to the classroom or a degree program. Learning is constant and requires engagement every day. The independent learning I have continued throughout my life has become the best way to keep myself connected to a changing world and to keeping my mind active and open to new ideas. The good news is that with a bit of discipline, these opportunities are virtually limitless.

Over the years when I worked during the day and attended graduate school at night, I consistently found that the best learning is rarely achieved only in the classroom. Growing up, my Uncle Blaine would often refer to "educated fools." He would illustrate this contrast by comparing a Harvard Ph.D. to a farmer with a high school education. My uncle likely gained more knowledge as a farmer tending to his cows, sheep, chickens, and horses in upstate New York than if he had solely engaged in the prestigious post-modern areas of study from the comfort of the ivory tower. By getting my hands dirty with real work and with the self-help of study to fill in some of the blanks, I have often benefited from greater lessons than those found in the theories of academia alone.

Common sense, hard work, and self-reliance are often implicitly dismissed by the "educated fools" of the establishment. In one notorious incident, former New York mayor, Democratic candidate for president, and Harvard M.B.A. Michael Bloomberg, once said: "I could teach anybody, even people in this room, no offense intended, to be a farmer. It's a process. You dig a hole, you put a seed in, you put dirt on top, add water, up comes the corn."[5]

The successful farmers I know have skills drawn from the disciplines of botany, mechanics, veterinary medicine, genetics, microbiology, and economics. In fact, the farmers I've known have come closer as a group to being Renaissance men and women than almost any other, with the possible exception of the military. As it turns out, it was Mayor Bloomberg who was "schooled" by millions of Americans living in farm states who did not buy his ignorance and arrogance. For many years on Wall Street, I had an expensive Bloomberg terminal on my desk. It's debatable where one could learn more, at a Bloomberg terminal or working hard on a farm.

Bloomberg closed his mind to many of the extraordinary opportunities in life. He lacked an open mind to the possibility that people who are very different from him might know things he didn't. Unfortunately, this attitude doesn't just include elite politicians, but also elite centers of learning, the brand snobbishness of high-profile universities. The online world, however, gives us a richer world of possibilities. You can now hear the lectures of star professors on history or philosophy, earn valuable business or technical degrees from local and regional institutions, update your knowledge on the free-to-all Khan Academy, or just Google what you want to read about.

While elite law schools have effectively cornered the market for legal education for over a century, a handful of states, including California and Virginia have a more practical approach as well. These "law reader" programs allow prospective attorneys to study the law in conjunction with actual practitioners, rather than sitting in a classroom. Throughout my personal experience and as I've increasingly learned, such approaches can help bring to life many of the most essential aspects of most life callings.

As these examples help to demonstrate, the intrinsic rigors of developing practical solutions on your own often become the ultimate form of education. It doesn't only happen in a work context. I have found that just getting out into the environment, both within the borders of your own country and around the world, can offer some of the best learning available anywhere if you take advantage of it.

2. SURROUND YOURSELF WITH PEOPLE DEDICATED TO SERVICE, BUT ASSIST THOSE WHO HAVE FALLEN INTO THE SELF-CENTERED CREVASSE OF FEAR AND FRUSTRATION

Those Americans who make it a habit of surrounding themselves with people who generally try to grow and serve others tend to enjoy collateral benefits. I have consistently found that those committed to service find more joy in their own lives, from my fellow volunteers in the Trump campaign to the many men and women of the American military whom I served alongside. The incredible men and women I got to know as a Trump campaign volunteer in 2016 carried many of the specific benefits described in this chapter. Prior to the election interference, the things I learned from working with these Trump campaign volunteers changed my life. It became the apex of my experience in working with many other great leaders throughout my career. Such collaboration has consistently offered key benefits. Once again, this ties back to the principles of learning described above. Many of the military veterans who became my closest colleagues during the campaign benefited from what collectively amounted to centuries of practical real-world experience.

It strikes me that one of the problems in Washington, D.C., today is that it is all too easy to remain a Beltway bureaucrat or politician who never gets out, never works in the private sector, and spends little time mentally or physically outside the Pennsylvania Avenue corridor. That lifestyle is alien to most Americans. Indeed, Americans outside the Beltway share generally similar lives that weave our collective experiences together. That connectedness explains why we are often so upbeat as a people, and why most of us are so ready to work together to address crises. On a personal level, carefully and selectively developing relationships with others in our lives can help to reinforce good characteristics that we admire in others and ourselves. Often the hardest step in the process, all we typically need to do is look for them.

Thoughout much of the past several years, I have been forced to operate as a lone wolf vigilante, a one-man rebuttal squad facing down all the lies cast against me. As people called for my death, I fought for my life against the dishonest acts instigated by the Democrats' consultants that enabled abuses across the U.S. Intelligence Community. As with most challenges in life, bad experiences will eventually come to an end, and the truth should ultimately come out. In the meantime, all good boxers need to get back in the ring to keep fighting. Reengaging with friends and sparring with opponents can help one gain closure after any traumatic experience.

Although it takes courage, the development of such points of contact can and should include your enemies. Like a tough physical exercise routine that helps build strength, endurance, or speed, engaging with those you disagree with can build your personal power on many levels too.

But first, a word of caution. The original intention of my experiences with the Comey–McCabe FBI throughout the month of March 2017 was meant to help clarify the truth, not just for the FBI, but for the public. Consistent with their recent pattern though, the Bureau nonetheless used my eagerness against me and submitted even more lies to the Foreign Intelligence Surveillance Court the following month. While the approach is by no means foolproof, remaining a steadfast advocate for the truth remains the best option.

At around that same time in 2017, a Naval Academy classmate and I went to Easter Sunday mass at the Cathedral of St. Matthew the Apostle in Washington. An active duty Navy captain based near the Pentagon, she and I had previously served together overseas. When I reminded her three years later about our Easter together, I got this reply: "That's when we were spied on, right?"

She was right. "We." Just like President-elect Trump's statement on his victory night, "It's about us." She correctly recognized that anyone and everyone in my circle was also spied upon. Just a few days earlier, reporters at the *Washington Post* began to break the unfortunate news about the FISA spying against President Trump and me in 2016. Although the full story would only get worse over time, the original article directly alluded to these same implications in its first sentence: "The FBI obtained a secret court order last summer to monitor the communications of an adviser to presidential candidate Donald Trump."[6] Most people with common sense would never believe that these illicit acts were still continuing to that day, months after the Trump inauguration. Little did I know that James Comey had just signed his third false affidavit a few days earlier. Experiences like these hard knocks helped me to grow on many personal levels.

As my income was cut off and I suffered personal finance losses, I still found that certain values and tactical approaches helped me to navigate these challenges too. One of the secrets of my survival in the long haul was the self-discipline to redeploy extra income over the years into savings and investments. Later when I found my back up against the wall with Spygate and other intelligence scandals, my frugal lifestyle paid off. Without savings, it would have been much more difficult to endure these unexpected events in my life. By staying focused on things that mattered and pursuing a fairly modest lifestyle during the more normal years, my savings kept me from having to face more limited options in my battles with the government. In doing so I also avoided more dire economic consequences in the process.

Throughout these three years, I benefited from lessons learned at the U.S. Army John F. Kennedy Special Warfare Center and School, where I once studied basic survival tactics. That training taught me that with a bit of creativity, there are ways to find advantage even in the most challenging situations. Since this course included strategies for survival while you're either in dangerous geopolitical environments or largely cut off from society, it came with many unexpected silver linings that I hadn't expected when I originally completed my training at Fort Bragg. Back then, I expected to use what I had learned in the fight against terrorism overseas. But when forced to find new levels of efficiency in all areas of my life, this aerodynamic and nimble approach helped to make things move much more smoothly and quickly here at home.

3. KNOW YOUR ENEMY, BUT HAVE EMPATHY

To my benefit as well as my disadvantage, I have always believed in the importance of trying to help others. This can sometimes lead to abuse, as I experienced when the FBI manipulated records to hide years of prior support to the CIA from the FISA court. But understanding others, including those who try to do you wrong, frequently offers invaluable insight.

As a lifelong cross-country runner, engaging with one's adversaries is similar to the difference between training on a steep mountain and on a flat plain. The more rigorous course often proves to offer the best exercise in preparation for a challenging race in the future.

By many accounts there may have been certain disingenuous motivations in play at the University of Cambridge conference in the U.K. over the summer of 2016 when I first met Professor Stefan Halper. With many Democratic operatives from the United States in attendance, my seemingly innocuous interactions may have eventually contributed to a great cascade of dishonesty and abuses. But talking to my adversaries has helped me better understand the basis of their hostility. Interacting with my enemies often sheds light on potential cures for the longstanding disagreements at the root of our conflicts. As I was incessantly attacked by such political operatives, engaging with my adversaries often helped me find ways to avoid, remedy, and counter their arguments against me.

At Cambridge that summer and as I have done throughout much of my life, I tried to deescalate conversations with antagonistic people who not only disagreed with me, but insisted on being disagreeable characters as well. It often helps to have a sense of humor—about everything, including oneself. When I faced hostile interrogations by liberal journalists or politicized prosecutors, I never allowed myself to be lost in anger. Instead, I coolly observed the absurdity of what I was witnessing. Every time I was lambasted by a political prosecutor or a biased journalist with similar objectives, I simply smiled, told the truth, and rolled with the punches.

Not all the humor I discovered was mocking. I found good fellowship and laughs in some unexpected corners, with the likes of Chris Hayes at MSNBC, Anderson Cooper on CNN, and ABC News anchor George Stephanopoulos. Many of them eventually approached me in a spirit of good humor and friendliness too. Since the truth was on my side and I kept a constructive perspective, I believe the virtuous cycle of good spirits has proved mutually beneficial to each of us.

The late Peter Peterson, billionaire entrepreneur and former secretary of commerce, once spoke to a class I was teaching about his autobiography, *The Education of an American Dreamer.* He told my students something that has stayed with me ever since. Peterson suggested that one should "travel light." As he explained in his book, "Avoid accumulating baggage in your work situation that keeps you from acting independently and ethically."[7] One should not carry heavy burdens of guilt, resentment, or desire. At the time, that point was largely self-evident to me and represented the way I had lived my life, but the same idea has recently proved helpful in the context of my new reality. Traveling light is beneficial while under attack.

Whenever I had to escape New York City because of the nearly constant threats I was receiving, when no one from the FBI or other federal agencies heeded my calls for help, I packed light too. On the way to my temporary refuge in Greenwich, Princeton, and other short-term hideouts, I simply adapted, as I had no other choice. I had to figure out the most necessary items that would fit in my backpack as I rode my bike disguised down the Delaware and Raritan Canal State Park in New Jersey, through the back roads of Connecticut, or along other getaway routes.

As an unprecedented pandemic and civil unrest brought economic challenges towards the end of President Trump's first term, many Americans have been forced to make similar choices. When one considers the bare necessities needed for survival, some sources of assistance are easily within reach. With information technology increasingly ubiquitous nowadays, access to learning outlets, communications technologies, and other essentials such as fitness routines now allow most people to enjoy the many basic tools of continuous personal growth. Such possibilities almost always remain within reach regardless of our income, resources, geographic location, or personal challenges.

When unexpected circumstances arise whether they be a global health pandemic or a spiteful political attack by partisan actors, travelling light helps me to concentrate attention and save resources. While navigating enemy territory, I have often found traveling light to be a source of focus and competitive advantage.

4. CANDOR: TELL THE TRUTH

Despite many errors in the DOJ inspector general's FISA abuse report, it did note that the CIA, "had given a positive assessment of Page's candor."[8] The *Cambridge Dictionary* defines candor as: "The quality of being honest and telling the truth, especially about a difficult or embarrassing subject."[9]

Amidst the difficult and embarrassing allegations of this fabricated scandal, everyone warned me not to say anything and to just hire an attorney to talk for me. I took precisely the opposite approach. Many people I respected thought this daring approach would land me in jail. After all, I was walking through a series of perjury traps that were often an intriguingly sabotaged maze of deception and unpredictability. NYU Law Professor Ryan Goodman even added me to a "Perjury Chart" of political adversaries.[10] The speculative hope upon which he based his analysis? Goodman claimed that I "probably lied to Congress about [my] contacts with Russian officials." It was the same false hope that Mueller lieutenants had when they thought they might catch me saying something which contradicted some prior statement somewhere.

Once again, humor in the face of such attacks remained essential—just as I had frequently laughed at Mueller's prosecutors during our day together in the FISA Prettyman Courthouse. Self-styled scholars like Professor Goodman always seemed to lack self-awareness, and whether I laughed with them or at them might depend upon the given moment. But the behavior of the self-appointed guardians of truth in legal academia and the federal bureaucracy has always been a source of entertainment. In an odd way, I found some of their attacks so absurd that they proved uplifting.

Similar sources of encouragement have existed in the news business too. Sean Hannity at Fox News often assesses his contributions in a self-deprecating way by describing himelf as "Just a simple talk show host."[11] I don't find such a characterization demeaning at all, but a perfect example of the strategy that Sean and others have used for finding success by living an honest life.[12] In contrast to his prime time cable news competitor Rachel Maddow,[13] who has attacked me relentlessly,[14] Hannity's simply telling the truth has been refreshing throughout the continued drama.

Amidst this entire saga, I never changed the essential facts of my personal story. Characters like Halper, who I never imagined might have been enlisted by the Intelligence Community as domestic political spies, have nonetheless allegedly managed to find a way onto the stage of this theater of the absurd.[15] Amidst all the madness, many—like NYU Law Professor Ryan Goodman—might have hoped that I would not immediately recall some small and irrelevant bit of trivia that Adam Schiff or other Democrats craftily tried to catch me out with.

Both personally and in terms of policy, I have still found it essential not to become too stubbornly wedded to one narrative. Willingness to change is important when your initial suppositions turn out to be incorrect. Many journalists have managed to fundamentally destroy their personal credibility by clinging to false narratives even after an opposing one has been confirmed. There is no reason to do this. Everyone gets it wrong from time to time. They might even win some people back by admitting they made a mistake.

Perhaps the quintessential example of what not to do in this regard is Congressman Adam Schiff. To this day, he doubles down on discredited stories.[16] A humble perspective and the ability to admit errors is necessary when the facts turn out to be different than we thought.

5. WORK OUT EVERY DAY

In addition to my faith, staying active, healthy, and engaged has been among my most effective mental outlets in surviving it all. Yes, it's often exhilarating to get out into the great outdoors or to engage in a team sport, but even completing basic exercise routines on my own has provided an important daily boost.

In many ways and like so many other things, athletic exercise adds diversity and excitement to a daily routine. When you're cooped up at home, in an office, or a hotel room, moving your body gives a renewed sense of focus and well-being. Endorphins generated from exercise are often the ultimate God-given drug.

Perhaps my greatest "runner's high," and the best example of how valuable exercise can prove in keeping your sanity, came amidst one of my worst political and media lows, the day the Adam Schiff Show hit one of its initial apexes on March 20, 2017. I think that House Intelligence Committee meeting with then-FBI director James Comey will stand as one of my worst days ever, and not just for me, but for other members of my family as well. As Schiff began reading false allegations from the DNC's Dodgy Dossier on national television, I watched it all with my headphones plugged into an elliptical machine at a gym in Arizona. As Schiff poured out his lies and the barrage of death threats continued, I responded by working out even harder on the machine. Like the famous quote from Charles Dickens at the start of *A Tale of Two Cities*, "It was the best of times, it was the worst of times." I could not have found a better outlet. Over four hours later and after a phone call from the FBI, I finally called it quits as the hearing and the live television commentary started to subside. It's hard to imagine how I might have otherwise felt at the end of that nonsense if I had not benefited from this physical release.

■ ■ ■

For many years, my signature has consisted of the first half of my first and last name. Written in cursive, simply CarPa. It's my own abbreviation for the Latin term *carpe diem*—the motto of my class of 1993 at the U.S. Naval Academy. The meaning is "seize the day."

As I learned when facing the relentless challenges of Spygate, it's important to make the most of each day. Despite a few imperfections and the unpleasant experiences caused by some corrupt actors lurking in the shadows of our nation's capital, America remains the best country on this planet.

Facing continued headwinds and with many questions still unanswered, it's not too late to take steps towards fully restoring our democracy. Many valuable lessons have already been learned on a national and personal level. In the future, an uncompromising approach to reestablishing justice and discovering the full truth may prevent a coup attempt like the one that sought to disrupt a historic election and obstruct the initial years of President Donald J. Trump's service in the White House.

ACKNOWLEDGMENTS

Over recent years, my friendly and constructive relationships with countless innocent Trump supporters have led to many of them getting saddled with large criminal defense attorney bills and incalculable levels of stress. This year's latest rounds of declassified FBI documents from the Witch Hunt mirror other illegal election-interference incidents involving the CIA and partner intelligence agencies worldwide. For example, university scholars of my acquaintance were often unexpectedly stopped by FBI special agents after getting off international flights. Such incidents frequently occurred at U.S. Customs and Border Patrol inspection checkpoints at John F. Kennedy International Airport in New York, as well as San Francisco International Airport in California and locations in between. Others were interrogated in their family homes.[1] The sole reason for these interrogations were the limited and inconsequential relationships they had with me. While I am grateful for such generous support, their affiliation with me only led to a politically

motivated target getting placed on their backs by some of the most powerful political operatives within the U.S. Intelligence Community and
the Justice Department. Parallel reputational assaults repeatedly happened in the media as well, carrying additional injurious ramifications.

With this precedent in mind, I want to limit future potential damage
and problems caused to other kind souls whose support I have long
cherished. At this point in the summer of 2020, some glimmers of hope
are visible on the distant horizon, but significant areas of uncertainty
remain. In the current election year, it is possible that many of the same
government officials who wreaked havoc on so many innocent lives will
find themselves in power once again. With the November election just a
few months away and the next presidential inauguration scheduled for
January 2021, many of the original cast of characters from the Democratic Party continue to raise money in a quest to reclaim enormous levels
of government power.[2] For this reason and with the exception of a few
of the most prominent public figures on the frontlines of these epic
battles, my acknowledgments here must remain cautiously reserved by
not naming names in the majority of instances.

First and foremost, President Trump may have said it best in his
post-impeachment acquittal press conference:

> I want to apologize to my family for having them have to go
> through a phony, rotten deal by some very evil and sick
> people....[3]

I want to express precisely the same sentiment to my own family.
After countless hours of our conversations were wiretapped and an
immense number of our emails hacked by corrupt government intelligence authorities, the titanic levels of pressure they have endured is
immeasurable. No words can express my gratitude for their heroic
strength and moral support. Amidst this unforgettable national tragedy,
their courage to do the right thing and their resolve to persevere amidst
unprecedented political crimes by government authorities armed with
new technologies was nothing short of a life-saving inspiration.

Near the front of the public arena, then-Chairman Devin Nunes of the House Intelligence Committee might stand as Exhibit A amongst those innocent individuals who paid a tremendous price for doing the right thing. His eponymous Nunes Memo served as an initial impetus that led to many of the revelations discussed in this book. House colleagues including Jim Jordan and Louie Gohmert were often a breath of fresh air amidst the dark clouds of thick manufactured smoke. In parallel, the Senate Judiciary Committee first led by Senator Chuck Grassley and then Senator Lindsey Graham served as another essential force. After many lives were sidelined, former House leaders, including Mark Meadows and John Ratcliffe, have moved into senior executive branch positions this year, marking an encouraging start to a transition back to normalcy on the national level. Each of their brave efforts to expose the truth have collectively represented a major force for good in my life and the lives of countless Americans.

Much of this book describes unconscionable deeds by various media actors. In an earlier era, such individuals may have been labeled journalists. Against this backdrop and in contrast, my return corridor to a normal life was paved in no small part by a few rare broadcast giants including Sean Hannity, Maria Bartiromo, and Tucker Carlson. While the vast majority of the mainstream media misrepresented me as little more than a suspicious Russian spy or an alleged criminal, the careful digging and willingness of these few to question conventional wisdom represented a true turning point. Similarly appreciated were a small handful of elite journalists from other outlets including One America News, The Daily Caller, The Federalist, Epoch Times, and Just The News. If it weren't for their valiant reporting which broke down walls of information secrecy restrictions and seemingly insurmountable political disinformation campaigns through Freedom of Information Act requests and other investigations, it is hard to know where the American republic might be today.

Working with the incredible team at Regnery has marked another important milestone in my recovery path towards restoring a normal life. On all levels, the depth of their consummate professionalism was truly extraordinary from start to finish. Unquestionably, this ambitious endeavor would not have been possible without them.

To all of those who have supported me during these darkest of hours, as well as those whom I have either intentionally or unintentionally left off these acknowledgment pages, I send another very big thanks to you as well. I am confident that I will eventually be at liberty to say more, after future steps towards transparency within some of the top secret offices of the U.S. government.

Finally, I am eternally grateful for the revolution that President Donald J. Trump has created. The genie is out of the bottle, and no matter what further illicit steps may be taken by corrupt forces within the national political and intelligence infrastructure, his movement to Make America Great Again cannot be extinguished. Having never met him but based on extensive firsthand experiences, I personally have faith that President Trump will continue to lead America out of the dismal situation that has plagued our country since the time he was first elected four years ago.

NOTES

CHAPTER 1: THE BEST OF TIMES, THE WORST OF TIMES

1. Robert M. Gates, "Guarding Against Politicization," Transcript of Speech at CIA Auditorium, March 16, 1992, https://www.cia.gov/library/center-for-the-study-of-intelligence/kent-csi/volume-36-number-1/html/v36i1a01p_0001.htm.

2. Steven Mufson and Tom Hamburger, "Trump Adviser's Public Comments, Ties to Moscow Stir Unease in Both Parties," *Washington Post,* August 6, 2016, https://www.washingtonpost.com/business/economy/trump-advisers-public-comments-ties-to-moscow-stir-unease-in-both-parties/2016/08/05/2e8722fa-5815-11e6-9aee-8075993d73a2_story.html.

3. Glenn Greenwald, "The FBI Informant Who Monitored the Trump Campaign, Stefan Halper, Oversaw a CIA Spying Operation in the 1980 Presidential Election," The Intercept, May 19, 2018, https://theintercept.com/2018/05/19/the-fbi-informant-who-monitored-the-trump-campaign-stefan-halper-oversaw-a-cia-spying-operation-in-the-1980-presidential-election/.

4. Eric Lichtblau, "C.I.A. Had Evidence of Russian Effort to Help Trump Earlier Than Believed," *New York Times*, April 6, 2017, https://www.nytimes.com/2017/04/06/us/trump-russia-cia-john-brennan.html.

5. Jon Levine, "Ex-CIA Chief John Brennan Signs as MSNBC/NBC Contributor," The Wrap, February 2, 2018, https://www.thewrap.com/ex-cia-chief-john-brennan-signs-as-msnbc-nbc-as-contributor/.

6. "John Brennan: Trump Most Ignorant, Incompetent Individual to Hold Presidency," MSNBC, January 15, 2020, https://www.msnbc.com/hardball/watch/

john-brennan-trump-most-ignorant-incompetent-individual-to-hold-
presidency-76849733681.

7. Jacqueline Thomsen, "Brennan: I Didn't Mean That Trump Committed Treason,"
    The Hill, August 18, 2018, https://thehill.com/homenews/
    administration/402473-brennan-i-didnt-mean-that-trump-committed-treason.

8. Lichtblau, "C.I.A. Had Evidence of Russian Effort."

9. Harry Reid, "Letter to FBI Director Comey," U.S. Senate, August 27, 2016, https://
    www.documentcloud.org/documents/3035844-Reid-Letter-to-Comey.html.

10. Ibid.

11. Kimberley Strassel, "Brennan and the 2016 Spy Scandal," *Wall Street Journal*, July
    19, 2018, https://www.wsj.com/articles/
    brennan-and-the-2016-spy-scandal-1532039346.

12. "Trump to Home Builders: We'll Cut Regulation, Taxes," CBS Miami, August 11,
    2016, https://miami.cbslocal.com/2016/08/11/
    trump-to-home-builders-well-cut-regulation-taxes/.

13. Dana Priest and William M. Arkin, "A Hidden World, Growing beyond
    Control," *Washington Post*, July 19, 2010, https://www.pulitzer.org/cms/sites/
    default/files/content/washpost_tsa_item1.pdf.

14. Tim Weiner, *Legacy of Ashes: The History of the CIA* (New York: Anchor Books,
    2007).

15. Michael Breen, email message to author, March 23, 2016.

CHAPTER 2: WHO IS MALE-1?

1. "The Rachel Maddow Show, Transcript, 4/3/2017," MSNBC, April 3, 2017, http://
    www.msnbc.com/transcripts/rachel-maddow-show/2017-04-03.

2. Ibid.

3. Elias, Groll, "Russian Spy Met Trump Advisor Carter Page and Thought He Was an
    Idiot," *Foreign Policy*, April 4, 2017, https://en.wikipedia.org/wiki/Foreign_Policy.

4. Chuck Ross, "Adam Schiff Says He Has No Sympathy for Carter Page," The Daily
    Caller, December 21, 2019, https://dailycaller.com/2019/12/21/
    adam-schiff-no-sympathy-carter-page/.

5. Radio Free Europe republished many of the core allegations from the 2016 Yahoo!
    report in the English language: "Report: U.S. Intelligence Officials Examining
    Trump Adviser's Russia Ties," Radio Free Europe, September 24, 2016, https://
    www.rferl.org/a/report-us-intelligence-probes-trump-advisers-russia-ties-
    kremlin/28010062.html. RFE also published many of the core allegations from the
    2016 Yahoo! report in the Russian language with an article entitled "В США
    проверяют советника Трампа относительно связей с Россией" via the U.S.
    Government's Radio Svoboda propaganda website (Радио Свобода) on September
    24, 2016: https://www.svoboda.org/a/28011337.html. They also published a
    Ukrainian language article entitled "Спецслужби США з'ясовують контакти
    радника Трампа з Кремлем – Yahoo News" via the U.S. Government's Ukrainian
    Radio Svoboda propaganda website too: https://www.radiosvoboda.org/a/
    news/28010275.html.

6. Erica Ritz, "Why Some Say Ronald Reagan's Wardrobe Choice on This Trip Helped
    End the Soviet Union," The Blaze, May 14, 2014, https://www.theblaze.com/
    news/2014/05/14/
    ready-why-some-say-ronald-reagans-wardrobe-choice-on-this-trip-helped-end-the-
    soviet-union.

7. John F. Kennedy, "Remarks at the U.S. Naval Academy, Annapolis, Maryland, August 1, 1963," John F. Kennedy Presidential Library and Museum, https://www. jfklibrary.org/archives/other-resources/john-f-kennedy-speeches/ united-states-naval-academy-19630801.
8. Napoleon Hill, *Think and Grow Rich* (Meriden, Connecticut: Ralston Society, 1937). Also found at https://theedge.solutions/wp-content/uploads/2018/09/Think-and-Grow-Rich-by-Napoleon-Hill.pdf.
9. Catherine Herridge, Pamela K. Browne, and Cyd Upson, "Comey's Memo Leak Contact Had 'Special Government Employee' Status at FBI," Fox News, April 25, 2018, https://www.foxnews.com/politics/comeys-memo-leak-contact-had-special-government-employee-status-at-fbi; Mike Levine, "McCabe Showed 'Lack of Candor' with Comey: DOJ Inspector General Report," ABC News, April 13, 2018, https://abcnews.go.com/Politics/mccabe-show-lack-candor-comey-doj-inspector-general/story?id=54450687.
10. Jan S. Prybyla, *The American Way of Peace: An Interpretation* (Columbia: University of Missouri, 2005), 115; Tom Toles, "Everybody Is Now Entitled to Their Own Facts," *Washington Post,* September 10, 2015, https://www.washingtonpost. com/news/opinions/wp/2015/09/10/everybody-is-now-entitled-to-their-own-facts/.
11. Daniel Patrick, Moynihan, *Pandaemonium: Ethnicity in International Relations* (New York: Oxford University Press, 1991), 174.
12. Ibid., 15.
13. Daniel Patrick Moynihan, *Secrecy* (New Haven: Yale University Press, 1999).
14. Carter Page, "Balancing Congressional Needs for Classified Information: A Case Study of the Strategic Defense Initiative," (Fort Belvoir, Virginia: Defense Technical Information Center, 1993), http://www.dtic.mil/dtic/tr/fulltext/u2/a271110.pdf.
15. Ibid., 109.
16. Ibid., 110.
17. Henry A. Kissinger, *White House Years* (New York: Little, Brown, 1979).
18. Francis Fukuyama, *The End of History and the Last Man* (New York: Free Press, 1992).
19. Mark Riebling, *Wedge: The Secret War between the FBI and CIA* (New York: Knopf, 1994).
20. Ibid., 299–300.
21. Aaron Maté, "The Brennan Dossier: All about a Prime Mover of Russiagate," RealClearInvestigations, November 15, 2019, https://www.realclearinvestigations. com/articles/2019/11/15/the_brennan_dossier_all_about_a_prime_mover_of_ russiagate_121098.html.
22. Terrence McCoy, "This Alleged Russian Spy Ring Was Interested in Some Very Dangerous Things," *Washington Post,* January 27, 2015, https://www. washingtonpost.com/news/morning-mix/wp/2015/01/27/ this-alleged-russian-spy-ring-was-interested-in-some-very-dangerous-things/.
23. *United States v. Evgeny Buryakov,* Southern District of New York, January 2015, https://www.courtlistener.com/recap/gov.uscourts.nysd.438190/gov.uscourts. nysd.438190.1.0.pdf.
24. Ibid.
25. Ibid.
26. Michael Horowitz, "Review of Four FISA Applications and Other Aspects of the FBI's Crossfire Hurricane Investigations," Office of the Inspector General, Department of Justice, December 2019, https://www.justice.gov/storage/120919-examination.pdf.
27. Hill, *Think and Grow Rich.*

CHAPTER 3: ENTERING THE ARENA

1. Horowitz, "Review of Four FISA Applications," 62.
2. "Open Letter on Donald Trump from GOP National Security Leaders," War on the Rocks, March 2, 2016, https://warontherocks.com/2016/03/open-letter-on-donald-trump-from-gop-national-security-leaders/.
3. Shaun Walker, "Trump Discusses Ukraine and Syria with European Politicians via Video Link," *The Guardian*, September 11, 2015, https://www.theguardian.com/us-news/2015/sep/11/donald-trump-ukraine-video-link. See also: Nick Gass, "Trump Bashes Obama before Ukrainian Audience," *Politico*, September 11, 2015. https://www.politico.com/story/2015/09/donald-trump-ukraine-foreign-policy-2016-21356.
4. James Carville and Ryan Jacobs, *We're Still Right, They're Still Wrong: The Democrats' Case for 2016* (New York: Penguin Random House, 2016), 210–211.
5. Michael Crowley, "Trump's Foreign Policy Team Baffles GOP Experts," *Politico*, March 21, 2016, https://www.politico.com/story/2016/03/donald-trump-foreign-policy-advisers-221058.
6. Amy Pereira and Jane C. Timm, "Behind the Scenes at MSNBC's Exclusive Town Hall with Donald Trump," MSNBC, February 17, 2016, http://www.msnbc.com/behind-the-scenes-msnbcs-exclusive-town-hall-donald-trump.
7. Carter Page, email to Sam Clovis, February 17, 2016.
8. David E. Sanger and Maggie Haberman, "In Donald Trump's Worldview, America Comes First, and Everybody Else Pays," *New York Times,* March 26, 2016, https://www.nytimes.com/2016/03/27/us/politics/donald-trump-foreign-policy.html.
9. Michael S. Schmidt, Matt Apuzzo, and Scott Shane, "Trump and Sessions Denied Knowing about Russian Contacts. Records Suggest Otherwise," *New York Times*, November 2, 2017, https://www.nytimes.com/2017/11/02/us/politics/trump-jeff-sessions-russia.html.
10. Susan Jones, "Sen. Cruz on FBI Abuse: 'How High Up the Chain Did This Go?'," Media Research Center, December 23, 2019, https://cnsnews.com/article/national/susan-jones/sen-cruz-fbi-abuse-how-high-chain-did-go.
11. "Meet the Press Transcript," NBC News, October 18, 2015, https://www.nbcnews.com/meet-the-press/meet-press-transcript-october-18-2015-n446721.
12. See also Jack Matlock, *Superpower Illusions: How Myths and False Ideologies Led America Astray—And How to Return to Reality* (New Haven: Yale University Press, 2010); Jack Matlock, "NATO Expansion: Was There a Promise?" April 3, 2014, JackMatlock.com, https://jackmatlock.com/2014/04/nato-expansion-was-there-a-promise/.
13. Philip D. Zelikow and Condoleezza Rice, *Germany Unified and Europe Transformed: A Study in Statecraft* (Cambridge: Harvard University Press, 1995).
14. Steve Levine, *Spies, Murder, and the Dark Heart of the New Russia* (New York: Random House, 2008), 160–62.
15. "Seven New Members Join NATO," NATO, March 29, 2004, https://www.nato.int/docu/update/2004/03-march/e0329a.htm.
16. Vincent Morelli *et al.*, "NATO Enlargement: Albania, Croatia, and Possible Future Candidates," Congressional Research Service, April 14, 2009. https://fas.org/sgp/crs/row/RL34701.pdf.
17. Jodi Kantor, "What to Expect When a Clinton Is Expecting," *New York Times*, April 18, 2014, https://www.nytimes.com/2014/04/19/us/politics/what-to-expect-when-a-clinton-is-expecting.html.

18. Robert Parry, "The Mess That Nuland Made," Consortium News, July 13, 2015, https://consortiumnews.com/2015/07/13/the-mess-that-nuland-made/.

19. Sergei L. Loiko, "Ukraine Announces $15-Billion Russia Loan, Gas Price Cut," *Los Angeles Times*, December 17, 2013, https://www.latimes.com/world/la-xpm-2013-dec-17-la-fg-ukraine-russia-20131218-story.html.

20. "US Blames Russia for Leak of Undiplomatic Language from Top Official," *The Guardian*, February 6, 2014, https://www.theguardian.com/world/2014/feb/06/us-russia-eu-victoria-nuland.

21. John Hudson, "The Undiplomatic Diplomat: Russia Hawks in Washington Love Victoria Nuland, the State Department's Point Person for the Ukraine Crisis. Many Europeans Can't Stand Her," *Foreign Policy*, June 18, 2015, https://foreignpolicy.com/2015/06/18/the-undiplomatic-diplomat/.

22. House of Commons Debate, Parliament of the United Kingdom, November 30, 1950, https://api.parliament.uk/historic-hansard/commons/1950/nov/30/foreign-affairs.

23. Steven Pifer, "The Budapest Memorandum and U.S. Obligations," Brookings Institution, December 4, 2014, https://www.brookings.edu/blog/up-front/2014/12/04/the-budapest-memorandum-and-u-s-obligations/.

24. "Memorandum on Security Assurances in Connection with Ukraine's Accession to the Treaty on the Non-Proliferation of Nuclear Weapons," United Nations, paragraph 3, https://treaties.un.org/doc/Publication/UNTS/No%20Volume/52241/Part/I-52241-0800000280401fbb.pdf

25. David A. Graham, "What Happened in Ukraine?" *The Atlantic*, September 25, 2019, https://www.theatlantic.com/ideas/archive/2019/09/biden-trump-corruption/598705/.

26. Eric Felten, "Victoria Nuland Tells All on Steele Dossier…Not," RealClearInvestigations, August 12, 2019, https://www.realclearinvestigations.com/articles/2019/08/12/victoria_nuland_tells_all_on_trump-russia__not_119932.html.

27. "Nuland Says NATO Must Install Command and Control Centers in All Six Frontline States," Interfax-Ukraine, January 28, 2015, https://www.kyivpost.com/article/content/war-against-ukraine/nuland-says-nato-must-install-command-and-control-centers-in-all-six-frontline-states-378744.html.

28. "Trump Administration Has Been Downsizing the National Security Council," "All Things Considered" transcript, NPR, January 10, 2020, https://www.npr.org/2020/01/10/795366669/trump-administration-has-been-downsizing-the-national-security-council.

29. Kathy Gilsinan, "How Is ISIS Still Making Money?" *The Atlantic*, November 21, 2015, https://www.theatlantic.com/international/archive/2015/11/how-is-isis-still-making-money/416745/.

30. Corey Lewandowski, email to author, June 19, 2016.

31. George Kennan, "Long Telegram," National Security Archive, George Washington University, February 22, 1946. http://www.gwu.edu/~nsarchiv/coldwar/documents/episode-1/kennan.htm.

32. Vladimir Putin, "Executive Order on Measures to Implement Foreign Policy," Kremlin, May 7, 2012, http://eng.kremlin.ru/acts/3764.

33. Matt Apuzzo and Sharon LaFraniere, "13 Russians Indicted as Mueller Reveals Effort to Aid Trump Campaign," *New York Times*, February 16, 2018, https://www.nytimes.com/2018/02/16/us/politics/russians-indicted-mueller-election-interference.html.

34. Scott Ritter, "How 'Reset' Man McFaul Helped Torpedo U.S.–Russia Relations," *American Conservative*, May 28, 2019, https://www.theamericanconservative.com/articles/how-reset-man-mcfaul-helped-torpedo-u-s-russia-relations/.

35. FOIA appendix to: Jason Leopold, "Mueller Memos Part 4: FBI Documents That Congress Had To Fight To Get," BuzzFeed, https://buzzfeed.egnyte.com/dl/QOyOORUMxw/.

36. CRASSH Cambridge, "Campaigns on the World Stage: Madeleine Albright and Vin Weber," YouTube, July 11, 2016, https://www.youtube.com/watch?v=wZSbzWYNMp0.

37. John Harwood, "Former Top Gingrich Ally Calls Trump Nom 'Mistake of Historic Proportions'," CNBC, August 4, 2016, https://www.cnbc.com/2016/08/03/former-top-gingrich-ally-calls-trump-nom-mistake-of-historic-proportions.html.

38. Jane Mayer, "Christopher Steele, the Man behind the Trump Dossier," *New Yorker*, March 5, 2018, https://www.newyorker.com/magazine/2018/03/12/christopher-steele-the-man-behind-the-trump-dossier.

39. Leslie H. Gelb, "Reagan Aides Describe Operation to Gather inside Data on Carter," *New York Times*, July 7, 1983, https://www.nytimes.com/1983/07/07/us/reagan-aides-describe-operation-to-gather-inside-data-on-carter.html.

40. Jeff Gerth, "A Bank That Banks on Conservative Dollars," *New York Times*, November 1, 1984, https://www.nytimes.com/1984/11/01/us/a-bank-that-banks-on-conservative-dollars.html.

41. Jonathan Turley, "FBI Source in Russia Probe Raises Alarms over Political Surveillance," *The Hill*, May 22, 2018, https://thehill.com/opinion/judiciary/388785-FBI-source-in-Russia-probe-raises-alarms-over-political-surveillance.

42. Margot Cleveland, "Did Spygate Source Stefan Halper Work for the Hillary Clinton Campaign?" The Federalist, March 13, 2020, https://thefederalist.com/2020/03/13/did-spygate-source-stefan-halper-work-for-the-hillary-clinton-campaign/.

43. "Grassley Continues to Press DoD over Mismanagement of Stefan Halper Contracts," Website of Senator Chuck Grassley, July 12, 2019, https://www.grassley.senate.gov/news/news-releases/grassley-continues-press-dod-over-mismanagement-stefan-halper-contracts.

44. Chuck Grassley, letter to James Baker, Director, Office of Net Assessment, Department of Defense, January 22, 2020, https://www.grassley.senate.gov/sites/default/files/documents/2020-01-22%20CEG%20to%20ONA%20%28Halper%20Follow%20Up%29.pdf.

45. Tobias Hoonhout, "Grassley Expands Probe into DoD Contracts Awarded to Stefan Halper over Spying Concerns," *National Review*, January 23, 2020, https://www.nationalreview.com/news/grassley-expands-probe-into-dod-contracts-awarded-to-stefan-halper-over-spying-concerns/.

46. Stefan Halper, email to author, August 15, 2016.

47. Ibid.

48. Elizabeth Cusma, "Global Partners in Diplomacy," Global Cleveland, July 28, 2016, https://globalcleveland.org/global-partners-in-diplomacy/.

49. Steve Reilly, "Exclusive: Two Other Trump Advisers Also Spoke with Russian Envoy during GOP Convention," *USA Today*, March 2, 2017, https://www.usatoday.com/story/news/2017/03/02/exclusive-two-other-trump-advisers-also-spoke-russian-envoy-during-gop-convention/98648190/.

50. Kyle Cheney, "Trump Foes Make New Push to Unbind GOP Convention Delegates," *Politico*, June 24, 2016, https://www.politico.com/story/2016/06/gop-unbind-convention-delegates-224774.

51. Tatiana Vorozhko and Iuliia Iarmolenko, "Proposed GOP Stance on Ukraine Sparks Controversy," Voice of America, July 21, 2016, https://www.voanews.com/usa/proposed-gop-stance-ukraine-sparks-controversy.

52. J.D. Gordon, email to Trump foreign policy volunteer team, July 14, 2016.

53. Carter Page, email to Trump foreign policy volunteer team, July 14, 2016. See also Horowitz, "Review of Four FISA Applications," 265.

54. Stephen Boyd, "October 21, 2016, FISA Application and FISC Order Related to Carter Page," Office of the Assistant Attorney General, U.S. Department of Justice, February 7, 2020, https://www.judiciary.senate.gov/imo/media/doc/FISA%20Warrant%20Application%20for%20Carter%20Page.pdf.

55. Horowitz, "Review of Four FISA Applications," 170.

56. Carter Page, Cambridge meeting notes, July 2016.

57. Alexander Burns and Maggie Haberman, "Donald Trump Hires Paul Manafort to Lead Delegate Effort," *New York Times,* March 28, 2016, https://www.nytimes.com/politics/first-draft/2016/03/28/donald-trump-hires-paul-manafort-to-lead-delegate-effort/; Josh Voorhees, "Team Trump Embraces the Theory of Two Donalds," *Slate*, April 22, 2016, https://slate.com/news-and-politics/2016/04/paul-manafort-tells-rnc-that-trump-been-just-playing-a-part.html.

58. Carter Page, email to Trump campaign officials, April 23, 2016.

59. Ibid.

60. Del Quentin Wilber, "In FBI Agent's Account, 'Insurance Policy' Text Referred to Russia Probe," *Wall Street Journal*, December 18, 2017, https://www.wsj.com/articles/in-fbi-agents-account-insurance-policy-text-referred-to-russia-probe-1513624580.

CHAPTER 4: THE START OF THE INTERNATIONAL FUGITIVE YEARS

1. "Assessing Russian Activities and Intentions in Recent US Elections'," Office of the Director of National Intelligence, January 6, 2017, https://www.dni.gov/files/documents/ICA_2017_01.pdf.

2. Damian Paletta, text message to author, August 26, 2016.

3. Justin Scheck, James Marson, and Damian Paletta, "Global Deals That Made Exxon's CEO Now Pose Big Test," *Wall Street Journal*, December 13, 2016, https://www.wsj.com/articles/deals-with-vladimir-putin-helped-fuel-rise-of-secretary-of-state-nominee-rex-tillerson-1481626925.

4. Ruptly, "Former Trump Adviser Carter Page Holds Presentation in Moscow," YouTube, December 12, 2016, https://www.youtube.com/watch?v=MEmg4DNVFSE.

5. Martin Longman, "Revisiting Carter Page and the Rosneft Deal," *Washington Monthly,* March 30, 2018, https://washingtonmonthly.com/2018/03/30/revisiting-carter-page-and-the-rosneft-deal/.

6. Ken Bensinger, Miriam Elder, and Mark Schoofs, "These Reports Allege Trump Has Deep Ties to Russia," BuzzFeed, January 10, 2017, https://www.buzzfeednews.com/article/kenbensinger/these-reports-allege-trump-has-deep-ties-to-russia.

7. Mufson and Hamburger, "Trump Adviser's Public Comments."

8. David J. Kramer, McCain Institute for International Leadership website, Arizona State University, https://www.mccaininstitute.org/staff/david-j-kramer/.
9. Mufson and Hamburger, "Trump Adviser's Public Comments."
10. Rowan Scarborough, "David Kramer Spread Steele Dossier around Washington during Trump Transition," *Washington Times*, March 14, 2019, https://www.washingtontimes.com/news/2019/mar/14/david-kramer-spread-steele-dossier-around-washingt/.
11. Chuck Ross, "John McCain Associate Gave Dossier To BuzzFeed," The Daily Caller, December 19, 2018, https://dailycaller.com/2018/12/19/buzzfeed-mccain-associate-dossier/.
12. Jerry Dunleavy and Daniel Chaitin, "John McCain Associate behind Dossier Leak Urged BuzzFeed to Retract Its Story: 'You Are Gonna Get People Killed!'" *Washington Examiner*, March 14, 2019, https://www.washingtonexaminer.com/news/john-mccain-associate-behind-dossier-leak-urged-buzzfeed-to-retract-its-story-you-are-gonna-get-people-killed.
13. Democratic Leader Harry Reid's Letter to FBI Director James Comey, August 27, 2016, https://www.documentcloud.org/documents/3035844-Reid-Letter-to-Comey.html.
14. Mufson and Hamburger, "Trump Adviser's Public Comments."
15. Carter Page, email to Hope Hicks, August 6, 2016.
16. Charles Grassley, "ODNI Declassification of Horowitz Investigation Footnotes, Line 379," April 15, 2020, https://www.grassley.senate.gov/sites/default/files/2020-04-15%20ODNI%20to%20CEG%20RHJ%20%28FISA%20Footnote%20Declassification%29.pdf.
17. Lezlee Brown Halper and Stefan Halper, *Tibet: An Unfinished Story* (Oxford: Oxford University Press, 2014).
18. Horowitz, "Review of Four FISA Applications," 317.
19. Stephen Boyd, "October 21, 2016, FISA Application and FISC Order."
20. Michael Isikoff, "U.S. Intel Officials Probe Ties between Trump Adviser and Kremlin," Yahoo! News, September 23, 2016, https://www.yahoo.com/news/u-s-intel-officials-probe-ties-between-trump-adviser-and-kremlin-175046002.html.
21. Carter Page, letter to FBI Director James Comey, September 25, 2016, https://www.washingtonpost.com/r/2010-2019/WashingtonPost/2016/09/26/Editorial-Opinion/Graphics/2016.09.25_FBI_letter.pdf.
22. Ibid.
23. Brooke Singman, "Top Mueller Investigator's Democratic Ties Raise New Bias Questions," Fox News, December 7, 2017, https://www.foxnews.com/politics/top-mueller-investigators-democratic-ties-raise-new-bias-questions.
24. Josh Rogin, "Trump's Russia Adviser Speaks Out," *Washington Post*, September 26, 2016, https://www.washingtonpost.com/news/josh-rogin/wp/2016/09/26/trumps-russia-adviser-speaks-out-calls-accusations-complete-garbage/.
25. David Corn, "A Veteran Spy Has Given the FBI Information Alleging a Russian Operation to Cultivate Donald Trump," *Mother Jones*, October 31, 2016, https://www.motherjones.com/politics/2016/10/veteran-spy-gave-fbi-info-alleging-russian-operation-cultivate-donald-trump/; "Judicial Watch Releases Email Exchange between State Department Official and Bruce Ohr Targeting Trump with Steele Dossier Material," Judicial Watch, May 15, 2019, https://www.judicialwatch.org/press-releases/judicial-watch-releases-email-exchange-between-state-department-official-and-bruce-ohr-targeting-trump-with-steele-dossier-material/.

26. Josh Gerstein, "FBI Releases Bruce Ohr Interview Reports," *Politico*, August 8, 2019, https://www.politico.com/story/2019/08/08/fbi-releases-bruce-ohr-interview-reports-1454402.

27. Horowitz, "Review of Four FISA Applications," xv.

28. Josh Campbell, "'No Turning Back Now': The Inside Story of James Comey's Trip to Trump Tower," CNN, September 16, 2019, https://www.cnn.com/2019/09/15/politics/crossfire-hurricane-josh-campbell-james-comey-trump-tower/index.html; Erik Ortiz and Dafna Linzer, "Who Is Daniel Richman, the Columbia Professor Who Leaked Comey's Trump Memo?" NBC News, June 8, 2017, https://www.nbcnews.com/politics/politics-news/who-daniel-richman-columbia-professor-who-leaked-comey-s-private-n769846.

29. Allan Smith, "Inspector General Says Comey Violated Policy by Leaking Memos, but DOJ Declines to Prosecute," NBC News, August 29, 2019, https://www.nbcnews.com/politics/justice-department/department-justice-declines-prosecute-comey-over-leaked-memos-n1047706.

30. Andy Sullivan, "DOJ Declines to Prosecute Comey despite Finding That He Leaked Info," Reuters, August 29, 2019, https://www.reuters.com/article/us-trump-russia-comey/doj-declines-to-prosecute-comey-despite-finding-that-he-leaked-info-idUSKCN1VJ1UO; Dan Mangan and Kevin Breuninger, "Ex-FBI Director Comey Violated DOJ Policies in Handling Trump Memos, Inspector General Says," CNBC, August 29, 2019, https://www.cnbc.com/2019/08/29/ex-fbi-director-james-comey-violated-fbi-policies-and-employment-pact.html.

31. Adam Goldman, "Andrew McCabe, Ex-F.B.I. Official, Will Not Be Charged in Lying Case," *New York Times*, February 14, 2020, https://www.nytimes.com/2020/02/14/us/politics/andrew-mccabe-fbi.html.

32. Mufson and Hamburger, "Trump Advisers' Public Comments."

33. Rogin, "Trump's Russia Adviser Speaks Out."

34. I documented these election interference abuses as part of my human rights appeal to an international organization in Vienna the next month: "As a further related form of their retaliation, I have learned from a reliable source that a law firm close to the Clinton campaign has hired a London-based private investigator to investigate my trip to Russia." See Carter Page, letter to Dr. Frank-Walter Steinmeier, Chairman-in-Office of the Organization for Security and Co-operation in Europe, October 28, 2016, https://www.scribd.com/document/371381223/Carter-Page-October-2016-letter.

35. "Federal Convention Elects the Federal President," Bundespräsidialamt, February 12, 2017, http://www.bundespraesident.de/SharedDocs/Berichte/EN/Frank-Walter-Steinmeier/2017/170212-Election-of-the-Federal-President.html.

36. Ben Wofford and Ben Oreskes, "The 320 Europeans Out to Protect America's Elections," *Politico*, November 7, 2016, https://www.politico.com/magazine/story/2016/11/2016-election-observers-monitors-us-voting-osce-foreign-214430.

37. See also: "Election Observation Mission Press Conference," OSCE, November 9, 2016, https://www.osce.org/odihr/elections/usa/246356.

38. Carter Page, Letter to Dr. Frank-Walter Steinmeier.

39. "Hillary for America Statement on Bombshell Report about Trump Aide's Chilling Ties To Kremlin," Hillary for America, September 23, 2016, https://www.presidency.ucsb.edu/documents/hillary-for-america-statement-bombshell-report-about-trump-aides-chilling-ties-kremlin.

40. Ciara McCarthy and Claire Phipps, "Election Results Timeline: How the Night Unfolded," *The Guardian,* November 9, 2016, https://www.theguardian.com/us-news/2016/nov/08/presidential-election-updates-trump-clinton-news.

41. Chuck Ross, "Trump Team Asked Carter Page to 'Cease' Calling Himself a Campaign Advisor," The Daily Caller, April 22, 2017, https://dailycaller.com/2017/04/22/trump-team-asked-carter-page-to-cease-calling-himself-a-campaign-advisor/.

42. Carter Page, letter to Don McGahn, December 22, 2016; Megan Twohey, "How Hillary Clinton Grappled with Bill Clinton's Infidelity, and His Accusers," *New York Times*, October 2, 2016, https://www.nytimes.com/2016/10/03/us/politics/hillary-bill-clinton-women.html.

43. Amie Parnes, "Mook: Trump Aides 'Should Be Prosecuted for Treason' If They Conspired with Russia," *The Hill*, March 20, 2017, https://thehill.com/homenews/administration/324772-mook-trump-aides-should-be-prosecuted-for-treason-if-they-conspired.

44. "Meet the Press," NBC News, December 18, 2016, https://www.nbcnews.com/meet-the-press/meet-press-12-18-2016-n697546.

45. Olivia Beavers and Megan R. Wilson, "Podesta Group One of the Companies Mentioned in Manafort Indictment: Report," *The Hill*, October 30, 2017, https://thehill.com/policy/national-security/357884-podesta-group-is-one-of-the-companies-mentioned-in-manafort.

46. Paul Crookston, "When Bill Clinton Was Paid $500,000 to Speak in Russia, Hillary Opposed State Dept. Sanctions," Washington Free Beacon, July 18, 2017, https://freebeacon.com/politics/bill-clinton-paid-500000-speak-russia-hillary-opposed-state-dept-sanctions/.

47. Marc A. Thiessen, "Yes, the Clintons Should Be Investigated," *Washington Post,* November 19, 2017, https://www.washingtonpost.com/opinions/yes-the-clintons-should-be-investigated/2017/11/19/d88bb652-cb15-11e7-b0cf-7689a9f2d84e_story.html.

48. "Assessing Russian Activities and Intentions in Recent US Elections," Office of the Director of National Intelligence, January 6, 2017, https://www.dni.gov/files/documents/ICA_2017_01.pdf.

49. Tim Hains, "Clapper Confirms: '17 Intelligence Agencies' Russia Story Was False," RealClearPolitics, July 6, 2017, https://www.realclearpolitics.com/video/2017/07/06/clapper_confirms_17_intelligence_agencies_russia_story_was_false.html.

50. Michael S. Schmidt *et al.*, "Intercepted Russian Communications Part of Inquiry into Trump Associates," *New York Times*, January 19, 2017, https://www.nytimes.com/2017/01/19/us/politics/trump-russia-associates-investigation.html.

51. Horowitz, "Review of Four FISA Applications," 188. See also: Jerry Dunleavy, "Senate Judiciary Investigation Zeros in on FBI and DOJ Officials Who Questioned Steele Dossier Sub-Source," *Washington Examiner*, March 23, 2020, https://www.washingtonexaminer.com/news/senate-judiciary-investigation-zeros-in-on-fbi-and-doj-officials-who-questioned-steele-dossier-sub-source.

52. Carter Page, text message to Steve Bannon, January 20, 2017.

53. Ibid.

54. "The Library Lions," New York Public Library, https://www.nypl.org/help/about-nypl/library-lions.

55. Scott Shane, Nicholas Confessore, and Matthew Rosenberg, "How a Sensational, Unverified Dossier Became a Crisis for Donald Trump," *New York Times*, January

11, 2017, https://www.nytimes.com/2017/01/11/us/politics/donald-trump-russia-intelligence.html.

56. Carter Page, letter to U.S. Senate Select Committee on Intelligence, March 5, 2017.

57. Katya Golubkova, "Russia Signs Rosneft Deal with Qatar, Glencore," Reuters, December 10, 2016, https://www.reuters.com/article/us-russia-rosneft-privatisation-idUSKBN13Z0QB.

58. "The Controversial Pardon of International Fugitive Marc Rich," House Committee on Government Reform, 2001, https://www.govinfo.gov/content/pkg/CHRG-107hhrg75593/html/CHRG-107hhrg75593.htm.

59. "An Indefensible Pardon," *New York Times*, January 24, 2001, https://www.nytimes.com/2001/01/24/opinion/an-indefensible-pardon.html.

60. Jo Becker and Mike McIntire, "Cash Flowed to Clinton Foundation amid Russian Uranium Deal," *New York Times*, April 23, 2015, https://www.nytimes.com/2015/04/24/us/cash-flowed-to-clinton-foundation-as-russians-pressed-for-control-of-uranium-company.html.

61. Joy Reid, "Donald Trump Campaign Associate Investigated for Russian Ties," interview with Michael Isikoff and MSNBC contributor Michael McFaul, MSNBC, September 24, 2016. https://www.msnbc.com/msnbc-news/watch/donald-trump-campaign-associate-investigated-for-russian-ties-772556867514.

62. Shane Harris, Carol E. Lee, and Julian E. Barnes, "Mike Flynn Offers to Testify in Exchange for Immunity," *Wall Street Journal,* March 30, 2017, https://www.wsj.com/articles/mike-flynn-offers-to-testify-in-exchange-for-immunity-1490912959.

63. Catherine Herridge, Pamela K. Browne, and Christopher Wallace, "Ex-Trump Adviser Carter Page Rips 'False Narrative' on Russia Collusion," Fox News, March 30, 2017, https://www.foxnews.com/politics/ex-trump-adviser-carter-page-rips-false-narrative-on-russia-collusion.

CHAPTER 5: TERROR THREATS AND THE ADAM SCHIFF SHOW

1. Abigail Tracy, "Carter Page Finally Realizes He'd Better Stop Talking," *Vanity Fair,* January 29, 2018, https://www.vanityfair.com/news/2018/01/carter-page-finally-realizes-he-should-stop-talking.

2. "Burbank: City Proclaims Itself 'Media Capital of World'," *L.A. Times,* October 16, 1992, https://www.latimes.com/archives/la-xpm-1992-10-16-me-354-story.html.

3. Maya Rodan, "Comey Hearing: Read Rep. Adam Schiff's Opening Statement," *Time,* March 20, 2017, https://time.com/4706721/comey-hearing-adam-schiff-transcript/.

4. "Correcting the Record—The Russia Investigation, Memorandum for All Members of the House of Representatives," HPSCI Minority, January 29, 2018. https://docs.house.gov/meetings/ig/ig00/20180205/106838/hmtg-115-ig00-20180205-sd002.pdf.

5. Judge Rosemary M. Collyer, United States Foreign Intelligence Surveillance Court, December 17, 2019, Docket No. Misc. 19-02.

6. "ICYMI: House Judiciary Committee RM Nadler Shares Analysis of Nunes Memo," Office of Congressman Jerrold Nadler, February 5, 2018, https://nadler.house.gov/news/documentsingle.aspx?DocumentID=391344.

7. Kim Wehle, "The House Is Making This Fight Too Easy for Trump," *The Atlantic,* December 2, 2019, https://www.theatlantic.com/ideas/archive/2019/12/house-democrats-need-better-subpoena-strategy/602782/.

8.   Zack Budryk, "Schiff: Trump Could Be Impeached for Bribery," *The Hill*, November 12, 2019, https://thehill.com/homenews/house/470165-schiff-trump-could-potentially-be-impeached-for-bribery.

9.   Tal Axelrod, "Schiff Hauls in $2.5M in Q4," *The Hill*, February 1, 2020, https://thehill.com/homenews/house/481024-schiff-hauls-in-25-million-in-q4.

10. Austin Wright, "Pelosi, Schiff Call on Nunes to Recuse Himself from Russia Probe," *Politico*, March 27, 2017, https://www.politico.com/story/2017/03/schiff-calls-on-nunes-to-recuse-himself-from-russia-probe-236565.

11. Jason Zengerle, "What (If Anything) Does Carter Page Know," *New York Times Magazine*, December 18, 2017, https://www.nytimes.com/2017/12/18/magazine/what-if-anything-does-carter-page-know.html.

12. "McCain Diagnosed with Skin Cancer," ABC News, January 6, 2006, https://abcnews.go.com/Politics/story?id=123110.

13. Jacob Gallagher, "The Bucket Hat: Not Just for Gilligan Anymore," *Wall Street Journal*, August 2, 2018, https://www.wsj.com/articles/the-bucket-hat-not-just-for-gilligan-anymore-1533221832.

14. Kristina Wong, "Unanswered Senate Intel Leaker Questions Haunt Russia Probe," Breitbart, June 11, 2018, https://www.breitbart.com/politics/2018/06/11/unanswered-senate-intel-committee-leaker-questions-haunt-russia-probe/.

15. Michael M. Grynbaum, Scott Shane, and Emily Fitter, "How an Affair Between a Reporter and a Security Aide Has Rattled Washington Media," *New York Times*, June 24, 2018, https://www.nytimes.com/2018/06/24/business/media/james-wolfe-ali-watkins-leaks-reporter.html.

16. Ibid.

17. Ibid.

18. *United States v. James A. Wolfe*, 1:18-cr-00170, June 7, 2018, https://fas.org/sgp/news/2018/06/wolfe-indict.pdf.

19. Aaron Mak, "How Did Investigators Read James Wolfe's Signal Messages?" *Slate*, June 8, 2018, https://slate.com/technology/2018/06/signal-how-did-fbi-read-james-wolfe-encrypted-messages-reporters.html.

20. "Ex-Senate Aide James Wolfe Turns Himself In over 'FBI Leaks'," BBC, June 11, 2018, https://www.bbc.com/news/world-us-canada-44444139; "Veteran of Senate Intel Committee Charged with Lying to Investigators in Leak Investigation," CNN, June 8, 2018, https://lite.cnn.com/en/article/h_dae65447108c21d74ac5dc43d1330bb9.

21. *United States v. James A. Wolfe*, 1:18-cr-00170.

22. Ali Watkins, "A Former Trump Adviser Met with a Russian Spy," BuzzFeed, April 3, 2017, https://www.buzzfeednews.com/article/alimwatkins/a-former-trump-adviser-met-with-a-russian-spy.

23. Brian Ross *et al.*, "Trump Campaign Adviser Says Info Provided to Russian Spies Was 'Immaterial'," ABC News, April 4, 2017, https://abcnews.go.com/Politics/trump-campaign-adviser-info-provided-russian-spies-immaterial/story.

24. Morgan Windsor, "Carter Page: 'Something May Have Come Up in a Conversation' with Russians about US Sanctions," ABC News, April 13, 2017, https://abcnews.go.com/Politics/carter-page-conversation-russians-lifting-us-sanctions/story.

25. Brian Ross and Matthew Mosk, "Trump Campaign Adviser Carter Page Targeted for Recruitment by Russian Spies," ABC News, April 4, 2017, https://abcnews.go.com/Politics/trump-campaign-adviser-info-provided-russian-spies-immaterial/story.

26. Michael Winship, "There's a Smell of Treason in the Air," HuffPost, March 21, 2017, https://www.huffpost.com/entry/theres-a-smell-of-treason-in-the-air_b_58d1837ee4b0537abd957598.

27. Jennifer Sabin, "All the President's Traitors," HuffPost, March 23, 2017, https://www.huffpost.com/entry/all-the-presidents-traitors_b_58d4266de4b002482d6e6fa2.

28. Elana Schor, "Ethics Committee Clears Rep. Devin Nunes," *Politico*, December 7, 2017, https://www.politico.com/story/2017/12/07/ethics-committee-clears-rep-devin-nunes-287125.

29. H.R.1—115th Congress (2017–2018), November 2, 2017, https://www.congress.gov/bill/115th-congress/house-bill/1.

30. Robert S. Mueller, "Report on the Investigation into Russian Interference in the 2016 Presidential Election," Volume I of II, U.S. Department of Justice, March 2019, 101, https://assets.documentcloud.org/documents/5955379/Redacted-Mueller-Report.pdf.

31. Ryan Goodman, "Did Carter Page Perjure Himself over His Russian Links?" *Newsweek*, November 7, 2017, https://www.newsweek.com/did-carter-page-perjure-himself-over-his-russian-links-704082.

32. Anthony Leonardi, "Trey Gowdy Admits 'Mistake' in Defending FBI during Russia Investigation," *Washington Examiner*, May 11, 2020, https://www.washingtonexaminer.com/news/trey-gowdy-admits-mistake-in-defending-fbi-during-russia-investigation.

33. Natasha Bertrand, "Carter Page's Testimony Is Filled with Bombshells—and Supports Key Portions of the Steele Dossier," *Business Insider*, November 6, 2017, https://www.businessinsider.com/carter-page-congressional-testimony-transcript-steele-dossier-2017-11.

34. James Freeman, "Who Is Kevin Clinesmith?" *Wall Street Journal*, January 30, 2020, https://www.wsj.com/articles/who-is-kevin-clinesmith-11580417909.

35. Harris, Lee, and Barnes, "Mike Flynn Offers to Testify."

36.   H. G. Wells, *The War of the Worlds*, Project Gutenberg Literary Archive Foundation, 1992, https://www.gutenberg.org/files/36/36-h/36-h.htm.

37. Nicholas Fandos, "Al Franken Issues Apology after Accusation of Forcible Kissing and Groping," *New York Times,* November 16, 2017, https://www.nytimes.com/2017/11/16/us/politics/al-franken-sexual-harassment-groping-forcible-kissing.html.

38. Leeann Tweeden (@LeeannTweeden), "I've decided it's time to tell my story too. #MeToo," Twitter, November 16, 2017, 10:06 a.m., https://twitter.com/LeeannTweeden/status/931176738586890241; Dartunorro Clark, "Al Franken Accused of Forcibly Kissing, Groping Leeann Tweeden," NBC News, November 17, 2017, https://www.nbcnews.com/politics/congress/sen-al-franken-accused-forcibly-kissing-groping-woman-n821381.

39. Daniella Diaz, "Sessions, Franken Get Heated at Hearing: 'The Ambassador from Russia Is Russian'," CNN, October 18, 2017, https://www.cnn.com/2017/10/18/politics/al-franken-jeff-sessions-capitol-hill-hearing-russia/index.html.

40. Natasha Bertrand, text message to author, November 16, 2017.

CHAPTER 6: WHAT'S IN MY POCKET? A DAY IN MUELLER'S WITCH HUNT DUNGEON

1. Andrew Kirell, "Mueller Will Not Talk about Steele Dossier in His Testimony," Daily Beast, July 24, 2019, https://www.thedailybeast.com/mueller-testimony-special-counsel-will-not-talk-about-steele-dossier-in-congressional-hearing.

2. Joseph A. Wulfsohn, "Trump Shares Satirical Image of Obama Spying on Him at Trump Tower amid FISA Abuse Developments," Fox News, January 23, 2020, https://www.foxnews.com/media/trump-obama-spying-trump-tower-fisa.

3. Sean Rossman, "Nearly 500 Witnesses, 675 Days: The Mueller Investigation by the Numbers," USA Today, March 24, 2019, https://www.usatoday.com/story/news/politics/2019/03/24/mueller-report-trump-campaign-investigation-numbers/3263353002/.

4. Horowitz, "Review of Four FISA Applications," 7.

5. Charles Creitz, "Alan Dershowitz: Some Democrats Channeling Soviet Minister's 'Show Me the Man, I'll Show You the Crime' Maxim," Fox News, December 8, 2019, https://www.foxnews.com/media/alan-dershowitz-some-democrats-channeling-soviet-ministers-show-me-the-man-ill-show-you-the-crime-maxim.

6. Jordain Carney, "Senate GOP Eyes Probes into 2016 Issues 'Swept under the Rug'," The Hill, March 26, 2019, https://thehill.com/homenews/senate/435723-senate-gop-eyes-probes-into-2016-issues-swept-under-the-rug.

7. Noah Weiland, Emily Cochrane, and Troy Griggs, "Robert Mueller and His Prosecutors: Who They Are and What They've Done,'" New York Times, January 25, 2019, https://www.nytimes.com/interactive/2018/11/30/us/mueller-investigation-team-prosecutors.html.

8. L. Rush Atkinson, "Subpoena 1501," The Special Counsel's Office, U.S. Department of Justice, October 10, 2017.

9. Rod Rosenstein, "Rod Rosenstein's Letter Appointing Mueller Special Counsel," New York Times, May 17, 2017, https://www.nytimes.com/interactive/2017/05/17/us/politics/document-Robert-Mueller-Special-Counsel-Russia.html.

10. Austin Wright, "Republicans Jump on Special Prosecutor Bandwagon," Politico, May 17, 2017, https://www.politico.com/story/2017/05/17/special-prosecutor-republicans-mueller-238527.

11. Carter Page, text message to CBS News, May 18, 2017.

12. Adam Goldman and Michael S. Schmidt, "Rod Rosenstein Suggested Secretly Recording Trump and Discussed 25th Amendment," New York Times, September 21, 2018, https://www.nytimes.com/2018/09/21/us/politics/rod-rosenstein-wear-wire-25th-amendment.html.

13. Michael Marshall, "Terrorism, International Crime Transforming Legal Scene, Mueller Tells Law Graduates," University of Virginia School of Law, May 19, 2003, https://www.law.virginia.edu/news/2003_spr/mueller_grad.htm.

14. Robert S. Mueller, "Report on the Investigation into Russian Interference."

15. "Attorney General Holder Announces Charges against Russian Spy Ring in New York City," U.S. Department of Justice, January 26, 2015, https://www.justice.gov/opa/pr/attorney-general-holder-announces-charges-against-russian-spy-ring-new-york-city.

16. Gregg Re and Brooke Singman, "Carter Page FISA Warrant Lacked Probable Cause, DOJ Admits in Declassified Assessment," Fox News, January 24, 2020, https://

www.foxnews.com/politics/
carter-page-fisa-warrant-lacked-probable-cause-declassified-doj-order-finds.

17. Byron York, "Next Step: House Intel Asks Trump to Declassify Rest of FISA Application; Tantalizing Clues about Pages 10–12 and 17–34," *Washington Examiner,* July 24, 2018, https://www.washingtonexaminer.com/opinion/columnists/byron-york-house-intel-asks-trump-to-declassify-rest-of-fisa-application.

18. "Statement from the Press Secretary," The White House, September 17, 2018, https://www.whitehouse.gov/briefings-statements/statement-press-secretary-34/.

19. Michael D. Shear and Katie Benner, "In Reversal, Trump No Longer Demands Declassification of Russia Documents," *New York Times,* September 21, 2018, https://www.nytimes.com/2018/09/21/us/politics/trump-classification-russian-documents.html.

20. Nicholas Fandos, "Democrats, Eyeing a Majority, Prepare an Investigative Onslaught," *New York Times,* September 3, 2018, https://www.nytimes.com/2018/09/03/us/politics/democrats-trump-impeachment.html.

21. Noah Weiland, "Meet the Special Counsel Team: So Careful They Won't Even Disclose Their Shake Shack Orders," *New York Times,* August 16, 2018, https://www.nytimes.com/2018/08/16/us/politics/special-counsel-investigation-mueller.html.

22. Katelyn Polantz, "Mueller Investigation Cost $32 Million, Justice Department Says," CNN, August 2, 2019, https://www.cnn.com/2019/08/02/politics/mueller-report-cost/index.html.

23. "What Is the Average Journalist Salary by State," ZipRecruiter, https://www.ziprecruiter.com/Salaries/What-Is-the-Average-Journalist-Salary-by-State.

24. Danny Cevallos "Cohen's Guilty Plea Offers Stark Reminder: Lying to Congress Can Be a Crime," NBC News, November 30, 2018, https://www.nbcnews.com/politics/politics-news/cohen-s-guilty-plea-offers-stark-reminder-lying-congress-can-n942136.

25. Jerry Lambe, "Senate Dems Investigating Former Federalist Society Leader's Influence over Trump Admin's Judicial Nominees," Law&Crime / MSN, March 7, 2020, https://www.msn.com/en-us/news/politics/senate-dems-investigating-former-federalist-society-leaders-influence-over-trump-admins-judicial-nominees/ar-BB10R1WV.

26. Rebecca R. Ruiz *et al.,* "Trump Stamps G.O.P. Imprint on the Courts," *New York Times*, March 15, 2020, https://www.nytimes.com/2020/03/14/us/trump-appeals-court-judges.html.

27. "2017 National Lawyers Convention," Federalist Society, https://fedsoc.org/conferences/2017-national-lawyers-convention.

28. Paul Rosenzweig, "Comparative Counterterrorism Surveillance and Cooperation," Lawfare, November 21, 2017, https://www.lawfareblog.com/comparative-counterterrorism-surveillance-and-cooperation.

29. Ewen MacAskill, "GCHQ Chief Robert Hannigan Quits," *The Guardian,* January 23, 2017, https://www.theguardian.com/uk-news/2017/jan/23/gchq-chief-robert-hannigan-quits.

30. Michelle Mark, "Meet the All-Star Team of Lawyers Robert Mueller Has Working on the Trump-Russia Investigation," *Business Insider,* May 17, 2018, https://www.businessinsider.com/lawyers-robert-mueller-hired-for-the-trump-russia-investigation-2017-6.

31. Kenneth P. Vogel, "The Trump Dossier: What We Know and Who Paid for It," *New York Times,* October 25, 2017, https://www.nytimes.com/2017/10/25/us/politics/steele-dossier-trump-expained.html.

32. "Why Jeff Sessions Recused," *Wall Street Journal*, July 27, 2017, https://www.wsj.com/articles/why-jeff-sessions-recused-1501111108.

33. Brooke Singman, "Mueller Probe: Meet the Lawyers Who Gave $$ to Hillary, Now Investigating Team Trump," Fox News, September 27, 2017, https://www.foxnews.com/politics/mueller-probe-meet-the-lawyers-who-gave-to-hillary-now-investigating-team-trump.

34. Chris Perez, "Robert Mueller Hounded by MSNBC Reporters after Easter Service," *New York Post*, April 21, 2019, https://nycom/2019/04/21/robert-mueller-hounded-by-msnbc-reporters-after-easter-service/.

35. Darren Samuelsohn, "'What's the Point?' Lawmakers Fess Up to Not Fully Reading the Mueller Report," *Politico*, July 9, 2019, https://www.politico.com/story/2019/07/09/congress-read-mueller-report-1402232.

36. Erin Kelly, "Adam Schiff: 'There is Ample Evidence of Collusion between Trump Campaign, Russians,'" *USA Today*, February 14, 2018, https://www.usatoday.com/story/news/politics/2018/02/14/adam-schiff-there-ample-evidence-collusion-between-trump-campaign-russians/336786002/.

37. Dana Milbank, "So This Is Why Mueller Didn't Want to Testify," *Washington Post*, July 24, 2019, https://www.washingtonpost.com/opinions/trump-was-right-testifying-was-a-disaster-for-robert-mueller/2019/07/24/7d3af2a4-ae58-11e9-8e77-03b30bc29f64_story.html.

CHAPTER 7: A HEIGHTENED DUTY OF CANDOR

1. Devin Nunes, letter to Rod Rosenstein, December 28, 2017, https://www.scribd.com/document/368046067/Devin-Nunes-letter-to-Rod-Rosenstein.

2. "James Clapper," IMDb, https://www.imdb.com/name/nm5724080/?nmdp=1&ref_=nm_ql_flmg_2#filmography; "John Brennan," IMDb, https://www.imdb.com/name/nm5039606/?nmdp=1&ref_=nm_ql_flmg_2#filmography; "Andrew McCabe," IMDb, https://www.imdb.com/name/nm8645833/?nmdp=1&ref_=nm_ql_flmg_2#filmography.

3. "Triangle of Sino-American Energy Diplomacy: A Symposium," Asia Society, January 18, 2013, https://asiasociety.org/new-york/events/triangle-sino-american-energy-diplomacy-symposium.

4. Stephanie Condon, "Hillary Clinton: The 'Vast, Right-Wing Conspiracy' Is 'Even Better Funded' Now," CBS News, February 3, 2016, https://www.cbsnews.com/news/hillary-clinton-the-vast-right-wing-conspiracy-is-even-better-funded-now/.

5. Luke Harding, "Why Carter Page Was Worth Watching," *Politico*, February 3, 2018, https://www.politico.com/magazine/story/2018/02/03/carter-page-nunes-memo-216934.

6. Ibid.

7. John Solomon, "New Evidence Shows Why Steele, the Ohrs and TSA Workers Never Should Have Become DOJ Sources," *The Hill*, August 15, 2019. https://thehill.com/opinion/white-house/457628-new-evidence-shows-why-steele-the-ohrs-and-tsa-workers-never-should-have.

8. John Solomon, "Nellie Ohr's 'Hi Honey' Emails to DOJ about Russia Collusion Should Alarm Us All," *The Hill*, May 1, 2019, https://thehill.com/opinion/white-house/441580-nellie-ohrs-hi-honey-emails-to-doj-about-russia-collusion-should-alarm-us.

9. Tristan Justice, "CNN Just Paid Off Another Corrupt Deep State Leaker with TV Contract," The Federalist, August 23, 2019, https://thefederalist.com/2019/08/23/cnn-just-paid-off-another-corrupt-deep-state-leaker-tv-contract/; Solomon, "New Evidence Shows Why Steele."

10. Solomon, "New Evidence Shows Why Steele."

11. Eric Tucker and Chad Day, "AP Sources: Lawyer Was Told Russia Had 'Trump over a Barrel,'" AP News, September 1, 2018, https://apnews.com/4ac772445073491aa7d3ca9e558e0144/AP:-Justice-lawyer-was-told-Russia-had-'Trump-over-a-barrel.

12. Rowan Scarborough, "Duty as a Citizen: Bruce Ohr Concealed Efforts to Spread Steele Dossier," Washington Times, January 5, 2020, https://m.washingtontimes.com/news/2020/jan/5/bruce-ohr-hid-mission-spread-anti-trump-steele-dos/.

13. Mike Levine, "Frequent Trump Target Bruce Ohr Is Heard from for the First Time," ABC News, March 8, 2019, https://abcnews.go.com/Politics/frequent-trump-target-bruce-ohr-heard-time/story.

14. Daniel Chaitin, "Bruce Ohr Names Andrew McCabe, FBI Officials Tied to Peter Strzok among his Trump Dossier Contacts: Reports," Washington Examiner, August 30, 2018, https://www.washingtonexaminer.com/news/bruce-ohr-names-andrew-mccabe-fbi-officials-tied-to-peter-strzok-among-his-trump-dossier-contacts-reports.

15. John Solomon, "Did FBI Get Bamboozled by Multiple Versions of Trump Dossier?" The Hill, July 10, 2018, https://thehill.com/hilltv/rising/396307-Did-FBI-get-bamboozled-by-multiple-versions-of-Trump-dossier%3F; Chuck Ross, "John McCain Associate Had Contact with a Dozen Reporters Regarding Steele Dossier," The Daily Caller, March 14, 2019, https://dailycaller.com/2019/03/14/john-mccain-dossier-steele-reporters/.

16. Scarborough, "Duty as a Citizen."

17. Ibid.

18. Brooke Singman, "Strzok-Page Texts Reveal Personal Relationship between FBI Official and Judge Recused from Flynn Case," Fox News, March 16, 2018, https://www.foxnews.com/politics/strzok-page-texts-reveal-personal-relationship-between-fbi-official-and-judge-recused-from-flynn-case.

19. Ibid.

20. Tara Francis Chan, 'Be Very Careful': Comey Was the First Person to Tell Trump about the Steele Dossier before the Inauguration," Business Insider, April 16, 2018, https://www.businessinsider.com/when-was-trump-told-about-the-steele-dossier-2018-4.

21. Ibid.

22. Alex Ward, "James Comey's Memos Shed More Light on Michael Flynn's Firing," Vox, April 20, 2018, https://www.vox.com/world/2018/4/20/17261770/james-comey-memo-trump-flynn; Jonathan Lemire and Sadie Gurman, "Comey's Release of Trump Memo to Newspaper, Was It Legal?" Associated Press, June 8, 2017, https://apnews.com/bda71db0b4ac4ceba09f4c1930f966f6/Comey%27s-release-of-Trump-memo-to-newspaper-draws-criticism.

23. Michael D. Shear and Matt Apuzzo, "F.B.I. Director James Comey Is Fired by Trump," New York Times, May 9, 2017, https://www.nytimes.com/2017/05/09/us/politics/james-comey-fired-fbi.html.

24. Louise Nelson, "Bannon: Trump Firing Comey Was Biggest Mistake in 'Modern Political History'," Politico, September 11, 2017, https://www.politico.com/story/2017/09/11/steve-bannon-trump-james-comey-firing-242549.

25. Mollie Hemingway, "Obama, Biden Oval Office Meeting On January 5 Was Key To Entire Anti-Trump Operation," The Federalist, May 8, 2020, https://thefederalist. com/2020/05/08/ obama-biden-oval-office-meeting-on-january-5-was-key-to-entire-anti-trump-operation/.

26. Horowitz, "Review of Four FISA Applications," ix.

27. Devin Nunes, "The Nunes Memo," HPSCI Majority, February 2, 2018, https:// www.theatlantic.com/politics/archive/2018/02/ read-the-full-text-of-the-nunes-memo/552191/.

28. Ibid.

29. Rosemary M. Collyer, "Accuracy Concerns Regarding FBI Matters Submitted to the FISC," Docket No. [Redacted], Order and Mem. Op. issued on April 3, 2007, at 14.

30. Ronn Blitzer, "Comey Admits 'I Was Wrong on FISA Conduct,'" Fox News, December 15, 2019, https://www.foxnews.com/politics/ comey-defends-fbis-fisa-process-after-scathing-ig-report.

31. Devin Nunes, "The Nunes Memo."

32. Ibid.

33. Tim Hains, "Adam Schiff on Nunes Memo Allegations: FBI 'Acted Completely Appropriately' with All FISA Warrants," RealClearPolitics, February 11, 2018, https://www.realclearpolitics.com/video/2018/02/11/adam_schiff_on_nunes_ memo_allegations_fbi_acted_completely_appropriately_with_all_fisa_warrants. html.

34. Rich Lowry, "The Schiff Memo Was a Disgrace," National Review, December 11, 2019, https://www.nationalreview.com/corner/the-schiff-memo-was-a-disgrace/.

35. Davis Richardson, "Devin Nunes Honored with 'Defender of Freedom' Award at CPAC as Schiff Memo Drops," The Observer, February 24, 2018, https://observer. com/2018/02/ devin-nunes-honored-with-defender-of-freedom-award-at-cpac-as-schiff-memo-drops/.

36. "Correcting the Record," HPSCI Minority.

37. Ibid.

38. Ibid.

39. Charles Grassley and Lindsey Graham, "Memorandum," Charles E. Grassley, U.S. Senate Committee on Judiciary, Lindsey O. Graham, Subcommittee on Crime and Terrorism to Rod J. Rosenstein, Deputy Attorney General, undated, https://www. judiciary.senate.gov/imo/media/doc/2018-02-02%20CEG%20LG%20to%20 DOJ%20FBI%20(Unclassified%20Steele%20Referral).pdf.

40. Ibid.

41. Ibid.

42. William McGurn, "A Job for Adam Schiff," Wall Street Journal, December 16, 2019, https://www.wsj.com/articles/a-job-for-adam-schiff-11576540574.

43. "Interview of Dan Coats, Director, DNI," Permanent Select Committee on Intelligence, U.S. House of Representatives, June 22, 2017, https://intelligence.house. gov/uploadedfiles/dc9.pdf.

44. Blitzer, "Comey Admits 'I Was Wrong on FISA Conduct.'"

45. Olivia Gazis, "House Intelligence Committee Transcripts Provide New Insight, Fuel Old Divisions," CBS News, May 9, 2020, https://www.cbsnews.com/news/ house-intelligence-committee-transcripts-provide-new-insight-fuel-old-divisions/.

46. Rich Lowry, "The Slippery James Comey Gets Nailed," National Review, December 16, 2019, https://www.nationalreview.com/2019/12/ james-comey-evades-dodges-chris-wallace-interview/.

47. Horowitz, "Review of Four FISA Applications," vi.
48. Ibid., v.
49. Ibid., vi.
50. Ibid., x.
51. Ibid., xi.
52. Ibid., ix.
53. Ibid., xii.
54. Ibid., ix.
55. Charles Creitz, "Gowdy Lauds Nunes for 'Phenomenal Job' with His Own Russia Probe, Says Trusting FBI Was 'Mistake'," Fox News, May 12, 2020, https://www.foxnews.com/media/trey-gowdy-devin-nunes-phenomenal-job-russia.
56. Adam Entous, Ellen Nakashima, and Greg Miller, "Sessions Discussed Trump Campaign–Related Matters with Russian Ambassador, U.S. Intelligence Intercepts Show," *Washington Post,* July 21, 2017, https://www.washingtonpost.com/world/national-security/sessions-discussed-trump-campaign-related-matters-with-russian-ambassador-us-intelligence-intercepts-show/2017/07/21/3e704692-6e44-11e7-9c15-177740635e83_story.html.
57. Devin Nunes, letter to Rod Rosenstein, December 28, 2017, https://www.scribd.com/document/368046067/Devin-Nunes-letter-to-Rod-Rosenstein.
58. "Correcting the Record," HPSCI Minority.
59. Horowitz, "Review of Four FISA Applications," vi.
60. Michael Caputo, "Death Threats and Drained Bank Accounts: Life on the Wrong End of the Mueller Probe," *Politico,* March 28, 2019, https://www.politico.com/magazine/story/2019/03/28/mueller-investigation-michael-caputo-trump-first-person-226336.

CHAPTER 8: A LEGACY OF LAWSUITS

1. James Freeman, "Obama's FBI and the Press: The Media Establishment Congratulated Itself for Getting Duped into Supporting an Abuse of Power," *Wall Street Journal,* December 16, 2019, https://www.wsj.com/articles/obamas-fbi-and-the-press-11576534979; Kaylee McGhee, "Yes, Hillary Clinton and the DNC's Ties to the Steele Dossier Matter," *Washington Examiner,* December 9, 2019, https://www.washingtonexaminer.com/opinion/yes-hillary-clinton-and-the-dncs-ties-to-the-steele-dossier-matter; Sonam Sheth, "'He Was Right, I Was Wrong': Former FBI Director James Comey Says He Was Wrong to Defend FBI's Use of the FISA Surveillance Process," *Business Insider,* December 15, 2019, https://www.businessinsider.com/james-comey-admits-he-was-wrong-to-defend-fbis-fisa-2019-12.
2. Daniel Chaitin, "Did Sally Yates Enable DOJ Official Tied to Trump Dossier? GOP Investigators Want to Know," *Washington Examiner,* August 19, 2018, https://www.washingtonexaminer.com/news/did-sally-yates-enable-doj-official-tied-to-trump-dossier-gop-investigators-want-to-know; Carlos Christian, "CORRUPT AS HELL! FBI Attorney Dana Boente Signed FBI Response to FISA Court Abuse," Union Journal, January 12, 2020, https://theunionjournal.com/corrupt-as-hell-fbi-attorney-dana-boente-signed-fbi-response-to-fisa-court-abuse/.
3. Philip Ewing, "Big Questions in Russia Case May Be Answered If FISA Documents Are Unredacted," NPR, September 14, 2018, https://www.npr.org/2018/09/14/646379749/big-questions-in-russia-case-may-be-answered-if-fisa-documents-are-unredacted.

4.   "Scaramucci and Other Alumni among Trump's Recent Appointees," Harvard Law Today, July 26, 2017, https://today.law.harvard.edu/ alumni-among-trumps-recent-appointees/.

5.   David Rutz, "Scaramucci to Trump: Don't Fire Rosenstein Over the Memo," Washington Free Beacon, February 4, 2018, https://freebeacon.com/politics/ scaramucci-to-trump-dont-fire-rosenstein-over-the-memo/.

6.   Tessa Berenson, "Jeff Sessions Is Recusing Himself. What Does That Mean?" *Time*, March 3, 2017, https://time.com/4689877/ recuses-meaning-jeff-sessions-donald-trump/.

7.   "Pro Se," Black's Law Dictionary Free Online Legal Dictionary, 2nd Ed., https:// thelawdictionary.org/pro-se/.

8.   5 U.S. Code § 552a(b).

9.   Carter Page, letter to FOIA/PA Mail Referral Unit, U.S. Department of Justice, May 21, 2017.

10.   Jerry Dunleavy, "FBI Lawyer under Criminal Investigation Altered Document to Say Carter Page 'Was Not a Source' for Another Agency," *Washington Examiner*, December 14, 2019, https://www.washingtonexaminer.com/news/ fbi-lawyer-under-criminal-investigation-altered-document-to-say-carter-page-was-not-a-source-for-another-agency.

11.   "A Career Counselor's Guide to Lateral Hiring at DOJ," Office of Attorney Recruitment and Management, U.S. Department of Justice, https://www.justice.gov/ oarm/images/lateralhiringguideforweb.pdf.

12.   Sally Q. Yates, "Protect the Justice Department from President Trump," *New York Times,* July 28, 2017, https://www.nytimes.com/2017/07/28/opinion/sally-yates-protect-the-justice-department-from-president-trump.html.

13.   C. Ryan Barber, "FBI Director Wray Banked $14M from King & Spalding since 2016," Law.com, December 20, 2018, https://www.law.com/ nationallawjournal/2018/12/20/ fbi-director-wray-banked-14m-from-king-spalding-since-2016/.

14.   H.Res. 1028 (115th): "Impeaching Rod Rosenstein, the Deputy Attorney General of the United States, for High Crimes and Misdemeanors," https://www.govtrack.us/ congress/bills/115/hres1028/text/ih.

15.   Laura Jarrett, "Rod Rosenstein Bids Farewell to Justice Department," CNN, May 9, 2019, https://www.cnn.com/2019/05/09/politics/rod-rosenstein-doj-goodbye/index. html.

16.   Sarah N. Lynch, "Former Deputy Attorney Rod Rosenstein Joins the Law Firm King & Spalding," Reuters, January 8, 2020, https://www.reuters.com/article/us-usa-moves-rosenstein/ former-deputy-attorney-rod-rosenstein-joins-the-law-firm-king-spalding-idUSKBN1Z72EO.

17.   "Birthday of the Day: Rod Rosenstein, Partner at King & Spalding," *Politico*, January 13, 2020, https://www.politico.com/news/2020/01/13/ playbook-birthday-rod-rosenstein-098094.

18.   Harry Reid, letter to James Comey, August 27, 2016, https://assets.documentcloud. org/documents/3035844/Reid-Letter-to-Comey.pdf.

19.   "Senator Harry Reid, Distinguished Fellow in Law and Policy," University of Nevada, Las Vegas William S. Boyd School of Law, https://law.unlv.edu/faculty/ senator-harry-reid.

20.   "MGM Resorts Public Policy Institute at UNLV," University of Nevada, Las Vegas, https://www.unlv.edu/mgmppi/about.

21. Glenn Thrush and Sarah Wheaton, "Boehner and Obama: Caught in a Bad Bromance," *Politico*, September 25, 2015. https://www.politico.com/story/2015/09/obama-boehner-bromance-214094.

22. *Erickson v. Pardus*, 551 U. S. Reports 94, 127 S.Ct. 2197 (internal quotation mark omitted) (quoting *Estelle v. Gamble*, 429 U. S. Reports 97, 106, 97 S.Ct. 285, 50 L.Ed.2d 251 [1976]).

23. Ken Woods, "Retired Maj. Gen. Discusses War Prevention," U.S. Army, June 15, 2016, https://www.army.mil/article/169717/retired_maj_gen_discusses_war_prevention.

24. Horowitz, "Review of Four FISA Applications," vi.

25. Carter Page, email to Philip Alston, September 17, 2017.

26. "Strategic Human Rights Litigation Seminar," New York University Law School, https://its.law.nyu.edu/courses/description.cfm?id=25112.

27. Philip Alston, email to author, September 19, 2017.

28. Philip Alston, email to author, October 3, 2017.

29. Philip Alston, email to author, October 1, 2017.

30. Philip Alston, email to author, October 3, 2017.

31. See *Bean LLC d/b/a Fusion GPS v. Defendant Bank and Permanent Select Committee on Intelligence* (D.D.C., 17-cv-02187), October 20, 2017.

32. "Bob Bauer," New York University Law School, https://its.law.nyu.edu/facultyprofiles/index.cfm?fuseaction=profile.overview&personid=36322.

33. "Lisa Monaco and Michael Bosworth to Join NYU Law," New York University Law School, https://www.law.nyu.edu/news/Lisa-Monaco-Michael-Bosworth-senior-fellows-national-security-criminal-justice.

34. Ken Bensinger, Miriam Elder, and Mark Schoofs, "These Reports Allege Trump Has Deep Ties To Russia," BuzzFeed, January 10, 2017, https://www.buzzfeednews.com/article/kenbensinger/these-reports-allege-trump-has-deep-ties-to-russia.

35. "NSD Organization Chart," U.S. Department of Justice, https://www.justice.gov/nsd/national-security-division-organization-chart.

36. Jodi Kantor, "Teaching Law, Testing Ideas, Obama Stood Slightly Apart," *New York Times*, July 30, 2008, https://www.nytimes.com/2008/07/30/us/politics/30law.html.

37. Kenneth P. Vogel, "Clinton Campaign and Democratic Party Helped Pay for Russia Trump Dossier," *New York Times*, October 24, 2017, https://www.nytimes.com/2017/10/24/us/politics/clinton-dnc-russia-dossier.html.

38. Horowitz, "Review of Four FISA Applications," 7.

39. "Counterterrorism, Cybersecurity, and Homeland Security," Council on Foreign Relations, January 10, 2017, https://www.cfr.org/event/counterterrorism-cybersecurity-and-homeland-security.

40. ChuckGrassley (@ChuckGrassley), "All of the delays and excuses why the Horowitz IG FISA report isn't public yet after several months of anticipation of its issues leads me to the suspicion it's going to be 'deep six' by the deep state," Twitter, October 21, 2019, 8:59 p.m., https://twitter.com/ChuckGrassley/status/1186446951967068160.

41. Jerry Dunleavy, "DOJ Inspector General Finds 17 'Significant Errors or Omissions' in Carter Page FISA Applications," *Washington Examiner*, December 9, 2019, https://www.washingtonexaminer.com/news/doj-inspector-general-finds-17-significant-errors-or-omissions-in-carter-page-fisa-applications.

42. "Andrew Weissmann," Reiss Center on Law and Security, https://www.lawandsecurity.org/mission/team/andrew-weissmann/.

43. Sidney Powell, "Judging by Mueller's Staffing Choices, He May Not Be Very Interested in Justice," *The Hill*, October 19, 2017, https://thehill.com/opinion/white-house/356253-judging-by-muellers-staffing-choices-he-may-not-be-very-interested-in.

44. Ryan Goodman, "Dissecting the Grassley–Graham Letter's Criticisms of the Carter Page FISA Application," Just Security, February 7, 2018, https://www.justsecurity.org/51956/dissecting-grassley-graham-letter-criticisms-carter-page-fisa-application/.

45. Max Kutner, "Senate Investigators Turn Focus to Carter Page and Trump Campaign's Foreign Policy Team," *Newsweek*, November 29, 2017, https://www.newsweek.com/senate-feinstein-grassley-russia-page-clovis-phares-gordon-726175; Greg Evans, "Carter Page: Al Franken Gropes Preferable to 'Groundless Witch Hunt'," Deadline, December 15, 2017, https://deadline.com/2017/12/carter-page-al-franken-grope-preferable-groundless-witch-hunt-dianne-feinstein-1202228084/.

46. Ryan Goodman, "Testimony from the Senate Judiciary Committee's Hearing on Election Interference," Just Security, June 12, 2018, https://www.justsecurity.org/57611/testimony-senate-judiciary-committees-hearing-election-interference/.

CHAPTER 9: OVERCOMING THE ABUSES AGAINST AMERICAN DEMOCRACY

1. Calvin Coolidge, *Messages to the General Court, Official Addresses, Proclamations, and State Papers*, Commonwealth of Massachusetts, June 23, 1920, 163.

2. "Management Advisory Memorandum for the Director of the Federal Bureau of Investigation Regarding the Execution of Woods Procedures for Applications Filed with the Foreign Intelligence Surveillance Court Relating to U.S. Persons," Office of Inspector General, U.S. Department of Justice, March 2020, https://oig.justice.gov/reports/2020/a20047.pdf.

3. Ellen Nakashima, "Repeated Mistakes in Phone Record Collection Led NSA to Shutter Controversial Program," *Washington Post*, June 26, 2019, https://www.washingtonpost.com/world/national-security/repeated-mistakes-in-phone-record-collection-led-nsa-to-shutter-controversial-program/2019/06/25/f256ba6c-93ca-11e9-b570-6416efdc0803_story.html.

4. Alex Hern, "Phone Call Metadata Does Betray Sensitive Details about Your Life—Study," *The Guardian*, March 13, 2014, https://www.theguardian.com/technology/2014/mar/13/phone-call-metadata-does-betray-sensitive-details-about-your-life-study. Study: https://www.pnas.org/content/113/20/5536.

5. Mana Azarmi, "The NSA Shuttered the Call Detail Records Program. So Too Must Congress," Center for Democracy and Technology, August 16, 2019, https://cdt.org/insights/the-nsa-shuttered-the-call-detail-records-program-so-too-must-congress/.

6. "*Entick v. Carrington* (1765) 19 St. Tr. 1030," *Loveland: Constitutional Law, Administrative Law and Human Rights 8e: Online Casebook*, https://oup-arc.com/static/5c0e79ef50eddf00160f35ad/casebook_19.htm.

7. David Snyder, "The NSA's 'General Warrants': How the Founding Fathers Fought an 18th Century Version of the President's Illegal Domestic Spying," Eff, https://www.eff.org/files/filenode/att/generalwarrantsmemo.pdf.

8. Michael E. DeVine, "Intelligence Community Spending: Trends and Issues," Congressional Research Service, November 6, 2019, https://fas.org/sgp/crs/intel/R44381.pdf.

9. Dana Priest and William M. Arkin, "A Hidden World, Growing beyond Control," *Washington Post*, July 19, 2010, https://media.washingtonpost.com/wp-srv/special/nation/tsa/static/articles/hidden-world.html.

10. Beverly Gage, "What an Uncensored Letter to MLK Reveals," *New York Times*, November 11, 2014, https://www.nytimes.com/2014/11/16/magazine/what-an-uncensored-letter-to-mlk-reveals.html.

11. "Schiff's Surveillance State: The Democrat Demands, and Then Discloses, the Call Logs of His Opponents," *Wall Street Journal*, December 4, 2019, https://www.wsj.com/articles/schiffs-surveillance-state-11575506091.

12. "The Intelligence Gathering Debate," NBCUniversal Archives, YouTube, January 23, 2014, https://www.youtube.com/watch?v=YAG1N4a84Dk.

13. Neema Singh Guliani, "The Inspector General's Report Makes It Clear: We Need to Reform the Government's Secret Intelligence Court," *Washington Post*, December 13, 2019, https://www.washingtonpost.com/opinions/2019/12/13/inspector-generals-report-makes-it-clear-we-need-reform-governments-secret-intelligence-court/.

14. "Sen. Burr Claims EO 12333 Permits Mass Surveillance 'without Congress's Permission'," C-SPAN, March 12, 2020, https://www.c-span.org/video/?c4860932/user-clip-sen-burr-claims-eo-12333-permits-mass-surveillance-without-congresss-permission.

15. Glenn Greenwald, "NSA Collecting Phone Records of Millions of Verizon Customers Daily," *The Guardian*, June 6, 2013, https://www.theguardian.com/world/2013/jun/06/nsa-phone-records-verizon-court-order.

16. Aaron Blake, "Sen. Wyden: Clapper Didn't Give a 'Straight Answer' on NSA Profiles," *Washington Post*, June 11, 2013, https://www.washingtonpost.com/news/post-politics/wp/2013/06/11/sen-wyden-clapper-didnt-give-straight-answer-on-nsa-programs/.

17. Allen Smith, "Comey Takes Responsibility for FBI 'Sloppiness' Revealed in DOJ Watchdog Report," NBC News, December 15, 2019, https://www.nbcnews.com/politics/justice-department/comey-takes-responsibility-fbi-sloppiness-revealed-doj-watchdog-s-report-n1102436.

18. Ryan Lucas, "Justice Department IG Finds Widespread Problems with FBI's FISA Applications," NPR, March 31, 2020, https://www.npr.org/2020/03/31/824510255/justice-department-ig-finds-widespread-problems-with-fbis-fisa-applications.

19. James Freeman, "Who Is Kevin Clinesmith," *Wall Street Journal*, January 30, 2020, https://www.wsj.com/articles/who-is-kevin-clinesmith-11580417909.

20. John Solomon, "Leaking Lovers and FBI Smear Job of Carter Page," *The Hill*, September 10, 2018, https://thehill.com/opinion/white-house/405956-leaking-lovers-and-an-fbi-smear-job-of-carter-page.

21. "Peter Strzok's Attorney Denies Media Leak Strategy to Harm Trump Administration," CNN, September 11, 2018, http://transcripts.cnn.com/TRANSCRIPTS/1809/11/sitroom.01.html.

22. Chuck Ross, "Isikoff Stunned That His Carter Page Article Was Used to Justify Spy Warrant," The Daily Caller, February 2, 2018, https://dailycaller.com/2018/02/02/isikoff-stunned-carter-page/.

23. Maya Rhodan, "Read Rep. Adam Schiff's Opening Statement on Russian Meddling in the Election," *Time*, Marc 20, 2017, https://time.com/4706721/comey-hearing-adam-schiff-transcript/.

24. James A. Gagliano, "The FBI Didn't Learn from Its Disastrous Richard Jewell Mistake," CNN, December 28, 2019, https://www.cnn.com/2019/12/28/opinions/richard-jewell-fbi-confirmation-bias-gagliano/index.html.

25. Scott Shane and Eric Lichtblau, "Scientist Is Paid Millions by U.S. in Anthrax Suit," *New York Times*, June 28, 2008, https://www.nytimes.com/2008/06/28/washington/28hatfill.html.

26. Joe Concha, "Scarborough: Trump Is Either 'an Agent of Russia' or 'a Useful Idiot'," *The Hill*, November 14, 2019, https://thehill.com/homenews/media/470446-scarborough-trump-is-either-an-agent-of-russia-or-a-useful-idiot.

27. George Orwell, *1984* (New York: Signet Classics, 1950).

28. Aaron Blake, "'One of the Greatest Travesties in American History': Barr Drops All Pretense about Ongoing Probe of Russia Investigation," *Washington Post*, April 9, 2020, https://www.washingtonpost.com/politics/2020/04/09/one-greatest-travesties-american-history-barr-drops-all-pretense-about-ongoing-probe-russia-investigation/.

29. Samantha Raphelson, "FBI Apologizes to Court for Mishandling Surveillance of Trump Campaign Adviser," NPR, January 11, 2020, https://www.npr.org/2020/01/11/795566486/fbi-apologizes-to-court-for-mishandling-surveillance-of-trump-campaign-adviser.

30. Margaret Taylor, "The Senate Proposes Five Amendments to FISA Reform," Lawfare, May 12, 2020, https://www.lawfareblog.com/senate-proposes-five-amendments-fisa-reform.

31. Tobias Hoonhout, "FISA Hawks Lee, Leahy Say 'Damning' Horowitz FBI Audit 'Makes Clear Our Work Is Not Done'," *National Review*, April 1, 2020, https://www.nationalreview.com/news/fisa-hawks-lee-leahy-say-damning-horowitz-fbi-audit-makes-clear-our-work-is-not-done/.

32. "Press Release: Lee–Leahy Introduce Bipartisan FISA Reform Bill," Website of Senator Mike Lee, March 9, 2020, https://www.lee.senate.gov/public/index.cfm/2020/3/lee-leahy-introduce-bipartisan-fisa-reform-bill.

33. Mike Lee, "It's Time for Congress to Bring Accountability to Intelligence Community's Surveillance Power," Fox News, March 3, 2020, https://www.foxnews.com/opinion/sen-mike-lee-congress-surveillance.

34. Brett Tolman, "Congress Must Rein in FISA Surveillance in the Wake of Abuses," *Washington Examiner*, March 11, 2020, https://www.washingtonexaminer.com/opinion/op-eds/congress-must-rein-in-fisa-surveillance-in-the-wake-of-abuses.

35. "Carter Page Surveillance Documents Released," *The Rachel Maddow Show*, MSNBC, July 23, 2018, http://www.msnbc.com/transcripts/rachel-maddow-show/2018-07-23.

36. "Another FISA Fiasco: The Judges Hire an FBI Apologist to Restore the Secret Court's Credibility," *Wall Street Journal*, January 13, 2020, https://www.wsj.com/articles/another-fisa-fiasco-11578958028.

37. Samuel Woodhams, "Huawei Says Its Surveillance Tech Will Keep African Cities Safe but Activists Worry It'll Be Misused," Quartz, March 20, 2020, https://qz.com/africa/1822312/huaweis-surveillance-tech-in-africa-worries-activists/.

38. Ellen Nakashima, "Inspector General Who Handled Ukraine Whistleblower Complaint Says 'It Is Hard Not to Think' He Was Fired by Trump for Doing His Job," *Washington Post*, April 6, 2020, https://www.washingtonpost.com/politics/inspector-general-who-handled-ukraine-whistleblower-complaint-says-its-hard-not-to-think-he-was-fired-by-trump-for-doing-his-job/2020/04/06/083166de-77b4-11ea-b6ff-597f170df8f8_story.html.

39. Michael K. Atkinson, "Statement of Nominee for Inspector General of the Intelligence Community," U.S. Senate Select Committee on Intelligence, January 17,

2018, https://www.intelligence.senate.gov/sites/default/files/documents/os-matkinson-011718.pdf.

40. Zachary Cohen, "Whistleblower Controversy Thrusts Little-Known Trump Appointee into the Limelight," CNN, September 30, 2019, https://www.cnn.com/2019/09/23/politics/ic-ig-michael-atkinson-whistleblower-complaint/index.html.

41. "John Carlin," Charlie Rose Show, October 12, 2016, https://charlierose.com/videos/29298.

42. Jeff Carlson, "John Carlin—The Former NSD Head Who Enabled the FBI's Carter Page FISA Warrant," Themarketswork, May 21, 2018, https://themarketswork.com/2018/05/21/john-carlin-the-former-nsd-head-who-enabled-the-fbis-carter-page-fisa-warrant/.

43. "Release of the FISC Opinion Approving the 2016 Section 702 Certifications and Other Related Documents," Office of the Director of National Intelligence, https://www.intelligence.gov/ic-on-the-record-database/results/3-release-of-the-fisc-opinion-approving-the-2016-section-702-certifications-and-other-related-documents.

44. Josh Rogin, "Trump's Russia Adviser Speaks Out."

CHAPTER 10: WINNING IN TROUBLED TIMES

1. "Isaiah 60," Bible Gateway, http://web.mit.edu/jywang/www/cef/Bible/NIV/NIV_Bible/ISA+60.html.

2. "Here's the Full Text of Donald Trump's Victory Speech," CNN, November 9, 2016, https://www.cnn.com/2016/11/09/politics/donald-trump-victory-speech/index.html.

3. Judy Kurtz, "Trump Dances to 'My Way' at Inaugural Ball," The Hill, January 20, 2017, https://thehill.com/blogs/in-the-know/in-the-know/315430-trump-dances-to-my-way-at-inaugural-ball.

4. Jason Zengerle, "The Happy Martyrdom of Carter Page," New York Times, February 6, 2018, https://www.nytimes.com/2018/02/06/magazine/the-happy-martyrdom-of-carter-page.html.

5. Tyler Olson, "Bloomberg Implied Farming Doesn't Take Intelligence in 2016 Comments," Fox News, February 17, 2020, https://www.foxnews.com/politics/bloomberg-implied-farming-is-easy-in-2016-comments.

6. Ellen Nakashima, Devlin Barrett, and Adam Entous, "FBI Obtained FISA Warrant to Monitor Trump Adviser Carter Page," Washington Post, April 12, 2017, https://www.washingtonpost.com/world/national-security/fbi-obtained-fisa-warrant-to-monitor-former-trump-adviser-carter-page/2017/04/11/620192ea-1e0e-11e7-ad74-3a742a6e93a7_story.html.

7. Peter G. Peterson, The Education of an American Dreamer: How a Son of Greek Immigrants Learned His Way from a Nebraska Diner to Washington, Wall Street, and Beyond (New York: Twelve, 2009), 355.

8. Horowitz, "Review of Four FISA Applications," ix.

9. "Candor," Cambridge Dictionary website, https://dictionary.cambridge.org/dictionary/english/candor.

10. Ryan Goodman, "Perjury Chart: Trump Associates' Lies, False, or Misleading Statements on Russia to Federal Authorities," Just Security, December 3, 2018, https://www.justsecurity.org/61682/perjury-chart-trump-associates-lies-false-statements-russia-federal-authorities/.

11. "Carter Page Has His Day," The Sean Hannity Show, Bullhorn FM, December 9, 2019, https://www.bullhorn.fm/theseanhannityshow/posts/carter-page-has-his-day.

12. Mark Joyella, "Sean Hannity Extends Win Streak over Rachel Maddow to 52 Weeks," *Forbes,* March 10, 2020, https://www.forbes.com/sites/markjoyella/2020/03/10/sean-hannity-extends-win-streak-over-rachel-maddow-to-52-weeks/.

13. Mike Brest, "Fox News Sweeps Top Five Most-Watched Cable News Programs for First Quarter of 2020," *Washington Examiner,* March 31, 2020, https://www.washingtonexaminer.com/news/fox-news-sweeps-top-five-most-watched-cable-news-programs-for-first-quarter-of-2020.

14. Rachel Maddow, *Blowout: Corrupted Democracy, Rogue State Russia, and the Richest, Most Destructive Industry* (New York: Crown, 2019).

15. Toby Harnden, "Cambridge Don Stefan Halper Named in Donald Trump Spy Row," *The Times,* May 20, 2018, https://www.thetimes.co.uk/article/stefan-halper-named-in-donald-trump-spy-row-tv9dhbn6d.

16. Jeff Mordock, "Schiff Protects Intel 'Status Quo' Power by Sinking Wide-Reaching FISA Reform," *Washington Times,* March 15, 2020, https://www.washingtontimes.com/news/2020/mar/15/adam-schiff-fisa-reform-intervention-protects-fbi-/.

ACKNOWLEDGMENTS

1. Jason Leopold, "Mueller Memos Part 4: FBI Documents That Congress Had to Fight to Get," BuzzFeed, January 17, 2020, https://www.buzzfeednews.com/article/jasonleopold/mueller-report-secret-memos-4.

2. Ryan Lovelace, "Ex-Mueller Prosecutor to Headline Biden Fundraiser: Report," *Washington Times,* May 21, 2020, https://www.washingtontimes.com/news/2020/may/21/ex-mueller-prosecutor-headline-joe-biden-fundraise/.

3. "President Trump Statement on Senate Acquittal," C-SPAN, February 6, 2020, https://www.c-span.org/video/?469059-1/president-trump-statement-senate-acquittal.

INDEX